The novels of Wells,
Bennett and Galsworthy

For Sara

Acknowledgments

The idea for this study arose largely out of a discussion I had with Tony Tanner in 1965. I am most grateful to Dr Tanner for that original guidance and for his help and encouragement subsequently. I owe thanks also to Dr J. B. Beer for advice and constructive criticism over a period of several years, and to Dr J. M. Newton and Dr J. R. Northam, each of whom has given me valuable support both in this and in other enterprises.

Part I
Introductory

I

Introduction

W. W. Wagar has written that 'for students of English literature' H. G. Wells has 'shrunk to the dimensions of a minor
novelist, fit for sweeping into the literary dustbin nowadays
shared by Hilaire Belloc, Arnold Bennett, and John Galsworthy'.[1]
Since 1961, when that Wellsian sentence was published, some
critics have rummaged among the trash; but although
Bernard Bergonzi has effected a major change in the general
response to Wells's early science fiction,[2] nothing else of any significance has been added to the critical view of Wells, Bennett
and Galsworthy since D. H. Lawrence and Virginia Woolf
made their classic indictments of the three Edwardians in the
1920s.

Caught up as we have been until now in a modernism
dating from and relevant for the 1920s, our criticism of Edwardians has been fixed in the direction established, for example, by the collection of iconoclastic essays called *Scrutinies*,
in which Lawrence's attack on Galsworthy was first published.[3]
We have been flattered by Virginia Woolf's insight that 'in or
about December, 1910, human character changed',[4] and have
perhaps felt that her 'Mrs Brown', while establishing a typology
for the Edwardian world, lives more vividly than any of the
Bennett characters she parodies. Instead of looking from the
very thick of the changing dialectic of decades, however, we
ought now perhaps to look back over the long perspective of

the emergence of modernism between 1880, say, and the present time. It is the history of the modern psyche, and it begins for the purposes of this study with Havelock Ellis's early classic statement of the Darwinian aftermath: 'We need to . . . put a living soul in the clothed body.'[5] When Virginia Woolf talked about life escaping from the novels of Wells, Bennett and Galsworthy,[6] it may be that she was talking as much about her own sense of predicament[7] (and updating the terms of crisis, as it were), thus sharing with T. S. Eliot the perception that 'We'

> . . . are the hollow men
> We are the stuffed men
> Leaning together
> Headpiece filled with straw. Alas!

The present study seeks to establish a line of continuity in the English novel, arguing that the release and consolidation of the self in modern times has depended upon a gradually developing ability to confront the post-Darwinian crisis of consciousness. It may be suggested that this ongoing crisis was in a sense successfully assimilated by the Edwardians, who left human nature changed in 1910, ready for Virginia Woolf and, in particular, Lawrence, to produce their own therapies and to render more sharply their own new terms of crisis:

> My whole consciousness is cliché
> and I am null;
> I exist as an organism
> and a nullus.[8]

It is to Beckett that the line proceeds, and we shall find prototypes for his clowns in the destroyed pastoral of Galsworthy's London.

Clearly in a study of this kind it is easy to attribute a modernist 'sophistication' to Wells, Bennett and Galsworthy that their comparatively limited horizons do not admit, but at the same time too unquestioning an acceptance of a clean break, of a sharp discontinuity at 1910, may be equally dangerous. It will be argued here that, whether consciously or unconsciously, Wells, Bennett and Galsworthy depicted selves in a 'postcultural' crisis which is only an earlier stage of our own.

In 1963 Gerhard Masur wrote: 'There are few figures in twentieth-century fiction that have stirred the imagination of so many readers as have Irene and Soames.'[9] In 1970 one would have to change this to: '. . . so many readers and television viewers'. The implication may be, not that Galsworthy is on a level with the author of *Peyton Place* (though the two have certain features in common), but that *The Forsyte Saga*, in its own particular way of making sense of life, seems to be confronting, seriously and radically, an experience of universal relevance. That 'experience', for the definition of which a term like 'post-cultural crisis' seems appropriate, is what, I would argue, Wells, Bennett and Galsworthy are each concerned with.

It is difficult to wipe away the after-images projected by previous critics, but in order to establish afresh the precise character of the Edwardian 'social' novel, one might consider the first paragraphs of the three central novels by Wells, Bennett and Galsworthy. The first quotation is from Wells's *Tono-Bungay*:

Most people in this world seem to live "in
character;" they have a beginning, a middle and
an end, and the three are congruous one with
another, and true to the rules of their type.
You can speak of them as being of this sort of
people or that. They are, as theatrical people
say, no more (and no less) than "character
actors." They have a class, they have a place,
they know what is becoming to them and what is
due to them, and their proper size of tombstone
tells at last how properly they have played the
part. But there is also another kind of life that
is not so much living as a miscellaneous tasting
of life. One gets hit by some unusual transverse
force, one is jerked out of one's stratum and
lives crosswise for the rest of the time, and,
as it were, in a succession of samples. That
has been my lot, and that is what has set me
at last writing something in the nature of a
novel. I have got an unusual series of
impressions that I want very urgently to tell.

I have seen life at very different levels, and
at all these levels I have seen it with a sort
of intimacy and in good faith. I have been a
native in many social countries. I have been
the unwelcome guest of a working baker, my
cousin, who has since died in the Chatham
infirmary; I have eaten illogical snacks – the
unjustifiable gifts of footmen – in pantries, and
have been despised for my want of style (and
subsequently married and divorced) by the
daughter of a gasworks clerk; and – to go to my
other extreme – I was once – oh, glittering days! –
an item in the house-party of a countess. I've
seen these people at various angles. At the
dinner-table I've met not simply the titled
but the great. On one occasion – it is my
brightest memory – I upset my champagne over
the trousers of the greatest statesman in
the empire – heaven forbid I should be so
invidious as to name him! – in the warmth of
our mutual admiration.

The second quotation comes from Bennett's *The Old Wives'
Tale:*

Those two girls, Constance and Sophia
Baines, paid no heed to the manifold interest
of their situation, of which, indeed, they
had never been conscious. They were, for
example, established almost precisely on the
fifty-third parallel of latitude. A little
way to the north of them, in the creases of
a hill famous for its religious orgies, rose
the river Trent, the calm and characteristic
stream of middle England. Somewhat farther
northwards, in the near neighbourhood of the
highest public-house in the realm, rose two
lesser rivers, the Dane and the Dove, which,
quarrelling in their infancy, turned their
backs on each other, and, the one by favour
of the Weaver and the other by favour of the

Trent, watered between them the whole width
of England, and poured themselves respectively
into the Irish Sea and the German Ocean. What
a county of modest, unnoticed rivers! What a
natural, simple county, content to fix its
boundaries by these tortuous brooks, with
their comfortable names – Trent, Mease, Tern,
Dane, Mees, Stour, Tame, and even hasty
Severn! Not that the Severn is suitable to
the county! In the county excess is deprecated.
The county is happy in not exciting remark. It
is content that Shropshire should possess that
swollen bump, the Wrekin, and that the
exaggerated wildness of the Peak should lie
over its border. It does not desire to be a
pancake like Cheshire. It has everything that
England has, including thirty miles of Watling
Street; and England can show nothing more
beautiful and nothing uglier than the works of
nature and the works of man to be seen within
the limits of the county. It is England
in little, lost in the midst of England,
unsung by searchers after the extreme;
perhaps occasionally sore at this neglect,
but how proud in the instinctive cognizance
of its representative features and traits!

The Galsworthy passage is from *The Man of Property*:

Those privileged to be present at a
family festival of the Forsytes have
seen that charming and instructive sight –
an upper middle-class family in full
plumage. But whosoever of these favoured
persons has possessed the gift of psychological analysis (a talent without monetary
value and properly ignored by the Forsytes),
has witnessed a spectacle, not only
delightful in itself, but illustrative of
an obscure human problem. In plainer words,
he has gleaned from a gathering of this

family – no branch of which had a liking for
the other, between no three members of whom
existed anything worthy of the name
sympathy – evidence of that mysterious concrete
tenacity which renders a family so formidable
a unit of society, so clear a reproduction
of society in miniature. He has been admitted
to a vision of the dim roads of social progress,
has understood something of patriarchal life,
of the swarmings of savage hordes, of the rise
and fall of nations. He is like one who,
having watched a tree grow from its planting –
a paragon of tenacity, insulation, and success,
amidst the deaths of a hundred other plants
less fibrous, sappy, and persistent – one day
will see it flourishing with bland, full
foliage, in an almost repugnant prosperity,
at the summit of its efflorescence.

These three paragraphs, whether taken out of context or considered in their contexts, seem to present certain distinguishable common features which show them to be representative of a separable moment in the history of the English novel. There is in these excerpts, for example, a distinct contrast between the unwittingly *subject* characters (or 'types') and the detached, objective observer; and while this tendency would seem to be implicit in all fictional narrative, and hence to have characterized the English novel from its beginnings, the dichotomy between narrator and character-subjects is transformed here into something like the relation between an analytic scientist and his experimental apparatus, or, indeed, between a psychoanalyst and his patient. Anyone familiar with psychoanalytical 'protocols' will notice the resemblance. 'Technique', wrote Mark Schorer in an essay dealing mainly with *Tono-Bungay*, 'must – and alone can – take the place of the absent analyst';[10] in each of these paragraphs, it might be suggested, 'technique' in Schorer's sense suffers, and the intervening voice of an 'analyst' seems concerned to display its executive presence. There is a pointed contrast between (i) the unconsciously 'symptomatic' subjects (e.g Wells's people who are

'true to the rules of their type' and, in opposition to the narrator, not conscious of their own role-playing; Bennett's sisters,
who have 'never been conscious' of 'their situation'; Galsworthy's Forsytes lacking the 'talent' of 'psychological analysis'),
and (ii) the conscious observer who shares with the reader his
cognitive ability to stand outside the containing situation of the
characters he is describing (compare Wells's 'I have come to see
myself from the outside, my country from the outside . . .', in
the penultimate paragraph of *Tono-Bungay*).

Limitations in individual consciousness, in fact, seem to be in
each case an inseparable element of the novelist's interest. There
is the implied Spencerian idea that successful and serene adaptation to cultural environment (e.g. 'They have a class, they
have a place'; the sisters at one with their 'situation', and a
Staffordshire complacently proud; the Forsytes compared to a
successfully evolved and adapted tree) carries with it no
accompanying charge of self-consciousness. And 'instinctive
cognizance', as opposed to consciousness, seems to be endowed
with special merit. The analogy with Freudian analysis, then,
breaks down at this point, if it is true that the three writers are
depicting unconsciousness as in some sense 'better than' consciousness. In fact, however, as I shall try to show, the situation
is not as simple as that. For there is in addition the concomitant
implication that consciousness is an essential part of the human
adaptive process; or at any rate that it is emphatically present
only when derangement or maladaptation occur. There is a
marked contrast between (i) those content to remain in their
'situation' (e.g. 'they know what is becoming in them and what
is due to them'; Bennett's Staffordshire, and, later in the novel,
Constance, whose name fits this role; the Forsytes in 'full
plumage') and (ii) those more 'conscious' beings who for one
reason or another are disengaged from any specific environment and way of life ('one is jerked out of one's stratum'; the
element symbolized by the wayward, 'hasty Severn', not 'suitable to the county', which foreshadows Sophia's extremism; the
implied non-Forsyte narrator who finds the family's prosperity
'almost repugnant', and who has an implied talent for 'psychological analysis').

In each passage individual life is seen as subject to chance
and unsolicited conflict, and there is the implication of the

pervasiveness of this Darwinian state in society and in personal relationships. In accordance with this, the passages exhibit an evolutionary, 'biomorphic' approach to the focused section of society (e.g. 'this remarkable social range, this extensive cross-section of the British social organism' – fifth paragraph of *Tono-Bungay*; Staffordshire as living organism; Bennett's 'proud in the instinctive cognizance of its representative features and traits').

The central topic of each passage is the relation of individuals to whole ways of life – social, national, regional, familial (e.g. 'I have seen life at very different levels. . . . I have been a native in many social countries' – which foreshadows Wells's later treatment of England in *Tono-Bungay* as social organism; 'England in little'; 'reproduction of society in miniature'). And the sociological approach of each novelist is displayed in the writers' obvious interest in rendering the background to temperament and the dialectic that obtains between consciousness and environment. Symptomatic of the sociological bent is an element which appears to register a 'positivist' sensibility on the part of the writers, a classifying, analytical, mensurational habit ('the three are congruous' and 'proper size of tombstone'; 'fifty-third parallel'; 'a unit of society' and 'psychological analysis'). But this is accompanied by a kind of hopefully human anti-positivist element. And the positivist and anti-positivist modes appear to cohere in the generalizing and synthesizing sweep of the literary gesture ('Most people in this world . . .'; 'Those two girls . . .'; 'Those privileged to be present at . . .'), and in the implied permissiveness of temperament that seems to be recommended, or at least admitted, in the three paragraphs.

Thus far such an interpretation in terms of the depiction of social consciousnesses in evolution would not perhaps differ very much from the traditional view of the three writers. One has been encouraged to think of them in much the same quasi-sociological way, concerned more with Mrs Brown's clothing environment than with Mrs Brown. But if we take a second look at the passages we shall see that they do not at all deal *simply* with consciousnesses in their social or, to use the language of sociology, their cultural environments. The interesting truth, surely, is that the narrators of these novels (and their most 'advanced' characters, as we read through), seem to occupy no recognizable cultural environment at all. The fully released consciousness, the aware mind, in these passages, seems to be inhabiting a 'post-cultural' or 'acultural' world. The first-person narrator who has been 'a native of many social countries' is indicating that he has left these relative, 'cultural' environments behind. 'Cultures', in the sense of the Forsytes, or Staffordshire middle-class communities, or of 'many social countries', once defined, once known cognitively, no longer seem to work 'culturally' for the fully conscious mind. The artist-narrator is alienated in such a fictional world, not because he is anti-bourgeois, but apparently because the fully conscious mind in process of analysis must automatically proceed to a post-cultural level. In this context a 'culture' is essentially a paradise that the narrator (*qua* narrator) may be said to have lost. Much the same kind of 'degenerative' trajectory is shown in Lawrence's novel, *The Rainbow*, which starts in the relative unconsciousness of the 'cultural mode' at Marsh Farm, and proceeds by way of a series of evolutionary progressions to a state in which Ursula Brangwen and Anton Skrebensky become detached from society (though not, in Lawrence's sense, far enough detached), become post-cultural beings – in need now of Lawrentian therapy, as it were.[11]

In a sense, of course, all novels have dealt with this conflict between self and culture, which has been, as Lionel Trilling points out, the 'particular concern of the literature of the last two centuries'. It is appropriate that this quotation from Trilling comes from his collection called *Beyond Culture*, and the passage (from the essay on Freud) is worth quoting in full:

> In its essence literature is concerned with the
> self; and the particular concern of the literature
> of the last two centuries has been with the self in
> its standing quarrel with culture. We cannot
> mention the name of any great writer of the modern
> period whose work has not in some way, and usually
> in a passionate and explicit way, insisted on
> this quarrel, who has not expressed the bitterness
> of his discontent with civilisation, who has not
> said that the self made greater legitimate demands
> than any culture could hope to satisfy. This
> intense conviction of the existence of the self

apart from culture is, as culture well knows,
its noblest and most generous achievement. At
the present moment it must be thought of as a
liberating idea without which our developing
ideal of community is bound to defeat itself.
We can speak no greater praise of Freud than to
say that he placed this idea at the very centre
of his thought.[12]

It may be that the novel, far from acting as the mouthpiece for 'society' and embodying contemporary social values, has acted as a contributory instrument for the revolutionary substitution of what Trilling calls 'community' for an older order of 'society' supported by 'culture'. The denotative divisions between such terms are notoriously difficult to assign, but it is possible to conclude from Trilling's remarks that a certain kind of radical warms to the word 'community' in a way that he does not to 'culture'. For a certain type of mind, 'our developing ideal of community' seems to render 'culture' more and more outmoded. The paradoxical truth may be that in analysing, in consciously defining and refining cultural values, the novel has murdered to dissect, and has reinforced the process of cultural change whereby 'instinctive cognizance' seems to work less and less, and a positive 'talent for psychological analysis' becomes more and more a necessity of life. In this view Soames Forsyte lacks spontaneity and 'instinctive cognizance' not because he is a Forsyte, but because he is a newly *conscious* Forsyte, a Forsyte with a residual 'cultural' identity, but detached from the herd, as it were, and living through what I have called 'post-cultural crisis'.

Many novels, of course, seem to exhibit this pattern of the initially alienated self-defining existing conditions as in some sense unsatisfactory and attempting to reconstruct the world according to its own values. Jean Duvignaud has suggested where the relation in fiction between the transforming self and 'our developing ideal of community' might lie:

> . . . the aim of the classical novel is to
> organise reality, whether that of individual
> dramas and their partial values and
> resolutions or that of murky dream and
> psychic visions. Flaubert's imaginative

invention of a Madame Bovary is the fruit of
a Utopian experience, the reconstruction of a
living whole in and around a character who
becomes the momentary symbol of this assembling
process.[13]

It might then be argued that most novels give the impression of
presenting consciousnesses in process of revolutionizing the conditions of reality. Jane Austen's *Mansfield Park*, for example,
shows Fanny's consciousness apparently rendering obsolete
both her own parents' home and the initial state of Mansfield
Park in cultural crisis. The novel promotes the illusion that
Fanny transforms a disintegrating country-house society into a
tightly knit, intimately interconnected community. The same
movement from fragmented, chaotic 'society' to a warmly intimate 'community' characterizes many of the novels of Dickens
also. Critics of society in the novel tend to derive their criteria
for judging human organization from the quality of life finally
achieved by the revolutionary self in constructing its 'ideal of
community'. Novels before Wells, Bennett and Galsworthy,
however, make it a condition of catering for the self that the self
submits to 'higher purposes' which only indirectly ensure individual well-being. In Defoe's novels this process of sublimation
works so palpably in the ultimate material interests of the self
that an ironical conflict between claimed religious and 'underlying' socio-economic ends results. Addison and Steele, Samuel
Johnson and Jane Austen helped to synthesize a new range of
sublimated communal ends; in Jane Austen 'self-knowledge'
gives the self access to the general moral principles which
sustain the Utopian (often village) communities which are
created (as 'a living whole in and around a character') during
the course of her novels. The measure of the heresy of Wells,
Bennett and Galsworthy in this respect is that the values
inherent in the universes their characters attempt to synthesize
are only those which tend *directly* to ensure the well-being of the
self. Their heroes and heroines find 'communality' not in
culture, but in a neo-Vitalist cosmic process beyond culture.
Emma's ultimate well-being is not an end in itself, but a by-
product of the process whereby she achieves full moral realization within the new cultural order which her 'education for

reality' has helped to 'reconstruct'. The three Edwardians, however, are hardly at all concerned with the general principles of moral conduct which are important elements in the linguistic totality of Jane Austen's novels, for example. We may hesitantly define their predicament as one in which cultural 'sublimation' no longer seems to work; for them the guide-lines for a fuller implementation of 'humanity' in society must come not from morality, but from cognitive analysis.

John A. Lester has identified a stage in the development of English thought when the secularization of teleologies was carried through into a more overt socialization. He quotes Beatrice Webb: 'I suggest it was during the middle decades of the nineteenth century that, in England, the impulse of self-subordinating servitude was transferred, consciously and overtly, from God to man',[14] and comments: 'The good and evil of man's life become not divine, but social, values.'[15] Galsworthy carries the process one stage further, and is only ambiguously stating the same hypothesis when he says: 'Society stands to the modern individual as the gods and other elemental forces stood to the individual Greek.'[16] Here is implicit an Edwardian progression beyond mere *fin-de-siècle* 'self-subordination'. 'Community' (or 'Fraternity') is to be pursued only if it ensures freedom from social 'forces', from the sense of being, as it were, determined arbitrarily from above. The 'free' characters in Galsworthy's novels are the asocial types, the individuals like Irene and Bosinney, who, in defiance of the gods, enjoy what Philip Rieff identifies as 'The Triumph of the Therapeutic',[17] viz. 'an intensely private sense of well-being . . . generated in the living of life itself'.[18] In contra-distinction to Irene and Bosinney, then, Soames Forsyte is not so much 'immoral' as standing unwittingly in need of Freudian therapy. Indeed, the Edwardian novels of Wells, Bennett and Galsworthy seem to be specifically concerned with therapies for the self and for society which ultimately respect only the requirements of the post-cultural consciousness. They move towards the Rieffian position where salvation derives not from adjustment to a modified culture, but from an analytic, ateleological mode of life which operates 'beyond culture'. They move towards a mode perhaps implicit in the difficult passages at the end of *Tono-Bungay*: 'I have come to see myself from the outside, my country from the outside –

without illusions. We make and pass.'[19] This Rieffian attitude is what Mark Schorer seems to have been trying to describe when he wrote of a 'nihilistic vision' at the end of *Tono-Bungay*, 'quite opposite from everything that he [Wells] meant to represent'.[20] We shall come to examine the hypothesis that Wells's rejection of technique in Schorer's sense parallels his rejection of a 'cultural' solution for his heroes' sense of crisis. While apparently afflicted in his polemical writings by the related neuroses of optimism and pessimism, Wells seems to have been able in his finest Edwardian novels to transcend teleological considerations. Rejecting the premature 'objectification' of 'technique', he invites the reader to share with him the ongoing analytic process which alone seems able to sustain the self in post-cultural crisis.

The Utopian mode which may be implicit in all novels (positively in *Emma*, for example, and negatively in *Clarissa*) becomes totally acultural in Wells's novel, *In the Days of the Comet* (1906), where the apocalyptic comet is seen as explicitly 'therapeutic', inducing a new sense of well-being in individuals; cultural fragmentation is cured by a movement beyond culture. Sexual and social crisis, seen initially in a relative, cultural setting, is confronted after 'the Change' by an unwittingly para-Freudian[21] analytical reading of the love-triangle which is the central theme of the novel. A balance between reason and the passions is finally achieved, not with the finality of a 'happy ending', but as possible only as the result of constant ongoing analytic effort. In this novel country houses (resembling the Bladesover House of *Tono-Bungay*) undergo a transformation into what latter-day sociologists would call 'therapeutic communities', thus making explicit a movement which may have been anticipated in the mutual 'curing' of Mansfield Park and Fanny.

Therapy, however, has also been recognized as a function of culture itself. As Philip Rieff points out:

In general, all cultures have a therapeutic
function, in so far as they are systems of
symbolic integration – whether these systems be
called religious, philosophical, or by any
other name.'[22]

Berger and Luckmann have a related definition of therapy in their book, *The Social Construction of Reality*:

Therapy entails the application of conceptual
machinery to ensure that actual or potential
deviants stay within the institutionalised
definitions of reality.'[23]

But let us suppose that, as Rieff has argued in *The Triumph of the Therapeutic*, the individual consciousness, detached from culture, takes over from 'society' the task of defining reality. Then we have the pattern I have tried to outline in the Edwardian novel, where the well-being of self becomes the absolute, and reality is redefined accordingly. The primary means of survival for the 'post-cultural' self becomes the self's definition of a 'crisis in culture'.

But if 'therapy' can have these two meanings, one welcome and the other unwelcome to the radical, the word 'culture' can have many more. I have been using the word culture in the latter-day sociological sense, and not, for example, in the Arnoldian sense of the arts or 'High Culture'. A particularly suggestive definition for the purposes of this study is that of Cooley, Angell, and Carr:

Culture is the entire accumulation of
artificial objects, conditions, tools,
techniques, ideas, symbols, and behaviour-
patterns peculiar to a group of people,
possessing a certain consistency of its own,
and capable of transmission from one
generation to another. Culture, in other
words, is the sum total of the transmittable
results of living together.[24]

At certain points in history the cultural 'heritage' (as it is known in popular cliché) seems to have become less 'capable of transmission from one generation to another' than at others. A very serious cultural disinheritance occurred, for example, in the late-Victorian period, after the public assimilation of Darwin's *Origin of Species* and after what J. Hillis Miller has called 'The Disappearance of God'[25] from the nineteenth-century universe. With such an uncovering of inexorable process, with such a sudden removal of what Wells calls 'a beginning . . . and an

end'. With such a depletion of 'the sum total of the transmittable results of living together', it is hardly surprising that the
late Victorians came more and more under the domination of
the *fin-de-siècle* myth. Concepts like 'crisis', 'transition', 'decadence', 'renovation', 'sickness', and 'therapy', which have only
recently been fully exposed as functional conventions,[26] seem in
the 1890s partially to have superseded institutionalized 'values'
as the primary means man possessed of making sense of his life.
It is then understandable that *fin-de-siècle* man should seize upon
a new apocalyptic ending and beginning, appointed by the self
perhaps, but also offered conveniently by the calendar, to take
place in the year 1900, the dawn of the twentieth century. The
disquieting intensity and power of that 'naïve' myth in its determination of contemporary patterns of art and science has not
perhaps been fully acknowledged.[27]

A theory of the transition between the late-Victorian and the
modern world (in that limbo which lies between Arnold and
Eliot) ought perhaps to take this hypothesis into consideration:
that after Darwin, and with the lapsing of the seventeenth
century, the Augustan, and the High Victorian 'cultures', conventional 'positive' cultural ordering tended to be replaced by
negative apocalyptic myth – a functional dialectic involving
not only the convention of sickness which made sense of man's
time and place in the 1890s, but also the ensuing convention of
therapy which is pervasive in the Vitalist and health-conscious
Edwardian decade.[28]

This is the background against which George Ponderevo,
Sophia Baines and Soames Forsyte may be seen. The fictional
development of their respective autonomous consciousnesses
from the 'cultures' of varying kinds with which they are initially
associated may be seen as related to the great movement 'beyond culture' which Englishmen (and the Western world)
projected, somewhat prematurely, but perhaps prophetically,
on to the transition through the year 1900. In general (and in
specific reply to Virginia Woolf's 'Mrs Brown' typology) it
might be argued that Wells, Bennett and Galsworthy placed
emphasis upon the possessive and locative aspects of their
characters because the human type they were depicting found
himself, precisely, dispossessed and dislocated. Having defined
culture as in crisis in the 1890s and having claimed sickness of

the self, Englishmen were apparently able in the early years of the twentieth century to consolidate the demands of the self by turning the blame, as it were, on to society. The *fin-de-siècle* myth seems to have been, in this sense, ultimately functional, serving the purposes of human evolution, and exploiting the calendar in the most absurdly simple of ways. The Edwardian 'social' novel is not, therefore, a capitulation to the conditions of social reality, but a revolutionary step towards the creation of the acultural 'Brave New World' which Aldous Huxley satirized into existence in his novel.[29] Wells, Bennett and Galsworthy, in the Edwardian decade, are interested less in environment as such than in therapy for the post-cultural self in crisis.

Only perhaps in our own time, with the emergence of an 'Open Conspiracy' of youth and a world-wide generation gap, has the 'entire accumulation of artificial objects, conditions, tools, techniques, ideas, symbols, and behaviour patterns peculiar to a group of people, possessing a certain consistency of its own' been as incapable as it was at the beginning of this century of 'transmission from one generation to another'. The French, American and Russian revolutions appear to have had specific cultural aims. The aims implicit in the Edwardian revolution are not those of cultural revolution, but involve a moving beyond culture. It is not surprising that the cultural revisionists of the 1920s – Virginia Woolf, T. S. Eliot, Ezra Pound and D. H. Lawrence – reacted so strongly against the Edwardian novel. Nor need it be surprising that the world, having gone beyond 'Modernism', returns with fascination to the predicament of Soames Forsyte.

II

Since this discussion will on occasion depend for its terminology upon Philip Rieff's book, *The Triumph of the Therapeutic*, it is necessary at this point to say something about Rieff's theories. While his work contains much that is alien to the literary mind, he introduces some challenging and disturbing ideas.

Rieff prophesies the gradual emergence of a world which is a global hospital. Unlike most other writers on this subject[30] (who seem to follow the line established by Aldous Huxley in

Brave New World), Rieff thinks that this may not necessarily be a bad thing. 'Christian' culture, as Rieff calls it, is, in his view, very nearly at an end. 'Christian man' is being superseded by 'Psychological man' and the type he calls 'the therapeutic' (when Rieff uses the word 'therapeutic' as a noun he is thinking of 'therapeutic man', the type of the emerging new order). A problem of terminology arises when Rieff calls Christianity itself a therapy of sorts (a therapy, as we have seen, in the Berger and Luckmann sense); but he makes it clear that religion, in his view, is a 'commitment therapy' – that is, a therapy which works by 'committing' the individual to a 'superior communal end'.[31] Various post-Freudian therapies, notably Jung's, Reich's and Lawrence's, have been commitment therapies, offering tempting surrogates for religious faith. But the true, the pure and the triumphant therapy is, for Rieff, Freudian 'analytic' therapy, which is committed to no communal end, is acultural, and is to be the central therapy of the emerging new order. Unfortunately, Rieff is not definite or precise about the ways in which his 'true' therapy can remain finally uncommitted and atheoretical, though it might be argued that his activist methodology *is*, in a sense, his evidence. As Rieff writes:

> In the absence of news about a stable and
> governing order anywhere, theory becomes
> actively concerned with mitigating the daily
> miseries of living rather than with a therapy
> of commitment to some healing doctrine of the
> universe.' (p. 86).

And:

> The transformative cast of theorizing
> unlike the conformative cast, is silent
> about ultimate ends (p. 86).

Rieff does point out that: 'The dialectic of perfection, based on a deprivational mode, is being succeeded by a dialectic of fulfilment, based on the appetitive mode' (pp. 49–50). But it is difficult to imagine the social system which would operate if this 'therapy' really did triumph:

17

> The therapy of all therapies is not to
> attach oneself exclusively to any particular
> therapy, so that no illusion may survive of
> some end beyond an intensely private sense
> of well-being to be generated in the living
> of life itself (p. 261).

Unfortunately, Rieff deliberately dissociates himself from any attempt to discuss social change, so that the dubious reader must be content to analyse – in a Rieffian manner – the 'configurative' information that the total field of the book supplies. A major problem arises over the kind of 'well-being' involved. Such a statement as the following, for example, is difficult at first to accept:

> That a sense of well-being has become the
> end, rather than a by-product of striving
> after some superior communal end, announces
> a fundamental change of focus in the entire
> cast of our culture – towards a human condition
> about which there will be nothing further
> to say in terms of the old style of despair
> and hope (p. 261).

Perhaps a form of 'psychedelic' well-being is indicated, and not the more superficial 'happiness' of *Brave New World* (which does not seem psychologically plausible). It is the sense of well-being that comes, presumably, from adopting James Thurber's fashionable advice: 'Let us not look back in anger, nor forward in fear, but around in awareness.'[32]

Thus if the objection were brought against Rieff's work that it does not take account of the relativity of crisis in a Kermodean manner ('We think of our own crisis as pre-eminent, more worrying, more interesting than other crises'),[33] Rieff might well reply that 'the Triumph of the Therapeutic' would take us beyond 'crisis' to a period of transition which may be ended at any time by our not thinking 'in terms of the old styles of despair and hope'. 'The end' then becomes not imminent, nor immanent,[34] but irrelevant. Rieff's ateleological activism may be the most desperate of defence measures against cultural crisis, but its refusal to worry is entirely in line with James Thurber's remark, and with Frank Kermode's enlightened protests and, incidentally, with Marshall McLuhan's revolutionary passivity.

There is nothing so 'pure' as the Rieffian 'therapy of all therapies' in the overt thinking of Edwardians, but at times the ethic implicit in the novels of Wells, Bennett and Galsworthy is related to Rieffian activism, and Rieff's categories are helpful in drawing distinctions between the variety of therapeutic responses to post-cultural crisis that the Edwardian period has to offer. Rieff's admiration for Freud has also relevance for the turning of the century. Freud showed (at a date corresponding approximately to the year 1900, with the publication of *Die Traumdeutung*) that fears and wishes (responses in a sense to the urgent post-Darwinian question, 'Where will it all end?') have extreme powers of intervention in and disruption of the normal living of life. An activist desire to move beyond the old pervasive grip of 'despair and hope' is therefore a quite natural expedient in the face of a runaway world. The analytic activism Rieff identifies in Freud was not exclusive to Freud in the years before 1900, as John A. Lester points out:

> Activism at the close of the century could,
> in each of its aspects, override all systems,
> faiths, and ultimate principles and, in its
> impulsive resolve, become an end in itself.[35]

The Freudian therapy, as defined by Rieff, is perhaps closer to the non-theoretical work of Wells, Bennett and Galsworthy than critics have cared hitherto to admit. The three writers may have neither heard of nor read Freud before 1910, but Bennett's (1909) para-Freudian injunction is implicit in the organization of their novels:

> The facts of today, which in my unregeneracy,
> I regarded primarily as anxieties, nuisances,
> impediments, I now regard as so much raw
> material from which my brain has to weave a
> tissue that is comely.[36]

Bennett's para-Freudian advice on 'How to Live'[37] may relate to centurial transition in the way that Freud's does. It might be argued that the experience Freud sets out to analyse and cure is the experience of Western man brought under the pressure of post-Darwinian time, living in an ongoing process apparently unresponsive to human control or understanding, living under the constant anxiety of the question, 'Where is it all leading?'. The 'neurotic' reaction to this experience is to indulge wishes and fears so obsessively that the individual becomes 'sick' and abdicates from present time. If one engages in cognitive analysis of the processes whereby one's wishes and fears are being translated into obsessive activity, one has already, Rieff implies, been cured, since cognition involves an active involvement in present time and in 'reality'. In examining the mature works of Wells, Bennett and Galsworthy we shall come to see the relevance of Rieffian phrases like, 'The "end" or "goal" is to keep going' (p. 27) and 'The important thing is to keep going' (p. 41).

It is important, finally, to distinguish in this context between therapy as cultural conditioning and therapy as self-realization. A conflict of therapies has seemed to characterize modern radical works like Saul Bellow's *Herzog*;[38] a Herzogian anti-psychiatry has grown up because the self, seeking a purer, existential therapy, objects to the routine adjustment to the *status quo* that psychotherapy, once institutionalized, has appeared to produce. The therapeutic activism of the Edwardians is not at all propaganda for the *status quo*, but innovates a new order. Theirs is an imperialist realism, in which environment provides a field for action. The 'facts of today', in Bennett's passage, are not to be submitted to. On the contrary, they are 'so much raw material'. Wells's Mr Polly is cured when, after taking active steps to remain faithful to the claims of his own existence, he discovers that man can break 'through the paper walls of everyday circumstances'[39] and that *'Fishbourne wasn't the world'*.[40] Bennett's Sophia forsakes her home-culture and synthesizes a new world in Paris. And Galsworthy's negatively presented therapeutic ideal in the extreme intimacy of the relationship between Irene and Bosinney is specifically subversive of the existing cultural order. True (Rieffian) analysis is as inherently revolutionary, because as soon as it is called into action the self becomes isolated – indeed, 'alienated' – from culture.

While there is a note of oblivious optimism in the three paragraphs quoted at the beginning of this chapter, the three

Edwardians had been writing very differently as apprentices in the 1890s. For in that decade, as I have suggested, the conditions of cultural crisis were being defined, and a convention of 'ontological insecurity' spread across the Western world. The spectre that was haunting Europe might be thought of as the image of man's offended existence establishing its claims to therapy. It might further be argued that the work of Marx and Freud springs from the same predicament of the anxious self confronted with an unknown future. In 1895, for example, Wells published *The Time Machine*. It contained phrases typical of the period, such as 'I was oppressed with perplexity and doubt' and 'I had a feeling of intense fear'.[41] Bennett in the 1890s was writing: 'He had been born in the shadow, and after a fitful struggle towards emergence, into the shadow he must again retire. Fate was his enemy.'[42] In the 1890s, Galsworthy wrote not of Forsytes, but of drug-addicts, white men of tainted blood running amok in the tropics, outcasts, black sheep of the family, and the liberating deaths of lovers frustrated by reality.[43] An attempt has been made by Bernard Bergonzi to explain the special quality of Wells's pre-1900 fiction in terms of its 'mythic' character,[44] but the sudden transition in Wells's fiction from 'myth' to 'comic realism' is still difficult to understand. Such a transition can be more adequately apprehended, and the teasingly definite quality of the central Edwardian novels can be more usefully placed, if the three novelists are taken together, and if their strikingly parallel developments from *fin de sièclism* to Edwardianism are traced. I believe it is impossible to understand the 'Mrs Brown' element in Edwardian fiction without seeking its origins in the latter part of the nineteenth century, in what might be called the Darwinian aftermath. And the Darwinian aftermath, fine-sounding phrase as it is, will describe nothing unless it is placed in calendar time. It may be that not only have we managed to 'project our existential anxieties on to history',[45] but that, by exploiting the still potent myth of calendar apocalypse and the turning of a synthetically 'crucial' century, we found impetus in the first years of the twentieth century for new therapies and the renewed sense of a beginning. The description that Rieff applies to Lawrence might equally apply to any one of Wells, Bennett and Galsworthy if that 'triumvirate' is seen in terms of its *fin de sièclism*:

. . . . Lawrence's isolation was in a measure
self-imposed. As an isolate, desperately
seeking community, he self-consciously
transformed himself into an uncompromising
critic of our culture. Underneath the dead
levels of conformity which Lawrence recognised
decades before their knowledge became common-
place, he detected in himself the panic of
isolation that grips modern men, too much bound
up in themselves, even in the act of love (p. 192).

III

To claim that the Edwardians were, *en masse*, suddenly 'happy'
after the death of Queen Victoria and after the highly distressing
Boer War would hardly be accurate. But they were at least
beginning to be able to define themselves objectively in terms of
crisis by looking 'from the outside' at themselves and society.[46]
One might even say that by living through the turn of the
century they had 'learned to live with' crisis. The fantastic
escapes into inner alternative worlds that characterize the
literature of the 1890s in England seem to have prepared the
way for the activist creation of an improved society in the
twentieth century. And, indeed, the history of English society in
this century has largely been one of the gradual remedying of
social 'ills'. The Welfare State may be traced back to the last
years of Edward's reign.

These, then, are my themes. I see the 1890s' fiction of Wells,
Bennett and Galsworthy as an art to be defined most accurately
in terms of its rendering of the symptomatic nature of subjective
experience. It is a literature of offence. And I see the central
Edwardian fiction as an art characterized by its overt interest in
therapy – not simply therapy in the shape of social reform, but a
transference from teleologies to direct remedial action undertaken on behalf of the self. This later fiction might be called a
literature of exhortation.

One further concept is essential to my case. This is the idea
that fantasy (one of the two major modes of *fin-de-siècle* fiction),
while remaining symptomatic of a 'sick' refusal to accept or

make reality, can act in a way that is ultimately therapeutic. The indulged dreaming of Wells in the science-fiction romances, the fear-fantasies of Bennett's *The Curse of Love*[47] and *A Man from the North*,[48] and the romantic-comedy wishful thinking of *Jocelyn*[49] – such fantasy is not only indirectly therapeutic in that by being symptomatic it invites cure, but also directly curative. It is useful in understanding the developments of each of the three writers if we take note of Heinz Hartmann's comment on 'the positive value of the detour through fantasy':[50]

> . . . though fantasy always implies an
> initial turning away from a real situation,
> it can also be a preparation for reality
> and may lead to a better mastery of it.
> Fantasy may fulfill a synthetic function by
> provisionally connecting our needs and goals
> with possible ways of realizing them. It is
> well known that there are fantasies which,
> while they remove man from external reality,
> open up for him his internal reality.[51]

The post-1900 fiction of Wells, Bennett and Galsworthy is still perhaps responding too directly to sensed crisis to be 'great art' or even 'art' at all. Virginia Woolf said that after reading their books she felt that she ought to finish the process by joining a society or writing a cheque; and perhaps the extreme sanity of their reverence for actuality, for chosen objects, and for real life was positively destructive of their art. But the adaptive process which employed, as it were, the dialectical transition from art for art's sake to art for life's sake was necessary, I would argue, before the great movement for cultural revisionism became possible in the 1920s.

2

Fiction and the *fin de siècle*

'It is clear that if we must give up the Divine scheme of redress as a dream, redress is an obligation returned upon ourselves. All will not be well in another world: all must be put right in this world or nowhere and never'[1] – an insight that became a challenge after 1900, was in the pre-Edwardian years the source of much anxiety. The new responsibility lay heavily upon post-Darwinian man, who seems, in an engagingly direct way, to have felt the *fin du globe* to be the next logical step.[2] Wells's novel, *The Invisible Man*, for example, is an extremely suggestive image of man in post-cultural crisis, of man attempting to assume a godlike role. Having burnt his house and become free from cultural residues (in the form of his discarded clothes), Griffin becomes socially invisible. He has opted out of the social dimension; as he walks naked in the winter streets he finds himself 'out in the cold', inhabiting what we might now see as a post-cultural limbo. He has changed into dissociated existence, a prototype for existential man. Griffin's attempt at redress fails, and the novel becomes the projection of fears of isolation, alienation and loss of identity. At one suggestive point Kemp confronts the invisible Griffin, and sees only a bandage:

'I'm confused,' said Kemp. 'My brain is rioting. What has this to do with Griffin?'
'I *am* Griffin'.

Kemp thought. 'It's horrible', he said. 'But what devilry must happen to make a man invisible?'

'It's no devilry. It's a process, sane and intelligible enough ——'

'It's really horrible!' said Kemp. 'How on earth——?'

'It's horrible enough. But I'm wounded and in pain, and tired. . . . Great God! Kemp, you are a man. Take it steady. Give me some food and drink, and let me sit down here'.

Kemp stared at the bandage as it moved across the room. . . .[3]

The normal social process has been abolished; Griffin presents himself to Kemp as needing to enter into 'therapeutic community' with him: '"I'm wounded and in pain, and tired. . . . Great God! Kemp, you are a man. Take it steady. Give me some food and drink, and let me sit down here."' Griffin is giving Kemp the opportunity to humanize himself ('you are a man'). What he seems to be asking for is a kind of existential recognition ('"I *am* Griffin"'), free of societal conditioning. He is demanding in effect a more direct interpersonal application of Kemp's 'social instincts', and is forced into identifying himself in terms of crisis, in terms of symptoms which are tantalizingly difficult to demonstrate. Griffin is forced to *tell* Kemp about his wounds, his pain and his fatigue, just as *fin-de-siècle* man seems to have been urgently in need of expressing his intangible sickness. When Griffin puts his clothes on in an attempt to resocialize himself, it is too late: he is socially hollow. His loss of dimensionality and his 'search for authentic selfhood' may be related to J. Hillis Miller's general definition of post-Darwinian crisis:

When God is annihilated, at the same time man annihilates himself and annihilates also the world around him. He annihilates them in the sense of hollowing them out, emptying them of any substantial presence. When the gods 'came to nothing', as Wallace Stevens puts it, we 'shared likewise this experience of annihilation'. Human subjectivity comes more and more to be experienced

as a lack, as a devouring emptiness, as an un-
assuageable hunger for some lost plenitude of being.
At the same time, the external world is also emptied,
and man has, as Nietzsche says, the sense of
'straying through an infinite nothingness', the
sense of being 'breathed on by empty space'.

This evacuation of man's nature and of external
nature is associated with an additional transformation of man's sense of himself. To define
man as a lack, as a hunger for fulfillment, is to
define him as will, as a spontaneous energy of
volition which reaches out in longing to sub-
stantiate itself by the assimilation of something
outside itself. When God vanishes, man turns to
interpersonal relations as the only remaining arena
of the search for authentic selfhood. Only in his
fellow men can he find any longer a presence
in the world which might replace the lost
divine presence.[4]

When Griffin wears his clothes they are absurdly empty to the
eye; one remembers Havelock Ellis's insistence that we need 'to
put a living soul in the clothed body'.[5]

Griffin is activist enough, with 'a spontaneous energy of
volition', but in the *fin-de-siècle milieu* his step beyond culture
must result in the end of his world. Wells's romance, *The War of
the Worlds*,[6] might be interpreted as another image of the
attempt to synthesize a world that has lost culture. The Martians may reflect Wells's sense of an emerging new order which
seems to throw the older cultural organization of England into
chaos. The impersonal absoluteness of the Martians, as they
stride across the English countryside in their high machines, is
contrasted with the parochial, 'cultural' mode of villages in the
South of England. Before 1900, however, the operation of a
kind of 'Icarus complex' seems to have prevented these fictional
scientific rebellions from achieving their object. Griffin perishes
and the Martians are attacked by a fatal germ.

Bennett's first novel, *A Man from the North*, presents a similar
pattern of post-cultural crisis, as its title suggests. It shows the
hero, who has suffered cultural parturition, beginning to define

himself as suffering malady and as existentially deprived. Galsworthy's first novel, *Jocelyn*, depicts two selves in post-cultural
crisis. Only at the very last moment of the novel do they find the
remedy in a mutual curing of their own fevered consciousnesses,
in a kind of erotic reunion with the cosmos. At this stage of his
career, Galsworthy's erotic remedy is as much the mere projection of wishes as Wells's *The Invisible Man* is the projection of
fears, and the happy ending is very much a coda to the main
body of the novel, which describes protracted crisis.

When, in fact, we think of the important novels of the
1890s – and there are not many of them – we think above all
perhaps of novels whose predominant theme is personal predicament, the sense of crisis in the life of isolated and alienated
individuals: James's *The Tragic Muse* (1890), *The Spoils of
Poynton* (1897), *What Maisie Knew* (1897), and *The Awkward Age*
(1899); Conrad's *Almayer's Folly* (1895) and *An Outcast of the
Islands* (1896); Hardy's *Tess of the D'Urbervilles* (1892) and *Jude
the Obscure* (1895); the novels of Gissing and Moore; Oscar
Wilde's *The Picture of Dorian Gray* (1891). In these and other
novels of the period there seems to lie a curse on man, a sense
that 'Fate was his enemy'.[7] The obscure threat of malignant
evil in *The Turn of the Screw* (1898) typifies a mood which was
common to 'realism' and 'fantasy' alike.[8]

One technical outcome of this mood seems to have been the
fact that the novels of the 1890s are often hardly novels at all.
The *nouvelle* seems to have become as important a form as the
novel, and to have influenced the form of works long enough to
be properly called novels. But what the novel lost in centrality
in the period (with Hardy and Meredith fading out after 1895,
and James for the time being moving towards other forms), the
short story gained. What emerged in the serious novels as protracted negation and greyness was only the tip of the fictional
iceberg. For the massive centre of fiction, the submerged bulk,
was made up of a wide range of quasi-daydreams and, more
significantly in so far as literature is concerned, short stories.
What writers could not assert consciously, as it were, in the
extended and shaped form of the novel, they were able to express
in short stories which made fewer demands on their sense of
reality or their sense of sequence. Freud's tendency, never
adequately argued in his work, to relegate art to mere

27

daydream or wishful thinking, should therefore be understood against a European 1890s background: the distinctive stories of the period do indeed appear blindly or half-blindly to raise unconscious wishes and fears, translating them 'half-sublimated' into the material of fiction. There is very little 'neutral' realism in the fiction of the 1890s. Even Kipling, whose work is not so palpably the projection of anxieties as Gissing's and Moore's, seems often simply to be crudely sublimating his desire for 'the pleasure of confederacy'[9] in face of what C. S. Lewis called 'that bleak misgiving – almost that Nothingness – in the background'.[10]

The short story, in its very brevity and fragmentary, disengaged nature, seems to have been suited to the predominant 1890s theme of crisis; but the literary achievement is of a limited kind. It is almost as if the epistemological crisis of the late-Victorian period (for which Pragmatism came as a remedy) was such as to permit only an 'agnostic mode' in literature. The writer of fiction in the 1890s seems to have been equipped only to depict the process of life in fragments and 'subjectively'. He was as yet technically unable to organize the forces of disruption within himself and within society. The finely analytical extended fiction of the Edwardian period was as yet unattainable. In terms of the jargon of our day, contemporary cultural anxiety seems to have inhibited the full flowering of a great and positive art; *The Picture of Dorian Gray* and *The Nigger of the 'Narcissus'* and *The Time Machine* and *The Turn of the Screw* all suffer from a certain obsessional quality, a disinclination to render a full sense of cognitive possession.

In essence the short story genre of the 1890s involves a definite movement towards 'abstraction', and there is little evidence that short-story writers were other than pleased with the new form and confident in its use.[11] But the short story bears the same relation to Edwardian fiction as *Art Nouveau* bears to Analytical Cubism in the visual arts. The European transition from an *Art Nouveau* cult of line (which died out very shortly after the year 1900[12]) to a Cubist analytic mode (appearing around the year 1907) shows a cognitive maturation which is parallel to contemporary developments in English (and Continental) fiction.

The short story need not, of course, reflect 'agnosticism' in the author (though it might be argued that exponents of the form have often been those writers most urgently threatened with 'Nothingness'); Bennett's 1895 story, 'A Letter Home',[13] while itself exhibiting *fin-de-siècle Angst*, is incongruous, for example, in the context of the other (post-1900) stories in his *Tales of the Five Towns* (1905). It may still be true, however, that the special value attributed to the short story in the 1890s, and the special use made of the form in that period, may relate to cultural crisis. If Max Nordau[14] represents a 'scientific-therapeutic' objectivism to be found in the *fin de siècle*, the short stories may have represented a way of rendering in art the converse principle, the 'aesthetic-symptomatic'.

Not only do short stories, in focusing upon a small section of life, thus appear to be producing material 'symptomatic' of a larger, and for the time being undefined, reality, but the aesthetic role of actual pathological symptoms seems to have been widely refined in the 1890s to a Wildean extremism. It may seem an unfamiliar association, this linking of a morbid Aestheticism with Wells, Bennett and Galsworthy, but it is centrally applicable to their *fin-de-siècle* work, and helps to explain the obsessional, truncated quality of their pre-1900 novels.

Wells himself bears witness to the pervasiveness of the short-story movement in the 1890s, and makes a specific contrast with the post-1900 decade:

> The nineties was a good and stimulating period
> for a short-story writer. . . . Short stories broke
> out everywhere. Kipling was writing short
> stories; Barrie, Stevenson, Frank Harris; Max
> Beerbohm wrote at least one perfect one, 'The
> Happy Hypocrite'; Henry James pursued his
> wonderful and inimitable bent; and among other
> names that occur to me, like a mixed handful
> of jewels drawn from a bag, are George Street,
> Morley Roberts, George Gissing, Ella d'Arcy,
> Murray Gilchrist, E. Nesbit, Stephen Crane,
> Joseph Conrad, Edwin Pugh, Jerome K. Jerome,
> Kenneth Graham [*sic*], Arthur Morrison, Marriott
> Watson, George Moore, Grant Allen, George Egerton,

Henry Harland, Pett Ridge, W. W. Jacobs (who
alone seems inexhaustible). I dare say I could
recall as many more names with a little effort.
I may be succumbing to the influence of middle
age, but I do not think that the present decade
1900–1910 can produce any parallel to this list,
or what is more remarkable, that the later
achievements in this field of any of the survivors
from that time, with the sole exception of Joseph
Conrad, can compare with the work they did before
1900. It seems to me this outburst of short
stories came not only as a phase in literary
development, but also as a phase in the development of the individual writers concerned.[15]

Henry James's place in Wells's list is interesting, for, as Leon
Edel points out:

There was some . . . allegory of the self in
Henry James's work of the late 1890s.
Whether we call this a 'crisis of identity'
or a 'middle age crisis' the particular
sequence of stories he created reveals the
benign workings of the imagination – in
this instance in chronological fashion –
that moved from direct confrontation of
disaster through the death of the spirit
and to its re-emergence and growth in the familiar
shapes of the past. History may yet
record that as Proust discovered memory and
association at the very time that Freud was
asking his patients to 'associate' and
remember, so Henry James recorded acts of
insight into himself, in terms of childhood
memories, in an analogous way to Freud.[16]

Henry James also had a financial motive for turning to short
stories and the drama, and no doubt in each case the 'outburst
of short stories' came as a 'phase in the development of the
individual writers concerned', but perhaps the sudden flowering
of the short story has also some general connection with the

psychic condition of late-Victorian England. Bernard Muddiman wrote that '. . . . for the first time in English literature, the
short story came into its own',[17] but Wells is more suggestive as
to the psychic process involved:

> There was a time when life bubbled with short
> stories; they were always coming to the surface
> of my mind, and it is no deliberate change of
> will that has thus restricted my production.
> It is rather, I think, a diversion of
> attention to more sustained and more exacting
> forms.[18]

Such a passage would seem to support the idea that short stories
permitted more direct access than novels to the unconscious
interests of *fin-de-siècle* man. Max Nordau considered that it was
a mark of the contemporary melancholic 'to surrender himself
to the perpetual obfuscation of a boundless, aimless, and shoreless stream of fugitive ideas . . . capricious, and, as a rule, purely
mechanical association of ideas and succession of images'.[19]
Wells seems to have had a more constructive view of the relation
between the stream of consciousness and the unconscious mind:

> Mr. Hind's indicating finger had shown me an
> amusing possibility of the mind. I found that,
> taking almost anything as a starting point and
> letting my thoughts play about it, there would
> presently come out of the darkness, in a manner
> quite inexplicable, some absurd or vivid little
> nucleus. Little men in canoes upon sunlit oceans
> would come floating out of nothingness, incubating
> the eggs of prehistoric monsters unawares; violent
> conflicts would break out amidst the flower-beds
> of suburban gardens; I would discover I was
> peering into remote and mysterious worlds ruled
> by an order logical indeed but other than our
> common sanity.[20]

It may not be 'coincidence' that Freud's 'peering into remote
and mysterious worlds ruled by an order logical indeed but
other than our common sanity' should also have begun in the
1890s. By 'surrendering himself' to subjectivity, Wells has

recourse to a new experience of reality; he presents his dreams or stories both as 'symptomatic' (as 'aesthetic-symptomatic' material), and as having the status of fictional paradigms. A Freudian subject seems to submit himself to a similar process of 'mythologization'.

It might be argued that the associative activism of Wells the short-story writer and Freud the psychoanalyst relates to a post-Darwinian breakdown in man's sense of a sequential universe. For *fin-de-siècle* man, disinherited and in crisis, sequential logic fails:

One epoch of history is unmistakably in
its decline, another is announcing its approach.
There is a sound of rending in every tradition,
and it is as though the morrow would not link
itself with today.[21]

A Hamletian associative logic takes the place of linear organization; 'simultaneity', puns, word-play and the symbols derived from the stream of consciousness seem to offer a magic remedy for the lack of linear relations.[22] Writers of the *fin de siècle* seem to be offering a variety of responses to the newly non-sequential universe: Yeats and Hopkins move towards techniques for the assimilation of simultaneity. The lapsing of the novel may reflect a contemporary inability to deal with seriality, the sequential novel being replaced by the quasi-instantaneous stories which Wells describes. An exploratory explanation of the transition from the production of short stories in the 1890s to 'more exacting forms' in the 1900s might involve a recognition of the power of the pivotal year 1900 (as focused in contemporary myth) to influence fictional forms. Cultural crisis in the 1890s set the individual under the pressure of an ending; in terms of fictional form, novelists might have used Hermione's phrase from *The Winter's Tale*: 'I am now unhappy . . . more/ Than history can pattern.'[23] In other words, the cultural milieu which partly derived from the sense of an uncontrollable and imminent ending for European culture could hardly be expected to result in extended novelistic 'histories' in which plot is designed specifically to control the movement towards an ending designed to be emotionally satisfying. A long and well-constructed novel surely represents, in the cultural matrix from which it emerges, the ability to control time, to define a sense of 'where it is all going to end'. Such a confidence in the face of the future was unthinkable for the English writers of the 1890s. And despite certain superficial resemblances between the Edwardian novel and the Victorian, the truly sequential novel (as in Jane Austen or Charles Dickens) was perhaps no longer possible after the turn of the century.

This alienation from the novel cannot convincingly be described theoretically; we may turn, then, to Henry James's short story, 'The Middle Years', which is an indirect comment on the difficulty of writing long works of fiction in the 1890s. Dencombe is a novelist, ill and near his death. He has come to Bournemouth for a cure, and has brought with him a copy of his last novel, *The Middle Years*, which he has not yet opened:

> Though such promptitude on the part of his
> publishers was rare he was already able to draw
> from its wrapper his 'latest', perhaps his
> last. The cover of "The Middle Years" was duly
> meretricious, the smell of the fresh pages the
> very odour of sanctity; but for the moment he
> went no further – he had become conscious of a
> strange alienation. He had forgotten what his
> book was about. Had the assault of his old
> ailment, which he had so fallaciously come to
> Bournemouth to ward off, interposed utter
> blankness as to what had preceded it? He had
> finished the revision of proof before quitting
> London, but his subsequent fortnight in bed had
> passed the sponge over colour. He couldn't
> have chanted to himself a single sentence,
> couldn't have turned with curiosity or
> confidence to any particular page. His
> subject had already gone from him, leaving
> scarcely a superstition behind. He uttered
> a low moan as he breathed the chill of this
> dark void, so desperately it seemed to represent
> the completion of a sinister process.
> The tears filled his mild eyes; something

33

precious had passed away. This was the pang
that had been sharpest during the last few
years – the sense of ebbing time, of shrinking
opportunity; and now he felt not so much that
his last chance was going as that it was gone
indeed. He had done all he should ever do,
and yet had not done what he wanted. This was
the laceration – that practically his career
was over: it was as violent as a rough hand
at his throat. He rose from his seat nervously –
a creature hunted by a dread; then he fell back
in his weakness and nervously opened his book.[24]

Certain key phrases take us to the heart of the *fin-de-siècle* experience: 'conscious of a strange alienation'; 'this dark void';
'the completion of a sinister process'; 'the sense of ebbing time';
'a creature hunted by a dread'. The phrase which, above all,
seems to epitomize the predicament of post-cultural man is:
'He had forgotten what his book was about', but in a less general
and speculative way one might choose to define such an utterance and such 'a strange alienation' from the novel, as similar to
James's own movement towards the short story in this period. In
such a writer's predicament a novel might be said to represent
too great an effort of temporal extension; and an imaginative
poverty, the poverty of the James passage here, seems to have
manifested itself in the fiction of the period, which contains
many creatures 'hunted by a dread'. Unless writers like James
are seen in their 1890s setting, however, the great fiction of the
Edwardian decade will be only half understood. The great
technical triumph of *The Ambassadors* and *Nostromo* is not fully
to be appreciated if the relation of these novels to James's
earlier stories and Conrad's *nouvelles* is ignored.

II

If this analysis of the fictional media of the 1890s has some truth
in it, the psychic derangement of the period must have been
drastic. It might be argued that the *fin-de-siècle* type of 1890s
fiction, whether the sick hero of James's tale or the downtrodden

girls of the Cockney School, is only the most palpable feature of a pervasive convention of 'ailment' and 'alienation'. Max Nordau's contemporary account in *Degeneration* (London, 1895) represents a useful introduction to the problem of 1890s hypochondria.

Bernard Bergonzi has already demonstrated the relevance of Nordau to the early work of Wells,[25] but does not in his book pursue the psychological implications of *Degeneration* (being concerned rather with social decay and the idea of the *fin du globe*); but Nordau's book is in effect a thorough-going psychiatric study of the 'excesses' of the period, set in a clinical framework, viz. a schematic division of the book into sections corresponding to an account of symptoms, diagnosis, aetiology, prognosis and indicated therapeutic action. The gist of Nordau's case is that

> the physician, especially if he have devoted
> himself to the special study of nervous and
> mental maladies, recognises at a glance, in
> the *fin-de-siècle* disposition, in the tendencies
> of contemporary art and poetry, in the life and
> conduct of the men who write mystic, symbolic and
> 'decadent' works, and the attitudes taken by
> their admirers, in the taste and aesthetic instincts
> of fashionable society, the confluence
> of two well-defined conditions of disease,
> with which he is quite familiar, viz. degeneration
> (degeneracy) and hysteria, of which the minor
> stages are designated as neurasthenic.[26]

Degeneration is not a book only recently discovered and unknown at the time of publication. On the contrary, sales in 1895 were very high indeed, perhaps because of the intense public interest in the Wilde trial. Wildean Aestheticism, then, was not at all an aspect of an esoteric and publicly unknown cult, but seems to have focused public attention in general upon a fundamental preoccupation of the age. Freud's attempts to define and cure hysteria in the 1890s were contemporaneous with a widespread European discussion of the prevalence of the disease in 'modern life'. And it is no exaggeration to say that most short stories and novels of the period either diagnose or exhibit symptoms of what one might call, in a general way, psychic 'degeneration'. Certainly those of Wells, Bennett and Galsworthy are committed to such an interest, as we shall see in Chapters 3, 4 and 5.

Our latter-day approach to the Nordauesque position might be to identify it with Berger and Luckmann's 'therapy': 'Therapy entails the application of conceptual machinery to ensure that actual or potential deviants stay within the institutionalised definitions of reality'.[27] Wylie Sypher has attempted an explanation of the phenomenon whereby post-Romantic man turns to therapy instead of to the isolation and self-assertion of the Romantic mode:

> Meanwhile along with this consolidation of
> the majority there came a new anxiety, for if
> one is to conform, then one must be assured he
> is normal. Thus the need for freedom is
> replaced by a need for therapy.[28]

And in another place:

> What began as romantic assertion of the
> self – of a free, wilful, often isolated
> self – changed into a mistrust of the self,
> a need for communion, adjustment, or therapy.[29]

This is most useful for an understanding of the 'medicalization' of society which took place between 1890 and 1910, but what Sypher does not apparently see is that the declaration of sickness can work both for the conforming self and for the existential self. The conformist self welcomes societal commitment therapies, and is pleased to 'adjust' to society. The existential self promotes therapies for existence, therapies which conflict with and render obsolete the social conditioning of potential Brave New World systems. Thus although a societal health-norm is satisfyingly definable in pseudo-positivist terms in Nordau, we have already traced in the existentialist *The Invisible Man* the process wherein,

> What began as romantic assertion of the
> self – of a free, wilful, often isolated self –
> changed into a mistrust of the self, a need
> for communion, adjustment, or therapy,

and have noted that in Griffin's career 'the need for freedom is replaced by a need for therapy'. And this new order of 'communion, adjustment, or therapy' can be, as we have seen, not a dehumanization, but on the contrary a challenge for the release of humanity in a post-cultural setting, a 'readjustment' of the grounds of freedom. Griffin claims, 'I *am* Griffin', and he authenticates Kemp by providing him with an interpersonal role: 'You are a man'.

Paradoxically, Nordau's positivism acts ultimately in such a way as indirectly to consolidate the rebelling self; indeed, the Wildean rebellion, in its cultivation of hyper-sensitivity and 'beautiful sickness', would have been meaningless unless defined by the hostile criteria of 'scientific-therapeutic' writers like Nordau. The symbiotic relation between two modes, the 'scientific-therapeutic' and the 'aesthetic-symptomatic', helped to make sense of life in the *fin de siècle*.

Nordau was not alone in this Darwinization of the aesthete into degenerate. William James also stressed the dangers of artistic over-indulgence (in a quite Platonic way) in his *Principles of Psychology*:[30]

> There is no more contemptible type of human
> character than that of the nerveless senti-
> mentalist and dreamer, who spends his life in a
> weltering sun of sensibility and emotion, but
> who never does a manly concrete deed.

And James goes on to stress that the audience's participation may equally become pathogenic:

> The habit of excessive novel-reading and
> theatre-going . . .
>   Even the habit of excessive indulgence in
> music . . . has probably a relaxing effect upon the
> character. One becomes filled with emotions
> which habitually pass without prompting to any
> deed, and so the inertly sentimental condition is
> kept up.[31]

Despite his defence of 'The Sanity of Art',[32] Bernard Shaw's classic plea for 'puritanism' in the arts contains the charge that 'Ten years of cheap reading have changed the English from the most solid nation in Europe to the most theatrical and hysterical'.[33]

Because Nordau's psychology is firmly pre-Freudian, intent upon categorizing mental phenomena as functions of primary neurological processes, his aetiology of the *fin-de-siècle* 'sickness' is consequently limited and impaired, and its limitations again tend, in this respect, to reflect those of the positivist attitude of the 'scientist-therapist'. The most sophisticated part of his account of the sources of malady is framed in terms of the inability of the nervous system to assimilate the manifold stimulations provided by modern life. Works of an equivalent temper had been appearing since the beginning of the century and even before, but although Nordau's may not be an entirely invalid conclusion, standing alone it has limited powers of effective application to actual events and to historical processes. Nordau refuses to endow aberrational mental phenomena with a meaning beyond the merely biological; his assignation of mental causation is physiological, and neurological, and always directed towards the environmental shortcomings of modern civilization in so far as they affect the individual physically. Physiologically, modern man has suffered from 'organic impurities',[34] overcrowding, fatigue, and artificial stimulants, such as tobacco and alcohol. Neurologically, he has had to endure over-stimulation of the nervous system in urbanized industrial culture, and the oppressive excitements of mass communications of which Nordau writes:

> All these activities . . . even the simplest,
> involve an effort of the nervous system, and
> a wearing of tissue. Every line we read or
> write, every human face we see, every conver-
> sation we carry on, every scene we perceive
> through the window of the flying express, sets
> in activity our sensory nerves and our brain
> centres.[35]

It is clear from passages like this that Nordau's book itself has elements of hysteria in it. Nordau seems actively to have been contributing to the promotion of a universal hypochondria, a view of 'modern life' which, by the last years of the nineteenth century, had achieved the status of popular convention. Great communal solidity, however, was implicit in such a mood, and in the wide advertising of patent medicines which distinguishes the late-Victorian 'medicalization' of society. Wells's suspicion of 'Tono-Bungay' should be seen in the light of this widespread Nordauesque reaction against the aberrational self. The panacea 'Tono-Bungay' is in a sense a fraudulent surrogate for 'communion', and its therapy is in direct conflict with the more closely existential, activist therapy which is recommended at the end of Wells's novel. The absurdity of Nordau's position is only fully revealed when, for example, he claims that nystagmus or 'trembling of the eyeball'[36] is *invariably* to be found in 'impressionists'[37] (or those, in other words, whom Nordau calls, scornfully, 'stipplers', 'mosaists', 'papilloteurs' and 'quiverers').[38]

Pater, however, had already established the epistemological grounds for impressionism, and such an attitude must be confronted when one begins to consider what I have called the 'aesthetic-symptomatic' mode in late-Victorian England:

> At first sight experience seems to bury us
> under a flood of external objects, pressing upon
> us with a sharp and importunate reality, calling
> us out of ourselves in a thousand forms of action.
> But when reflexion begins to play upon those objects
> they are dissipated under its influence; the
> cohesive force seems suspended like some trick of
> magic; each object is loosed into a group of
> impressions – colour, odour, texture – in the
> mind of the observer. And if we continue to
> dwell in thought on this world, not of objects
> in the solidity with which language invests them,
> but of impressions, unstable, flickering, incon-
> sistent, which burn and are extinguished with our
> consciousness of them, it contracts still further:
> the whole scope of observation is dwarfed into the
> narrow chamber of the individual mind. Experience,
> already reduced to a group of impressions, is
> ringed round for each one of us by that thick wall
> of personality through which no real voice has ever
> pierced on its way to us, or from us to that which
> we can only conjecture to be without. Every one

of these impressions is the impression of the
individual in his own isolation, each mind keeping
as a solitary prisoner its own dream of a world.[39]

This, Pater's view, written in 1868, foreshadows F. H.
Bradley's concept of the individual as opaque sphere, quoted by
T. S. Eliot in his notes to *The Waste Land*:[40]

My external sensations are no less private
to myself than are my thoughts or my feelings.
In either case my experience falls within my
own circle, a circle closed on the outside;
and, with all its elements alike, every sphere
is opaque to the others which surround it. . . .
In brief, regarded as an existence which
appears in a soul, the whole world for each is
peculiar and private to that soul.[41]

Pater's protestations of inescapable subjectivity, of real life as
dream-experience, of isolation and of a potentially irremediable
alienation, are both philosophically doctrinaire and at the same
time recognition in a sense of malady. Nordau, on the other
hand, can see no purely epistemological sanction for the Hamletian 'incapacity for action' and 'inane reverie'[42] of what he
calls the 'melancholic':[43]

He allows his brain-centres to produce semi-
lucid, nebulously blurred ideas and inchoate
thoughts, and to surrender himself to the
perpetual obfuscation of a boundless, aimless,
and shoreless stream of fugitive ideas . . .
capricious, and, as a rule, purely mechanical
associations of ideas and succession of images.
. . . He rejoices in the faculty of imagination,
which he contrasts with the insipidity of the
Philistine.[44]

This unwitting rejection of the very 'stream of consciousness'
that Freud was contemporaneously exploiting represents one
pole of the *fin-de-siècle* polarization of the 'objective' and 'subjective' attitudes to life. The year 1895 focused attention on the
late-Victorian schizophrenia in its most extreme form; the

Wildean mode was in a sense on trial with Wilde himself, and the reaction of society against the threat of 'subjectivity' was epitomized by Nordau's ultra-'objective' book. Both extremes must seem to us, perhaps, as undesirable, and genuinely indicative of the 'unhealthiness' of late-Victorian 'culture'. And yet the predicament is still with us, if not in the 'Two Cultures', then certainly in the kind of experience Lawrence refers to in his essay, 'John Galsworthy':

> It seems to me that when the human being
> becomes too much divided between his subjective
> and objective consciousness, at last something
> splits in him and he becomes a social being.
> When he becomes too much aware of objective
> reality, and of his own isolation in the face
> of objective reality, the core of his identity
> splits, his nucleus collapses, his innocence
> or his naiveté perishes, and he becomes only a
> subjective-objective reality, a divided thing
> hinged together, but not strictly individual.[45]

It seems hard on Galsworthy to accuse him of depicting such characters when he had (together with Wells and Bennett) been confronting this very problem in an intense form in his pre-1900 fiction, and had evolved a fictional mode for rendering such a predicament in a vivid way during the Edwardian years. And it seems unfair also because it is so clearly owing to work like Galsworthy's that Lawrence was able to see more clearly the grounds of his discontent. In general it might be argued that such a 'schizophrenia', such a 'splitting' of the 'core of identity', was a pre-requisite for the Lawrentian 'therapy' which has the source of its impetus in the Edwardian years. There is an article by Edward Carpenter, significantly entitled 'Civilisation: Its Cause and Cure',[46] which is as much the basis of Wells's, Bennett's and Galsworthy's thought as the basis of Lawrence's:

> . . . during the civilization-period, the body
> being systematically wrapped in clothes, the
> *head* alone represents man – the little finnikin
> intellectual self-conscious man in contra-
> distinction to the cosmical man represented by

the entirety of the bodily organs. The body
has to be delivered from its swarthings in
order that the cosmical consciousness may once
more reside in the human breast.

Where the cosmic self is, there is no more
self-consciousness.[47]

Nordau makes adaptation to the *status quo* a rigorous discipline
never shared by the three Edwardians:

The degenerate is incapable of adapting
himself to existing circumstances. This
incapacity, indeed, is an indication of morbid
variation in every species, and probably a
primary cause of their sudden extinction. He
therefore rebels against conditions and views
of things which he necessarily feels to be
painful, chiefly because they impose upon him
the duty of self-control, of which he is incapable on account of his organic weakness of
will. Thus he becomes an improver of the world,
and devises plans for making mankind happy. . . .[48]

Bennett's Edwardian injunctions to the ordinary man, for example, may sound similar in temper, but they have proceeded
to a para-Freudian therapy which in effect resolves the *fin-de-
siècle* conflict of 'objective' and 'subjective':

This day is before me. The circumstances
of this day are my environment; they are the
material out of which, by means of my brain,
I have to live and be happy and to refrain
from causing unhappiness in other people. It
is the business of my brain to make use of
this material.

The facts of today, which in my unregeneracy
I regarded primarily as anxieties, nuisances,
impediments, I now regard as so much raw material
from which my brain has to weave a tissue of life
that is comely.[49]

Such a phenomenological 'Utopianization' of everyday reality
is the primary mode in the fiction of Wells, Bennett and Gals-

worthy; the degree to which the 'raw material' of life was felt to be susceptible to cognitive recreation increased as their careers progressed. While 'compromise' was the general mood of the pre-1900 fiction, the fiction of the years between 1905 and 1910 increasingly explores the potential of the self's ability to become 'cosmic' by a process of knowing which takes the individual beyond pathological self-consciousness, and heals the apparent schizophrenia of *fin-de-siècle* man. 'Cosmic consciousness' is not an odd luxury to be indulged by people more mystic than the average; it is, in the mature work of the three Edwardians, the only workable solution for the post-cultural self in crisis.

In a sense, what Lawrence diagnoses as a division between 'subjective and objective consciousness' is consciousness itself. And there is a case to be made for the view that the *fin-de-siècle* malady is, in the final analysis, an intense form of self-consciousness, a development of the Gulliverian schizophrenia[50] into an extreme post-Darwinian form. We might then see the 1890s as the history of consciousness and cure:

> Consciousness is like a fever which, if not
> excessive, hastens curative processes and so
> eliminates its source. Hence its transitory,
> wandering, and often strangely unreasonable
> character. Contrasted with the growth of a
> plant or an animal, persisting self-awareness
> is like an illness which continually provokes
> its own cure, and in the long run usually does
> so.[51]

This passage, from L. L. Whyte's book, *The Unconscious Before Freud*, is useful in putting Nordau's diagnosis in perspective. What Nordau depicts as pathological would seem simply to be manifestations of heightened consciousness:

> He allows his brain-centres to produce semi-
> lucid, nebulously blurred ideas and inchoate
> thoughts, and to surrender himself to the
> perpetual obfuscation of a boundless, aimless
> and shoreless stream of fugitive ideas. . . .[52]

It is just such a rich harvest of 'archetypal' material which Jung exploited in his simple post-1900 reversal of Nordau's hypothesis. Having Jung's insights to guide us, we may, with J. C. Flugel, see 'regression' (the kind of regression implicit in the psychology of *fin-de-siècle* man as Nordau sees him) in a more positive light:

> It may be too that, as Jung and his followers
> appear to hold, a temporary regression to a deep
> level of autistic thinking can sometimes act
> recuperatively, or perhaps even creatively, in
> such a way as to enable us to deal more
> efficiently with grave problems and difficulties,
> both those presented by the external world and
> by our own inner conflicts.[53]

This brings us very close to the concept of schizophrenia as cure, as outlined in extreme form in R. D. Laing's fashionable book, *The Politics of Experience*.[54] This book is unsatisfactory in many ways, but it has the advantage of being able to place what R. G. Collingwood calls 'the corruption of consciousness'[55] in existential terms. Once the existential crisis implicit in the 'corruption' of consciousness is understood, one can see that the heightened consciousness of the *fin de siècle* is a measure of the 'ontological insecurity' of post-Darwinian man. A case-history is perhaps required, and William James, brother of Henry, provides one. This is the order of experience which lies behind the mature novels of Wells, Bennett and Galsworthy:

> Whilst in this state of philosophic
> pessimism and general depression of
> spirits about my prospects, I went one
> evening into a dressing-room in the
> twilight to procure some article that
> was there; when suddenly there fell upon
> me without any warning, just as if it came
> out of the darkness, a horrible fear of my
> own existence. Simultaneously there arose
> in my mind the image of an epileptic patient
> whom I had seen in the asylum, a black-haired
> youth with greenish skin, entirely idiotic, who
> used to sit all day on one of the benches, or
> rather shelves against the wall, with his

knees drawn up against his chin, and the
coarse gray undershirt, which was his only
garment, drawn over them inclosing his entire
figure. He sat there like a sort of sculptured
Egyptian cat or Peruvian mummy, moving nothing
but his black eyes and looking absolutely non-
human. This image and my fear entered into a
species of combination with each other. *That
shape am I*, I felt, potentially. Nothing that
I possess can defend me against that fate, if
the hour for it should strike for me as it
struck for him. There was such a horror of
him, and such a perception of my own merely
momentary discrepancy from him, that it was
as if something hitherto solid within my
breast gave way entirely, and I became a mass
of quivering fear. After this the universe was
changed for me altogether. I awoke morning
after morning with a horrible dread at the pit
of my stomach, and with a sense of the insecurity
of life that I never knew before, and that I have
never felt since. It was like a revelation; and
although the immediate feelings passed away, the
experience has made me sympathetic with the morbid
feelings of others ever since. It gradually faded,
but for months I was unable to go out into the
dark alone.[56]

Under the circumstances James has nothing to turn to but his
religion; the passage continues:

In general I dreaded to be left alone. I
remember wondering how other people could
live, how I myself had ever lived, so unconscious of that pit of insecurity beneath
the surface of life. My mother in particular,
a very cheerful person, seemed to me a perfect
paradox in her unconsciousness of danger, which
you may well believe I was very careful not to
disturb by revelations of my own state of mind.
I have always thought that this experience of

45

melancholia of mine had a religious bearing. . . .
I mean that the fear was so invasive and
powerful that if I had not clung to scripture-
texts like 'The eternal God is my refuge',
etc., 'Come unto me, all ye that labor and are
heavy-laden', etc., 'I am the resurrection and
the life', etc., I think I should have grown
really insane.[57]

This comment, from a characteristic book of 1902, describes objectively the 'curing' of a psychic malady deriving from the intense 'ontological insecurity' of *fin-de-siècle* man. The abolition of God and the pervasiveness of Darwinian theory seems to have established the idea of existence as accident. The therapeutic nature of an almost pragmatically adopted 'clinging' to religion seems to be defined quite clearly in this passage; James's prophylactic against insanity and his remedy for *Angst* is a Rieffian 'commitment therapy' of a typically modern kind.

Such an insight as that described in the William James passage is a perception, almost, of the potential absurdity of existence. Such a perception seems to have been the basis of Wells's vision in *The Island of Dr. Moreau*:

Particularly nauseous were the blank
expressionless faces of people in trains
and omnibuses; they seemed no more my
fellow-creatures than dead bodies would be;
so that I did not dare to travel unless I
was assured of being alone. And even it
seemed that I, too, was not a reasonable
creature, but only an animal tormented with
some strange disorder in its brain, that sent
it to wander alone, like a sheep stricken with
gid.[58]

It seems to remain the basis, too, for the strange mixture of threat and fascination that Galsworthy later finds in *Fraternity*:

In the centre of the lane a row of elm-
trees displayed their gnarled, knotted roots.
Human beings were seated there, whose matted

hair clung round their tired faces. Their
gaunt limbs were clothed in rags; each had a
stick, and some sort of dirty bundle tied to
it. They were asleep. On a bench beyond,
two toothless old women sat, moving their eyes
from side to side. . . .[59]

Such images, which appear to derive from the extreme insecurity of the *fin de siècle*, are the source of many latter-day
images of deprived man. Statements like Lawrence's 'I am
null', and Eliot's 'We are the hollow men' link the *fin-de-siècle*
experience with the modern world, with the world, especially, of
Beckett. The philanthropic vision of the mature Wells, Bennett
and Galsworthy seems to have derived in part from their pre-
1900 recognition of a Kurtzian hollowness at the core, and from
a vivid perception of the menace of such a malaise.

Such was *fin-de-siècle* 'malady'; whether experienced in terms
of 'hysteria' or 'degeneration' or 'corruption of consciousness',
it seems to have been related to the birth-pangs of existential
man. Although modern developments in existential thought
have taken us back to and beyond the *Angst* of the 1890s, important areas of modern thought have also taken up the
Edwardian interest in placing the post-cultural self in its societal
matrix. The self has gained much of its power of determining
the external conditions of human organization from the harrow-
ing experience of the *fin de siècle*. Alan Sandison has pointed out
that 'the imperial idea becomes not an end in itself but a major
expression of the problems of self-consciousness'.[60] We could say
that, in a related way, the idea of a universe created according
to the self's needs ultimately derives from 'problems of self-
consciousness', i.e. from the invasiveness and power of post-
Darwinian images of the deprived self.

In this respect the development in Conrad through the turn
of the century parallels that of Wells, Bennett and Galsworthy.
In his book, *Conrad: The Psychologist as Artist*, Paul Kirschner sees
the year 1900 as the turning-point:

With *Lord Jim*, Conrad had followed the self
as far as he could in the isolation of its
dream. Society, although invoked for background and perspective, had been taken largely

47

for granted in the determination of the self's
aspirations. Conrad was beginning to feel that
'there was nothing more in the world to write
about' when there came 'a subtle change in the
nature of the inspiration'. The new inspiration
was the dependence of the self-idea on society
and the 'laws of order and progress'.[61]

Kirschner proceeds to give an account of *Nostromo*, and concludes: 'Thus does Conrad evolve a whole society out of his concept of the self.'[62] Kirschner is talking, of course, about Conrad's
fictionalization of 'a whole society', and this is precisely how the
transition from *fin de sièclism* to Edwardianism in Wells, Bennett
and Galsworthy may most profitably be viewed.

III

The English fiction of the *fin de siècle* is, then, influenced both in
form and in substance by the insertion of 'The Self in the
Dream'.[63] In manifesting itself in short stories or novels of a
generally negative cast, it exhibited symptoms of post-Darwinian cultural crisis. And in dealing largely with the ontologically
insecure self immersed in the dream world of its own intensified
consciousness, it presented a wide range of images of malaise.

Before coming to a study of the 'Utopianization' of experience
in the mature novels of Wells, Bennett and Galsworthy, we
shall need to examine the triumvirate's *fin-de-siècle* work more
closely. This earlier work is strikingly different from the fiction,
in the 'objective' mode, of the Edwardian years.

Part II
Wells, Bennett and Galsworthy in the 1890s

3
The Time Machine

The Time Machine is a highly characteristic Wellsian attempt to answer the question: 'Where is it all leading?' As Bernard Bergonzi has pointed out, it is as much concerned with contemporary process as with mere prophecy, presenting an interpretation of current social tendencies in evolutionary terms.[1] The fictionalization of self implicit in the novel, however, goes beyond the mythic structuring that Bergonzi identifies. There is indeed a sense in which the symbiotically related Eloi and Morlocks are mythic representations of certain social and psychological conflicts; but the vividness of the Eloi and Morlocks derives from their place in the living world of the Time Traveller's consciousness, and it as a model of consciousness that, in the context of this study, we shall view the novel.

Bernard Bergonzi has noted the relevance of Wells's earlier, unfinished, story, 'The Chronic Argonauts', as a source for *The Time Machine*.[2] In this story the polarized 'objective' and 'subjective' modes of *fin-de-siècle* experience are incorporated in a fictional scheme which holds the conflicting elements in tension. Fantasy, in so far as it becomes the enforced realization of subjective experience in terms of the universe created in the fiction, bears a direct relation to the ordinary condition of human consciousness, where events may take on the quality of a dream, and yet are felt to be undeniably 'there':

Who can fix the colours of the sunset? Who
can take a cast of flame? Let him essay to
register the mutations of mortal thought as it
wanders from a copper butterfly to the disembodied
soul, and thence passes to spiritual motions. . . .
   It seemed like a machine that had been crushed
or warped; it was suggestive, and not confirmatory,
like the machine of a disordered dream. The men,
too, were dreamlike. One was short, intensely
sallow, with a strangely-shaped head, and clad in
a garment of dark olive green; the other was,
grotesquely out of place, evidently a clergyman
of the Established Church, a fair-haired, pale-
faced, respectable-looking man.
   . . . the machine had vanished! It was an
illusion – a projection of the subjective – an
assertion of the immateriality of mind. 'Yes',
interpolated the sceptic faculty, 'but how comes
it that the clergyman is still there?'[3]

The existence of the clergyman ('Christian man' in crisis,
perhaps) becomes a matter of doubt. The tenuousness of subjective existence is registered in the stressed division in the story
between Part I, 'The Story from an Exoteric Point of View', and
Part II, 'The Esoteric Story based on the Clergyman's Deposi-
tions'. This structure corresponds roughly to the dream-within-
reality structure of *The Time Machine*. By the time that Wells came
to write *The Time Machine* he had learned enough to have both
'stories' told in the first person, thus setting one kind of subjectivity against another, and achieving a more complex embodiment of the condition of consciousness in *fin-de-siècle* England.
   The Time Machine embodies, necessarily, the dispossessed and
dislocated status of the Time Traveller as primary element. But
he is not the primary narrator of the story. The primary narrator, who speaks in the first person, and has participated in the
events he relates, describes the after-dinner atmosphere in
which a group of professional men, having gathered for a
dinner-party at the invitation of an affable but eccentric inven-
tor (given the anonymous epithet, 'the Time Traveller', from
the very beginning), are addressed by their host, and presented

with a theory and an experiment to support it. The exposition
of the scientific theory of time-travelling, and the experimental
sending of a model of a larger 'Time Machine', still under construction, into the future, are rendered by the narrator's remembering of dialogue. The first section ends with the declaration of
the Time Traveller's intention to travel into the future when the
Time Machine is complete.

In the second section a second meeting at the Time Traveller's
home is described. The narrator remembers the return of the
Time Traveller in 'an amazing plight',[4] his subsequent meal
eaten voraciously, and, finally, his account of what happened
to him in his journey into the future. This inset narrative occupies Sections III – XVI of the total work, and the final section
(XVI) consists of the transition back from the Time Traveller's
story to that of the narrator, who describes the guest's incredu-
lity in the face of such a 'gaudy lie' (p. 148), as the Editor puts it.
Upon returning next day, the narrator finds the Time Traveller
preparing for a second journey through time, and watches his
'ghostly, indistinct figure' disappear (p. 150). That, the narrator
informs us, was 'three years ago' (p. 151), and the Time
Traveller has 'never returned' (p. 151). In the short 'Epilogue'
the narrator considers where the Time Traveller might be now –
whether in the past or in the future – and refers to the 'manhood
of the race' (p. 152), a time in which men 'are still men, but with
the riddles of our own time answered and its wearisome problems solved!' (p. 152). The narrator declares that he cannot
believe the contemporary state to be 'man's culminating time',
and although the Time Traveller was not so optimistic about
the future of man, he – the narrator – has for his 'comfort'
(p. 152) the 'two strange white flowers' (p. 152) brought back by
the Time Traveller from the far-distant future – witness that
'even when mind and strength had gone, gratitude and a mutual
tenderness still lived on in the heart of man' (p. 152).

The dinner-party milieu in the novel is Kiplingesque in a
sense, and the sympathetic reader experiences 'the pleasure of
confederacy'[5] implicit in the small-group gathering beyond
which lies mystery. But on the other hand the 'gaudy lie' seems
to be Wells's analogy for individual existence itself in process
of defying and moving beyond the Kiplingesque 'in-group'
mode to a direct confrontation of 'that Nothingness – in the

background'.[6] When the Time Traveller becomes 'ghostly' and 'indistinct' he is following the path of social invisibility established by Griffin. Something is forcing him into post-cultural crisis, and we shall want to ask exactly what pressures are being exerted in the cosy atmosphere of the Time Traveller's Wimbledon house.

The story the Time Traveller tells describes briefly the sensations of time-travelling, and then presents, in a series of six or seven scenically distinct episodes, his experiences in the year 802,701, and – at much shorter length – in the more distant future. The focal experience of the whole work is the Time Traveller's discovery, in the year 802,701,[7] of a 'splitting of the human species' (p. 81) into two distinct types, the supra-human Eloi – a beautiful, child-like, effete and physically attenuated latter-day aristocracy – and the subhuman Morlocks – a repulsively albino, ape-like, subterranean species, providing technological support for the 'frail' (p. 36) Eloi, and taking as their share of the symbiosis the liberty to emerge from underground at night in order to capture and eat the 'Overworld' people (p. 82). Wells intensifies the effectiveness of these evolved species as comments upon the ultimately pathological state of late-Victorian social conditions, through the device of making the Time Traveller only gradually aware of the full horror of the Eloi-versus-Morlocks situation. It is part of the dramatic interest of the story that he should be able to account, more and more accurately, for the strange phenomena presented to him. The story then becomes a cognitive process, and the conditions of the world created by the Time Traveller's learning consciousness are constantly changing. The effect is to project the Time Traveller's 'present' consciousness far beyond the cultural modes represented by the Eloi and Morlocks. Although the Morlocks are the result of the down-trodden working classes going further and further underground, and the Eloi are derived from thousands of years of upper-class freedom from primary needs, there is no hint that Wells is assigning any class loyalties or is concerned at all with 'social justice'. His criteria are therapeutic rather than socio-economic or ethical, and his viewpoint is that of the detached observer whose intensified consciousness has transported him, like the Time Traveller, beyond the regions of cultural ordering. Wells's suspicion of cultural organization, as implicit in both the Eloi and the Morlocks (these latter have their machines and their blood-rituals), may originally derive from personal cultural deprivation, but, as we have seen, cultural deprivation was the natural state of all post-Darwinian men.

A vital element in the story is the intensity with which the Time Traveller's momentary sensations are registered (including his sense of alienation, his irrational fears, his sudden moods of unmotivated anger, his sense of dislocation and dispossession). The story takes on the attributes of a dream, with heightened emotional charges attaching to events which do not quite match them (so that the 'charges' are not, strictly, 'emotive'). Much of the material of the Time Traveller's tale is itself dreamlike, of course, and it is described – being sequentially disrupted – as if part of a dream. It is partly this, one might conclude, this charge of localized meaningfulness, that allows Bergonzi to attribute a mythic content to *The Time Machine*.[8]

The pessimistic view that emerges as one aspect of *The Time Machine* – the journey further forward in time finally reveals a world of frighteningly alien quality, empty of life except for a round black object, with tentacles, 'hopping fitfully' on a beach (p. 141) – is echoed in the isolated, alienated character of the Time Traveller himself, the first of Wells's detached novelistic selves. Paradoxically, the Time Traveller's Wimbledon home is on the surface of things as safe and secure, as comfortable and middle-class as an environment could be. But Wells's interpretation of social tendencies is, however, not only nightmarish in its imaginative reconstructions, but is unconsciously nightmarish in its piquant registration of the crisis in the cultural milieu of the Time Traveller's home. The quality of the fantasy-material (whose efficacy in making a comment on real social problems is not perhaps as great as Bergonzi, for instance, seems willing to claim) – the irrational fears, the blood-lusts, the cannibalism and the dehumanization of both Eloi and Morlocks – emerges as the predictable product of the human situation as defined in the relations between the primary narrator, the Time Traveller, and their friends. That world of Kiplingesque security, of 'sconces' (p. 1) and cigars and club-bable gatherings, that hypermasculine world of 'The Editor filled a glass of champagne and pushed it towards him' (p.

20) is not, if we come freshly to it, very far from a *fin-de-siècle* zoo – as if a later Wells had tried to imagine Bloomsbury and had filled it with apes instead of people. The Time Traveller himself – already defined by the identifying epithet as a species or type rather than an individual – takes his place at once as a grey-eyed organism, a sort of king of the jungle:

> The Time Traveller (for so it will be convenient
> to speak of him) was expounding a recondite matter
> to us. His grey eyes shone and twinkled, and his
> usually pale face was flushed and animated. The
> fire burned brightly, and the soft radiance of the
> incandescent lights in the lilies of silver caught
> the bubbles that flashed and passed in our glasses.
> Our chairs, being his patents, embraced and
> caressed us rather than submitted to be sat upon,
> and there was that luxurious after-dinner atmosphere
> when thought runs gracefully free of the trammels
> of precision. And he put it to us in this way –
> marking the points with a lean forefinger – as we
> sat and lazily admired his earnestness over this
> new paradox (as we thought it) and his fecundity
> (p. 1).

The Time Traveller fits – in his animalized form – somewhat incongruously into the refined 1890s atmosphere, with its *Art Nouveau* décor and its 'thought gracefully free of the trammels of precision', and its admiration of paradox; so that, although the dehumanization and animalization effected by phrases like 'His grey eyes shone' and 'flushed and animated' and 'lean forefinger' and 'we admired . . . his fecundity', is in a sense a part of the total *fin-de-siècle* mood, it is at the same time a source of apparently unacknowledged conflict; the author, one feels, is unconscious at this point of the Eloi-versus-Morlocks tension present, already, in the containing situation in Wimbledon.

The initial contrast between *Art Nouveau* effeteness and the Time Traveller's animation is echoed in his primitive pose upon returning to his civilized dining-room: '"Where's my mutton?" he said. "What a treat it is to stick a fork into meat again"' (p. 23). And while the reader readily associates this red-blooded Kiplingese with the macabre, meat-eating habits of the Morlocks, one wonders whether Wells himself saw the connection. Part of the force of the novel is, one might argue, connected with the fact that there are large areas of experience of which Wells remains unconscious, but which are given expression in the inset dream-like tale. Here, for instance, there might well be something in the theory that all the dining activities of the Time Traveller are only symptomatic gestures on the part of a Wells who is unwittingly over-compensating for his own 'social' inadequacies. We note the use of a decoying scientific approach to sanction the vulgarity:

> 'Story be damned!' said the Time Traveller. 'I want something to eat. I won't say a word until I get some peptone into my arteries. Thanks. And the salt.'
> 'One word', I said. 'Have you been time travelling?'
> 'Yes,' said the Time Traveller, with his mouth full, nodding his head. The Time Traveller . . . displayed the appetite of a tramp (pp. 23–4).

In this interesting (and surely unintentional) cameo-depiction of cultural crisis it is significant that the 'therapeutic' motive ('some peptone into my arteries') takes precedence over the 'cultural' (' . . . said the Time Traveller, with his mouth full').

The conflicts and class-inconsistencies in this dining-room domesticity have a distinct bearing upon the 'splitting of the human species' (p. 81) that occurs eight hundred thousand years later.[9] The Wilde-versus-Kipling mixture of the 'lilies of silver' paragraph, and the quite different attitudes to champagne, for instance, suggested in (i) ' . . . the soft radiance caught the bubbles that flashed and passed in our glasses' (p. 1) and (ii) 'The Editor filled a glass of champagne, and pushed it towards him. He drained it . . .' (p. 20), form an exact parallel to the Eloi-Morlocks design of the inset story.[10]

The very crux of the socio-psychological problem implicit in the Eloi-Morlocks situation is inherent in the terms of the Time Traveller's consciousness. And we note that that consciousness has not so much the enigmatic quality of mythic experience as the disorganized quality of schizoid dissociation. It is as if Wells were using, in their raw form, for the purposes of circumstantial psychological realism, those very ignorances that lie at the root of 'the riddles of our time' (p. 152):

The next night I did not sleep well.
Probably my health was a little disordered.
I was oppressed with perplexity and doubt.
Once or twice I had a feeling of intense fear
for which I could perceive no definite reason (p. 86).
   I think I must have had a kind of frenzy.
I remember running violently in and out among
the broken twigs. . . . 'Where is my Time Machine?'
I began bawling like an angry child . . . (p. 59).
   The freshness of the morning made me desire
an equal freshness. I had exhausted my emotion.
Indeed, as I went about my business, I found
myself wondering at my intense excitement
overnight (pp. 61–2).

It is, in a sense, in order to explore these conflicts, these hidings of one part of the psyche from another, that the Time Traveller sets out on his horrifying journey; these subjective problems of consciousness (which appear to be associated with post-Darwinian man's inability to come to terms with his instinctual self) are objectified in the projected fantasy of the Eloi-Morlocks conflict. There is a very good reason for the Time Traveller to choose to travel in time as a means of ordering his consciousness (though this is nowhere presented as his specific intention): '*There is no difference between Time and any of the three dimensions of Space*,' he points out, '*except that our consciousness moves along it*' (p. 3). In a way, then, *The Time Machine* is a direct analogue of the way in which the consciousness seeks its own cure. It depicts the self-aware but self-bemused psyche in process of exploring deep into the inner world of itself.

   The Time Traveller's psychological predicament seems to be a refinement of the Cartesian logic which works for the individual as 'I think, therefore I am not'. It reflects a modern disintegration of being. In Wells in the 1890s we seem to be seeing the institutionalization of a new doctrine of Original Sin, a doctrine perhaps reflected in William Golding's *The Lord of the Flies*, which has been developed from the Christian doctrine by the addition of evolutionary and anthropological elements. The Eloi and Morlocks are, seen in this light, the latter-day equivalents of the Houyhnhnms and the Yahoos, and Wells's special felicity in his novel is to have the anthropological fantasy exactly parallel the functional derangement manifest in his hero's consciousness. Elsewhere Wells defines his version of the Fall: 'There is no health in us, and it is only by effort, by wisdom and continence, by the suppression of instincts that are a part of us, that even a sufferable equilibrium may be maintained.'[11] The religious metaphor, 'There is no health in us', becomes a more nearly literal doctrine in secular therapy. Such a version of Original Sin is close to Freud's; and it is surely with Freud that the metaphor of ill-health is made literal, and established as a source of much modern thinking on the condition of man.

One way of describing the crisis Wells renders in *The Time Machine* is to view it as the more or less predictable result of the self dissociating under the threat of the future. The Time Traveller's account of the process of time travel seems similar to contemporary accounts of the experience of living in the 1890s:

> The unpleasant sensations of the start were
> less poignant now. They merged at last into a
> kind of hysterical exhilaration. I remarked
> indeed a clumsy swaying of the machine, for
> which I was unable to account. But my mind was
> too confused to attend to it, so with a kind of
> madness growing upon me, I flung myself into
> futurity. At first I scarce thought of stopping,
> scarce thought of anything but these new sensa-
> tions. But presently a fresh series of
> impressions grew up in my mind – a certain
> curiosity and therewith a certain dread – until
> at last they took complete possession of me.
> (pp. 30–1).

Wells is apparently creating a model of consciousness which, under threat from an over-valued future, opts out of present time, loses contact with what R. D. Laing calls its 'present self',[12] and undergoes a vertiginous dissociation. The 'kind of madness' in this case seems to be a kind of *fin-de-siècle* schizophrenia, in which the 'I' of the Time Traveller's account feels itself quite separate from the 'impressions' and 'emotions' which impinge, in a disturbingly alien way, on the experiencing 'I' from the outside. The total psychic state defined is pathological rather than sane, 'possessed' rather than 'self-possessed'. Indeed, the dispossession which we have identified as the state of post-Darwinian man is reflected in the fact that 'one' no longer is in possession of 'one's' 'self'. The primarily ontological nature of Edwardian fiction may be traced back to this 'splitting'; Wells comments on the process of identification in *First and Last Things*, where he implies that the Edwardian interest in physical environment is derived from the need for a field for action in which the educating self may enter into an integrative process of knowing:

> Necessarily when one begins an enquiry into
> the fundamental nature of oneself and one's
> mind and its processes, one is forced into
> biography. I begin by asking how the conscious
> mind with which I identify myself, began.
>   It presents itself to me as a history of a
> world of facts opening out from an accidental
> centre at which I happen to begin.[13]

The need to identify oneself with one's mind presupposes some initial sense of misidentity in that context, and that is, if one thinks of it, exactly how the personae of Wells's Edwardian novels are initially presented. The logic of these novels, of *Love and Mr. Lewisham*, *Kipps*, *Tono-Bungay* and *The History of Mr. Polly*, is that 'accidental' existences are 'forced into biography' and hence into fuller being. We may note that Wells's controlled prose of 1908 ('It presents itself to me as a history . . .') reflects a wider process of centurial maturation, whereby the 'fated', 'accidental' selves of the 1890s are given histories. Earlier, as I have suggested, *fin-de-siècle* man tended to be 'now unhappy . . . more/Than history can pattern'. And the existential overtones of Wells's later account ('an accidental centre at which I happen to begin') indicate the modernity of his characters, depicted in the 1890s, who felt the accidental nature of their existences in terms of severe ontological insecurity. Wells's Time Traveller, socially invisible in his own time, alienated from his 'present self', finding fearful images which analogize the conflicts of his own unconscious, is one of the most striking of modern fictional heroes. In him post-cultural man is vividly presented in process of coming into consciousness of his new dissociated existence:

> At once, like a lash across the face, came the
> possibility of losing my own age, of being left
> helpless in this strange new world. The bare
> thought of it was an actual physical sensation.
> I could feel it grip me at the throat and stop
> my breathing. In another moment I was in a
> passion of fear (p. 57).

II

There is a close relation between the *fin-de-siècle* crisis of consciousness and the assimilation of Darwinism into contemporary thought. That relation can be understood more readily if the condition of the 1890s is seen specifically as an existential predicament.

'Existential' is a loose term, but if we can agree on a fairly wide base for the meaning of the word, we may claim that in certain of his works Wells is an existentialist in all but name, and that in his prophetical writings he sets out quite clearly the basic tenets of existentialist thought.[14] From the very beginning he was acutely aware of the uniqueness of his own existence and of that of all objects external to him. Such an awareness was perhaps inevitable in a sensitive student of Darwinian biology, as the early essay on 'The Rediscovery of the Unique'[15] shows:

> The work of Darwin and Wallace was the clear
> assertion of the uniqueness of living things. . . .
> We are on the eve of man's final emancipation
> from rigid reasonableness, from the last trace
> of the trim clockwork thought of the seventeenth
> and eighteenth centuries.[16]

Together with this comprehension of the importance of the unique and the irrational stands his early vision of the insufficiency of science in the face of the unknown:

> Science is a match that man has just got
> alight. He thought he was in a room – in moments

of devotion a temple – and that his light would
be reflected and pillars carved with philosophical
systems wrought into harmony. It is a
curious sensation, now that the preliminary
splutter is over and the flame burns up clear,
to see his hands lit and just a glimpse of
himself and the patch he stands on visible,
and around him, in place of all that human
comfort and beauty he anticipated – darkness still.[17]

This essay also contains an account of the theory of essences
and points out the insupportability of that theory in the face of
what is in fact a universe of individually existing unique objects.
The theme is taken up again in the Appendix to *A Modern
Utopia*,[18] in which Wells refers somewhat contemptuously to the
earlier essay – 'That unfortunate paper, among other oversights
I can no longer regard as trivial, disregarded quite completely
the fact that a whole literature upon the antagonism of the one
and the many, of the specific ideal and the individual reality,
was already in existence'[19] – and proceeds to elaborate his
nevertheless continuing 'doubt of the objective reality of classification'[20] in this new no-nonsense style:

This idea of uniqueness in all individuals
is not only true of the classification of
material science; it is still true, and still
more evidently true, of the species of common
thought, it is true of common terms. Take the
word *chair*. When one says chair, one thinks
vaguely of an average chair. But collect
individual instances . . . and you will perceive
what a lax bundle in fact is this simple
straightforward term.[21]

We inhabit, according to Wells, 'an unlimited universe of
objective uniques'.[22] Thus Plato 'tended to regard the idea as the
something behind reality, whereas it seems to me that the idea
is the more proximate and less perfect thing, the thing by which
the mind, by ignoring individual differences, attempts to com-
prehend an otherwise unmanageable number of unique
realities'.[23]

In this Appendix, and in other places, Wells defines the process whereby he has come to see the Absolute in existentialist terms as 'nothingness':

> Our instrument of knowledge persists in
> handling even such openly negative terms as
> the Absolute, the Infinite, as though they
> were real existences. . . .
>   Let me try and express how in my mind this
> matter of negative terms has shaped itself.
> I think of something which I may perhaps best
> describe as being off the stage or out of
> court, or as the Void without Implications,
> or as Nothingness, or as Outer Darkness.
>   . . . . When you speak of the Absolute you
> speak to me of nothing.[24]

This 'nothingness' is, as Wells explains, 'a sort of hypothetical Beyond to the visible world of human thought, and thither I think all negative terms reach at last, and merge, and become nothing. . . . Not blue, not happy, not iron, all the not classes meet in that Outer Darkness.'[25]

An essential element of what Wells calls the 'Scepticism of the Instrument'[26] is its registration of paradox:

> Take life at the level of common sensation
> and common experience and there is no more
> indisputable fact than man's freedom of will,
> unless it is his complete moral responsibility.
> But make only the least penetrating of analyses
> and you perceive a world of inevitable consequences,
> a rigid succession of cause and effect.[27]

The existential nature of *The Time Machine*'s holding of the objectivity/subjectivity paradox is clear; the only answer to this kind of contradiction is to *accept* the paradox – not to deny one or both sides of it – and to recognize the limitations of one's ability to assign final truth to any idea. But

> This insistence upon the elements of uniqueness
> in being, this subordination of the class to the

individual difference, not only destroys the
universal claim of philosophy, but the universal
claim of ethical imperatives. . . .[28]

So – existentially again – the individual is forced to construct
his own 'imperatives'. And, since 'life has for its primordial
elements assimilation and aggression', we must not only try to
obey our 'imperatives', but must 'put them persuasively and
concisely into other minds'.[29]

As in many existential readings of experience, Wells's
approach to the potential chaos of life is to recommend some
kind of transcendent, supra-rational remedy:

The repudiation of demonstration in any but
immediate and verifiable cases that this scepticism
amounts to, the abandonment of any universal
validity for moral and religious propositions,
brings ethical, social, and religious teaching
into the province of poetry, and does something
to correct the estrangement between knowledge and
beauty that is a feature of so much mental
existence at this time. Such an opinion sets a
new and greater value on that penetrating and
illuminating quality of mind we call insight,
insight which when it faces towards the contradictions that arise out of the imperfections
of the mental instrument is called humour. In
these innate, unteachable qualities I hold – in
humour and the sense of beauty – lies such hope
of intellectual salvation from the original sin
of our intellectual instrument as we may entertain
in this uncertain and fluctuating world of unique
appearances.[30]

Wells's secularization of Original Sin once again implies that
consciousness is man's only recourse in the face of the incomprehensible. 'A Modern Utopia' must depend upon the 'Utopianization' of experience by the recreating consciousness. In
Wells, as in Dickens, humour becomes a revolutionary force, in
many cases apparently the last resort of the existential self; in
Wells, however, the benevolent Absurd is left behind; his

humour of crisis is bound up with the concept of alienation, and self-consciousness comes earlier to his heroes.

In 'The Purple Pileus', for example, Mr Coombes suffers nausea and 'despair'[31] – 'Mr. Coombes was sick of life. . . . He would stand it no longer.'[32] He has suffered a kind of Kafkaesque transmutation in his marriage, and to his wife he is 'a little grub';[33] he suffers total alienation from his wife and her friends and has had to flee the house. He swallows what he thinks is a poisonous toadstool, and, intoxicated with it, returns to the house for a confrontation with the unwelcome visitors. Having lost all moral inhibitions, he resorts to self-assertion in the form (characteristically existential) of violence. He succeeds in asserting his 'imperatives' upon his wife and has no further trouble with her. He becomes a person. The similarity with Mr. Polly's career is striking; both take a Kierkegaardian leap into the unknown, both attempt suicide and, by rejecting unacceptable situations, both attain selfhood. This use of a *fin-de-siècle* short-story motif within the extended fictional medium of the post-1900 novel is not uncommon in Wells, Bennett and Galsworthy. Here, characteristically, the earlier story contains a central core of fantasy, while the novel is given a more realistic structure. Mr. Coombes's short period of insanity might be said to correspond to the psychotic-existential therapy defined by R. D. Laing in *The Politics of Experience*, so that Wells ends the story by talking of the purple pileus 'maddening this absurd little man to the pitch of decisive action, and so altering the whole course of his life'.[34] Once again consciousness itself, though presented as hallucinated and temporarily pathological, effects the Utopianization.[35]

In Wells's thought may be distinguished anticipations of all the negative aspects of existentialism, all the traditional insights of the 'Outsider':[36] alienation; despair; the absurd; the absolute as nothingness; philosophical, religious and ethical anarchy; external reality as chaos or dream; the self as the only source of moral authority; the pragmatic sanctioning of 'sane madness'; violence and death as existential action. And on the other hand we may pick out some of the possible positive activities of existentialism: the decision to accept paradox; the opting for a faith acknowledged to be 'arbitrary' and 'mystical';[37] the accepted need for transcendental modes of experience. Taking these insights as a basis, then, we may return to the text of *The Time Machine.*

The Time Traveller asks his guests (he is host, set apart, given powers of insight not available to the common herd) to accept this 'new paradox' (p. 1), to leave everyday life and normal common-sense criteria behind, and to enter a new world, a fourth dimension. There is the suggestion that the Time Traveller's apparent eccentricity and insanity are more worthy of our respect than the 'sanity' of normal life ('A pork butcher could understand Filby', p. 17). In face of the unknown, when the model of the Time Machine disappears before his eyes, the Psychologist, already in the 1890s the guardian of sanity, finds the experience too much for him; he cannot prevent it from interfering in his actions: 'The Psychologist, to show that he was not unhinged, helped himself to a cigar and tried to light it uncut' (p. 13). In contrast, moreover, to the Time Traveller's obvious skill at narration, the Psychologist's attempt to describe the events of the previous week falls somewhat flat. And it is a point of irony that 'it was the Psychologist himself who sent forth the model Time Machine on its interminable voyage' (p. 12).

When the Time Traveller declares that he intends 'to explore time' (p. 16), his guests are open to the 'odd potentialities' (p. 18) and the 'curious possibilities of anachronism and utter confusion' (p. 18) that such a journey might involve. In fact, the Time Traveller plays the role of Outsider, and he is going to be able to see deep into the conditions of reality in ordinary life. His journey will show the common-sense normalities of his guests to be an aspect of an insane and schizophrenic society, 'this splitting of the human species' (p. 81).

The Time Traveller's description of his journey through time resembles that of a madman's account of a psychotic episode: 'The whole surface of the earth seemed changed – melting and flowing under my eyes. . . . With a kind of madness growing upon me, I flung myself into futurity' (p. 30). And some of the phrases in the central part of the story – read objectively – also sound psychotic: 'I felt hopelessly cut off from my own kind – a strange animal in an unknown world. I must have raved to and fro, screaming upon God and Fate' (p. 60)/'I had exhausted my emotion. Indeed, as I went about my business, I found myself wondering at my intense excitement overnight.'/'I had the hardest task in the world to keep my hands off their pretty laughing faces. It was a foolish impulse, but the devil begotten of fear and blind anger was ill curbed and still eager to take advantage of my perplexity.'/ "Patience," said I to myself. . . . "If they mean to take your machine away, it's little good your wrecking their bronze panels"' (p. 64). And when he has finished his story, the Time Traveller finds that 'the atmosphere of everyday is too much for my memory'. He is forced to ask himself: 'Did I ever make a Time Machine, or a model of a Time Machine? Or is it only a dream? They say life is a dream, a precious poor dream at times – but I can't stand another that won't fit. It's madness' (p. 147). In *The Time Machine* the *fin-de-siècle* resentment against dreams 'that won't fit' – that fundamental neurosis of the age – assumes psychotic shape. It is as if Wells's sense of 'offence' is so great that a straight account of neurosis (as in Bennett's *A Man from the North*) is not sufficient to express it.

The story of *The Time Machine* is the story of Wells himself – an expression of himself at the time of writing it. It is part wish-fulfilment, part fear-projection, part confession, part complaint. In common with much of the other distinctive fiction of the 1890s Wells's first novel represents the translation of specific personal predicament into literary terms. When the Time Traveller decides to investigate the Morlock exits into the upper world of the Eloi, it is almost as if he is exploring 'Wells': 'After a time, too, I came to connect these wells with tall towers standing here and there upon the slopes. . . . I was at first inclined to associate it with the sanitary apparatus of these people' (p. 68). A Freudian might argue that Wells's choice of 'wells' and 'tall towers' and his first free association of these things with 'sanitary apparatus' indicates an unconscious return to infantile confusion and to the Freudian source of his need to systematize experience so painstakingly. Again, when the Time Traveller explores the world beneath the 'wells', he finds the lower-class Morlocks eating the upper-class Eloi meat (though something like a transliteration of the dream-censor prevents him from recognizing it as such at first). What is striking is not simply that this might be seen as an unconscious analogization of Wells's own unconscious wishes, but that the analogization is only just sub-limated, and is on the verge, we feel, of breaking through into explicitness (as, for instance, in the murderous and conscious lower-class resentment against the upper classes felt by Leadford in the post-1900 *In the Days of the Comet* (1906)). A critic is normally justified in rejecting or minimizing the weight of 'Freudian' evidence, but this is a special case. Here is a hero specifically exploring the dimension of consciousness and doing so contemporaneously with Freud himself. The Time Traveller is so lost, so neurotic (almost psychotic) in the degree to which he is possessed by forces he cannot control (largely due to his fears in the face of an unknown future), that experience comes to him specifically in a form requiring analysis before it is to be comprehended. The Time Traveller commits himself finally to ongoing analysis of the material of consciousness.[38] The criteria by which the Time Traveller judges his environment are given as initially insufficient.

Certainly one cannot translate this quasi-insane experience of the Time Traveller with any precision into a schematized biographical 'meaning'; it is more useful to affirm that what Wells is doing is letting us share his 'insane' nightmare so that we may return to the world with a clearer, a saner understanding of humanity as insane. This is why the ending of *The Island of Dr. Moreau* is not just an imitation of Swift, but a genuine extension of the Swiftian experience:

I had to act with the utmost circumspection
to save myself from the suspicion of insanity. . . .
And, unnatural as it seems, with my return to
mankind came, instead of that confidence and
sympathy I had expected, a strange enhancement
of the uncertainty and dread I had experienced
during my stay upon the island.
  They say that terror is a disease, and,
anyhow, I can witness that, for several years
now, a restless fear has dwelt in my mind,
such a restless fear as a half-tamed lion
cub may feel. My trouble took the strangest
form. I could not persuade myself that the
men and women I met were not also another,
still passably human, Beast People, animals
half-wrought into the outward image of human

souls. . . . But I have confided my case to a
strangely able man, a man who had known Moreau,
and seemed half to credit my story, a mental
specialist – and he has helped me mightily. . . .[39]

The mental specialist is already there in the background,
ready to come to the aid of the sick consciousness. We may note
the closeness of the early Wells to the personae of the Outsider:

Particularly nauseous were the blank
expressionless faces of people in trains
and omnibuses; they seemed no more my fellow-
creatures than dead bodies would be; so that
I did not dare to travel unless I was assured
of being alone. And even it seemed that I, too,
was not a reasonable creature, but only an
animal tormented with some strange disorder
in its brains, that sent it to wander alone,
like a sheep stricken with gid.[40]

All the documentary containing apparatus of the early Wells
fiction is used to establish a proper aesthetic distance; so that we
may benefit from these apparently insane reveries without feeling that they represent too subjective (or pathological) an interpretation of the Wellsian predicament. This device enables
Wells to set the insanities of the inner world against the pseudo-
sane outer world, and to establish the equivocality of 'ordinary'
life.

The primary image of the absurd in *The Time Machine*
emerges when the Time Traveller tells of his experiences even
further in the future:

A horror of this great darkness came on me.
The cold that smote to my marrow, and the pain
I felt in breathing, overcame me. I shivered,
and a deadly nausea seized me. Then like a red-
hot bow in the sky appeared the edge of the sun.
I got off the machine to recover myself. I felt
giddy and incapable of facing the returning journey.
As I stood sick and confused I saw again the
moving thing upon the shoal – there was no mistake
now that it was a moving thing – against the red

water of the sea. It was a round thing, the size
of a football perhaps, or, it may be, bigger, and
tentacles trailed down from it; it seemed black
against the weltering blood-red water, and it was
hopping fitfully about. Then I felt I was fainting.
But a terrible dread of lying helpless in that
remote and awful twilight sustained me while I
clambered upon the saddle (p. 141).

Wells takes a contemporary cliché – the *fin du globe* – and
transforms it into a classic existential statement. The atmosphere
of this passage is very close to the description by Camus of
Meursault's walk on the Algerian beach.[41]

The Time Traveller is afflicted with a 'deadly nausea' – he is
'sick and confused', a prototype for Sartre's nauseated hero. In a
sense, also, Wells's 'round thing' represents an image, the prim-
eval registration, of human alienation, like Kafka's insect-man,
or Dostoevsky's beetle-man, or Wells's own Mr. Coombes – the
'little grub'. It is as if Wells is pointing to man in the universe.
This is our environment: the black ball 'hopping fitfully about'
in face of a sullied eternity. We are ultimately this biological
essence, absurdly at the mercy of the whim of evolution, of
chance mutation, of meaningless and inexorable change.[42]

The Time Machine – in common with much of the distinctive
fiction of the 1890s – represents the indirect transcription of
'abnormal' mental phenomena into literary terms. Aestheticism
itself has been epitomized as 'impressionisms of the abnormal by
a group of individualists',[43] but it is certain that such an interest
went outside the aesthetic inner group. *The Turn of the Screw* is an
example, as is Conrad's early fiction. The interest of these works
(though not always their intention), and of stories like *The
Picture of Dorian Gray*, is not that they describe a partitioned
world of insanity out of mere morbid interest in such a world,
but that they question the sanity and moral implications of *this*
world; the technique of ambiguity which employs Wellsian
equivocations about the 'truth' or 'falseness' of perceptions
leads the reader back to his own life wanting to see deeper and
question further. It is the reader who feels lonely when he learns
that 'the Time Traveller vanished three years ago. And as
everybody knows now, he has never returned' (p. 151).

4

A Man from the North

I

Like *The Old Wives' Tale*, *A Man from the North* is formally united and organized by four deaths (although in this case three are actual and one is metaphorical), the deaths which give Richard Larch's life its meaning, and to which he attributes his quite strikingly *fin-de-siècle* failure. The ultimate status of the hero's predicament in the novel is self-professed 'malady'[1] and the symbiotic pattern of (i) analytic objectivity in the narrative strategy and (ii) hypochondria (the hero as neurotic, sensitive to two main things – 'beauty' and himself as ill), is further indication of the central complementarity of the 'scientific-therapeutic' and 'aesthetic-symptomatic' modes in 1890s fiction.

After the death of his sister Mary (his only surviving relative – he has been living uncomfortably with her and her husband) and the still-birth of her first child, Richard Larch leaves the Potteries to take lodgings in London – the 'City of Pleasure'. He is a shy, rather sententious young man. Working as a clerk with a firm of City solicitors, he finds a friend in a young Cockney colleague called Albert Jenkins. Albert introduces him to the culinary delights of London, and Richard himself discovers some of its other attractions, overawed as he is by the romance of the metropolis, with its luxurious sins and splendours. Mary's death has thus had two results: first, it has cut Richard off from all familial support and left him isolated and alone in the world; and, second, it has indirectly enabled him to confront the seductive challenge of London and life. This first death of Richard's life (leaving aside the 'vague' (p. 15) absence of his father and mother, which is, however, archetypal for him) is thus responsible both for the initiation of his growth towards independent manhood and for his suspension in a newly-vulnerable position. He has evolved socially to a point at which he must sustain himself by some therapeutic course, part-conscious, part-unconscious. In order that therapy be applied most efficiently he (unwitting of this process) becomes ill.

The ambivalent consequences of death (or here, in archetypal terms, parent-loss) – it is both afflicting and freeing, destructive and revivifying – form the central motif for the novel, and the diversified recurrence of the primordial parent-loss conditions the 'rhythmic contour' that Bennett later referred to in *The Truth about an Author*.[2] When first submitted to John Lane in 1896, the novel bore the provisional title of *In the Shadow*, and the four deaths and aftermaths of death that it contains comprise, as novelistic rendering of that 'umbrage', as it were, a dramatic counterpart to the *fin-de-siècle* rhetoric of Richard's final self-analysis:

Why had nature deprived him of strength and
purpose? Why could not he, like other men, bend
circumstances to his own ends? He sought for a
reason, and he found it in his father, that
mysterious dead transmitter of traits, of whom
he knew so little, and on whose name lay a blot
of some kind which was hidden from him. He had
been born in the shadow, and after a fitful
struggle towards emergence, into the shadow he
must again retire. Fate was his enemy (p. 262).

The word 'umbrage' suggests the concept of 'offence'. If we bear in mind the relation of 'offence' to the development of existentialist thought,[3] we shall see that Bennett's novel is, in a sense, an existentialist document. It may also be said to create a psychiatric predicament for its hero, and in some sense to suggest a cure for it in terms of the pre-1900 deprivational mode.

At the beginning of the book Richard is shown in a romance-of-the-Metropolis setting; in terms of the text of the novel he might simply be about to have Babylonian adventures. But by the end, after he has come under the influence of the aged Mr Aked (whose literary career has itself been – conveniently – ruined by chronic dyspepsia), with his plan for writing a definitive 'Psychology of the Suburbs', not only is London potentially a 'psychiatric' city, with the hero doomed to a suburban domesticity in which he will soon require 'psycho-therapeutic' support from something like Bennett's own *How to Live on Twenty Four Hours a Day*,[4] but Richard is himself suffering from malady only just kept under control. No longer is Richard Larch simply a young man with romantic yearnings or even a deprived individual with unsatisfied desires – by the end of the book he has created himself as what Rieff calls a therapeutic, and has taken an adaptive course intended to improve the condition of his troubled consciousness. Richard's self-analysis, then, is not merely an ephemeral and idiosyncratic 'symptom' of the 1890s; on the contrary, it takes its place in the development of the chronic hypochondria of modern Western experience. For in terms of the externals of Richard's early life, and, indeed, in terms of the happenings described within the total extent of the novel, there is nothing that would seem to justify his lack of 'moral strength';[5] the only way that the final failure can derive a meaning from within its context of the events of the novel is for the hero to begin to advance beyond 'moral' thinking towards the ability to judge cognitively[6] – that is, *psychologically*. But this very ability to judge oneself cognitively is an inextricable part of the grounds of modern alienation; it is the scientific-therapeutic side of what we have distinguished as the 1890s' syndrome. Flugel, pointing to the Edwardian utterance of Graham Wallas that 'anger, previously part of the angry man, is now separable from him',[7] while stressing its contribution towards moral progress, naturally misses its dangers for the period just before 1900. When Richard is turning to Laura Roberts as his last hope in an alien universe, he feels that 'separable' passion is, ultimately, not passion at all:

His entity seemed to have become dual. One part of him was willingly enslaved to an imperious headstrong passion; the other stood calmly, cynically apart, and watched. There were hours when he . . . admitted that his passion

had been, as it were, artificially incited,
and that there could be no hope of an
enduring love. . . .[8]

Bennett's rendering of Richard's love is schizoid, partaking of
his own tendencies towards 'dissociated sensibility':

I see that at bottom I have an intellectual
scorn . . . for all sexual-physical manifestations. . . . I can feel myself despising them at
the very moment of deriving satisfaction from
them, as if I were playing at being a child. . . .[9]

The Freudian cure for this classic kind of alienation from one's
instinctive life works by the analytical setting of reality against
fantasy. Bennett developed two parallel cures for the predicament. The first was the para-Freudian facing up to reality that
is recommended in, for instance, *How to Live on Twenty Four
Hours a Day.* Bennett's alternative cure depends upon the transformation of one's material and social environment to match
one's ambitions and desires. This is an element of the achieved
equilibrium of *The Old Wives' Tale,* just as 'facing up to reality'
is. This kind of cure attempts to abolish the sense of offence
through a kind of self-seeking hedonism. Thus, in *A Man from the
North* Richard's success as clerk, his promotions, his 'aesthetic'
redecorating, and his gradually increasing social superiority,
help to compensate for the existential nullity of his life.

One day at lunch Richard meets Mr Aked – an old and
broken-down 'literary' clerk in the office – and as a result of the
latter's eccentric discourse, determines to pursue a literary
vocation. His sudden decision to do so follows a passage in
which Aked has been explaining how *his* literary potentialities
have been destroyed by chronic dyspepsia. So that Richard is
deliberately modelling himself upon a failure whose psychoso-
matic defection from life has provided him with the role of
littérateur without having actually to *be* an established writer,
and in so far as Richard's malady depends upon that identification it is self-sought. In the same restaurant Richard meets his
future wife, Laura Roberts, who is a waitress on good terms with
Aked. She – though not a pretty girl – has a 'magnificent
coiffure' (p. 51), and is one of several unattainable erotic images

haunting Richard's first diffident experiences of London. The obscure relationship that has existed between Aked and Laura is developed on more than one occasion, and seems to represent another version of the vaguely-absent-father-and-mother and William-and-Mary relationships.

In this first structural unit of the novel, then, Richard discovers versions of his mother/sister in the Ottoman Theatre girls, and makes first contact with his future mentor, Aked, and his future wife, Laura. He submits an article for publication and has it rejected. The second section – and second death – is introduced through the news of the death of Richard's brother-in-law. Although he is quite unsentimentally neutral about this, Richard is prompted to apprehend his utter isolation upon the face of the earth – 'he was now a solitary upon the face of the earth. It concerned no living person whether he did evil or good' (p. 58). The moral self-sufficiency which is thus forced upon Richard – he has no 'ruling relative' – makes his predicament existential and therapeutic. He is acutely aware of the isolation and independence of his own existence. It paves the way, moreover, for his development away from moralistic towards psychological life. The self-analysis which accompanies this new awareness sets the tone for those to follow. Although he still 'rejoiced in London . . . there was something to lack in himself. His confidence in his own abilities and his own character was being undermined' (p. 58). This second structural unit (there are four such units, each of around eight chapters long) begins with Richard's experiences on the train northwards to the funeral. This 'voyage' back to the roots, this returning to first things, as it were, is to be associated both with William's death and with the promotion of new creation and new hope. Richard's train journey seems to constitute an antidote to depression; as with the Time Traveller's voyage, a sense of disengaged motion, almost of vertigo, accompanies the experience:

He still experienced but little sorrow at
the death of Vernon. His affection for the man
had strangely faded. During the nine months that
he had lived in London they had scarcely written
to one another, and Richard regarded the long

journey to attend William's obsequies as a tiresome concession to propriety.

That was his real attitude, had he cared to
examine it.

At about four o'clock it was quite light, and
the risen sun woke Richard from a brief doze.
The dew lay in the hollows of the fields but elsewhere there was a new and virginal beauty – as
though that had been the act of creation itself.
The cattle were stirring, and turned to watch the
train as it slipped by.

Richard opened the window again. His mood had
changed and he felt unreasonably joyous. Last
night he had been too pessimistic. Life lay yet
before him, and time enough to rectify any in-
discretions of which he might have been guilty.
The future was his, to use as he liked. Magnificent, consoling thought! Moved by some symbolic
association of ideas, he put his head out of the
window and peered in the direction of the train's
motion. A cottage stood alone in the midst of
innumerable meadows; as it crossed his vision,
the door opened, and a young woman came out with
an empty pail swinging in her left hand.
Apparently she would be about twenty-seven, plump
and sturdy and straight. Her hair was loose about
her round, contented face, and with her disengaged
hand she rubbed her eyes, still puffed and heavy
with sleep. She wore a pink print gown, the
bodice of which was unfastened, disclosing a white
undergarment and the rich hemispheres of her bosom.
In an instant the scene was hidden by a curve of
the line, but Richard had time to guess from her
figure that the woman was the mother of a small
family. He pictured her husband still unconscious
in the warm bed which she had just left; he
even saw the impress of her head on the pillow,
and a long nightdress thrown hastily across a
chair.

He was deeply and indescribably affected by

this suggestion of peaceful married love set in
so great a solitude (pp. 59–61).[10]

This revelation of an Oedipal element in the dynamic of
Richard's life, through 'some symbolic association of ideas',
works for Richard in an ultimately therapeutic way. We
remember Heinz Hartmann's perception that

> ... though fantasy always implies an initial
> turning away from a real situation, it can also
> be a preparation for reality and may lead to a
> better mastery of it. Fantasy may fulfil a
> synthetic function by provisionally connecting
> our needs and goals with possible ways of
> realizing them.[11]

The field of action here is the hero's consciousness, and it is with
a kind of para-Freudian permissiveness that Bennett allows
Richard's mind to follow its desires. This daydreaming, detailed
and elaborated, is something new in the English novel, just as
'free association' was something new for European psychologists
in the 1890s.

Bennett's rendering of the regulating function of consciousness, then, has affinities with the clinical situation in Freudian
psychoanalysis, and is always related to the ontological status or
the hero at any given point, and to his success or failure in feeling in control of the future. The non-virginal beauty of this
bosomy pastoral idyll foreshadows the attractions of the 'pulsing'
(p. 125) breast of Adeline (Aked's daughter), who is 'part of
Nature, the great Nature which hides itself from cities' (p. 193),
and establishes itself as the archetypal maternal-marital image
for Richard's attitude towards marriage. Thus Laura, the girl
Richard finally decides, in desperation, to marry, is defined
towards the end of the book in relation to this earlier image; her
own identity is hidden behind her status as woman and her
correlative in Richard's fantasy-life:

> All the inessentials of her being were
> stripped away, and she was merely a woman,
> captured. She sat passive, expectant, the
> incarnation of the Feminine.
> He took her hand and felt it tremble. . . .

Then with inexplicable rapidity his mind went
unerringly back to that train-journey to
William's funeral. He saw the cottage in the
fields, and the young mother, half-robed and
with sleep in her eyes, standing at the door.
Exquisite vision! (p. 258).

Bennett's Freudianism in *A Man from the North* is thus of what
Wells would have called a 'poetic' kind. Bennett shows, for
example, that Richard's malady is defined by his tendency to
domesticate – in fantasies – a potential wife. He shows that it is a
condition of that domestic bliss that the wife also be a benign
mother, and juxtaposes access to the mother-wife with the death
of a father-husband (first with William and the country-wife,
and then with Aked and Adeline). The sexual (or near-sexual)
intimacy of the woman and her family is so strongly desired by
Richard as his own future state of existence that he opts out of
present life in what Nordau would have diagnosed as a degenerate swoon:

The woman and her hypothetical husband and
children were only peasants, their lives were
probably narrow and their intellects dormant,
yet they aroused in him a feeling of envy which
surged about his brain and for the moment
asphyxiated him (pp. 60–1).

The conventional nature of Bennett's image and the respect
implicitly paid to family life, seem old-fashioned when one
thinks of Freud's account of family relations, or Butler's,[12] or
even Bennett's own in the later novel, *Clayhanger*. But perhaps it
was precisely by seizing upon the family as set apart from and
unattainable by the deprived self that *fin-de-siècle* man contrived
its twentieth-century fall. What Richard Larch is seeking, after
all, is not a family as he himself has known it, but a Utopianized
family created by the conditions of his own consciousness.
Nordau, as we have seen, is critical of the Utopianizing bent of
fin-de-siècle man:

The degenerate is incapable of adapting
himself to existing circumstances. This incapacity, indeed, is an indication of morbid

variation in every species, and probably a
primary cause of their sudden extinction.
He therefore rebels against conditions and
views of things he necessarily feels to be
painful, chiefly because they impose upon
him the duty of self-control, of which he is
incapable on account of his organic weakness
of will. Thus he becomes an improver of the
world, and devises plans for making mankind happy.

Richard's first understanding of his Utopianizing consciousness
is that it is 'morbid', and he defines himself as a Nordauesque
degenerate:

> . . . with solitaries like Richard it is
> different. Debarred from fellowship with
> the opposite sex by circumstances and an
> innate diffidence which makes the control of
> circumstances impossible, their starved
> sensibilities acquire certain morbid
> tenderness. . . . Richard grasped this. In a
> luminous moment of self-revelation, he was
> able to trace the growth of the malady.
> From its first vague and fugitive symptoms,
> it had so grown that now, on seeing an
> attractive woman, he could not be content
> to say, 'What an attractive woman!' and have
> done with it, but he needs must build a fire
> in the room, place a low chair by the fire,
> put the woman in the chair, with a welcoming
> smile on her upturned lips – and imagine that
> she was his wife (pp. 248–49).

Set in a process which 'makes the control of circumstances
impossible', post-Darwinian man reacts to the unknowable
and threatening future by indulging wishes and fears. For
Richard to identify interfering wishes as 'malady' is for him to
fall not far short of the Freudian diagnosis of modern man's
'neurosis'. And just as his self-'asphyxiating' desires derive from
the threat of the future, so his self-analysis treads a para-
Freudian path into past family history:

Why had nature deprived him of strength and
purpose? Why could not he, like other men,
bend circumstances to his own ends? He sought
for a reason, and he found it in his father,
that mysterious dead transmitter of traits, of
whom he knew so little, and on whose name lay
a blot of some kind which was hidden from him.
He had been born in the shadow, and after a fitful
struggle towards emergence, into the shadow he
must again retire. Fate was his enemy (p. 262).

These 'blots' and 'traits' are never made explicit in the novel,
which thus presents evidence for the inscrutable sense of dam-
nation that *fin-de-siècle* man seems to have felt. The secularization of Heaven and Hell in the late-Victorian period seems to
have had drastic repercussions. A Darwinian fall from grace
seemed to introduce a new evolutionary Fall ('He sought for a
reason, and he found it in his father, that mysterious dead transmitter of traits'); in such a universe, Heaven seems to have been
the province of the Utopianizing consciousness, released from
the 'Hell' of given reality.

Bennett's careful juxtaposition of death and dream in the
train passage is akin to his rendering of the 'Freudian' relation in
Richard's mind between his sister's death and his erotic day-
dreams:

'Why the dickens didn't I say something to
that girl?'
    Between the candles on the mantelpiece was
a photograph of his sister, which he had placed
there before going out. He looked at it with
a half-smile, and murmured audibly several times:
    'Why the dickens didn't I say something to
that girl with her *chéri*?' (p. 13).

Here the imagery of deification, the suggestion of prayer, the
word 'Mary', the altar-mantelpiece, suggest a cult of eroticism
somehow associated with Richard's sister's death. The reason
for Richard's silence on the occasion he describes is given in the
direction of his gaze: he is still tied to his sister, even though her
death has released him erotically. A similar association of death

and stream of consciousness occurs at the beginning of the third
section, immediately following the apparently traumatic
(though, in a sense, trauma-releasing) experience Richard has
when watching his friend Aked dying. That experience forces
Richard to revise his ideas about life, and now, looking at life
once again from a window, he is again refreshed and allowed a
new lease of optimism:

> He stood leaning on the front of the balcony
> till the din of traffic had declined to an
> infrequent rumble, his thoughts a smiling,
> whirling medley impossible to analyse or
> describe. At last he came in, and leaving
> the window ajar, undressed slowly without a
> light, and lay down. He had no desire to sleep,
> nor did he attempt to do so; not for a ransom
> would he have parted with the fine, full
> consciousness of life which thrilled through
> every portion of his being. The brief summer
> night came to an end; and just as the sun was
> rising he dozed a little, and then got up
> without a trace of fatigue. He went to the
> balcony again, and drank in all the sweet
> invigorating freshness of the morning. The
> sunlit streets were enveloped in an enchanted
> silence (p. 163).

The paradoxical re-birth that the death of Aked provides is
manifested in the subsequent intensification of Richard's
relationship with Adeline, who, after nursing her father to his
end – she falls 'conveniently' ill with influenza – blossoms out.
Richard, attracted to her 'idiosyncrasy' (p. 127) and her isolation as well as to her 'tight black bodice' (p. 125), visits her
when she goes to Littlehampton for a holiday; but after Richard
has spent several weeks as her escort in London, Adeline informs
him that she is to go off to America to visit her uncles for an in-
definite period. At the last moment – by which time the panick-
ing Richard is beginning to appreciate what he will be missing
when she has gone – Adeline confesses that she would have
accepted her uncles' invitation sooner, but that she wanted to
see whether she and Richard 'cared for' (p. 213) each other.

Having been entirely dependent upon her, and having been somewhat desperately trying to fall in love with her, Richard is shattered:

> It had come, the explanation! He blushed red,
> and stuck to her hand. The atmosphere was suddenly
> electric. The station and the crowd were blotted
> out (p. 215).

Arriving back in London, he seeks 'solace' (p. 216) in a prostitute. After Mary's death he had not been quite able to raise the courage to reply to a girl who had 'twittered a phrase ending in *chéri*' (p. 12); now, when a kind-faced and entirely motherly whore solicits him with a murmured '*Chéri!*' he has 'no resistance' (p. 217).

Once again the initial release provided by the 'fatal' (p. 263) abandonment carried with it a recharge of energy, but again the outcome is failure. The alienation accompanying Richard's rejection by 'the opposite sex' (p. 248) is repeated in his attempts at literary creation:

> At the commencement of the year which was
> now drawing to a close he had attacked the
> art of literature anew, and had compassed
> several articles; but as one by one they
> suffered rejection, his energy had dwindled,
> and in a short time he had again entirely
> ceased to write (p. 219).

The period after Adeline's departure is one of apathy and lethargy – fourteen months during which a sense of social and sexual alienation is gradually generated in him. His failure to write increases his general sense of insecurity, and he experiences acute loneliness, especially feeling cut off from women. It is in this fourth section of the book, following upon the fourth 'death' – the departure of Adeline – that Richard defines the symptoms and traces the origins of his malady. Under the circumstances, it isn't surprising that, after seeing Laura Roberts on a bus, Richard decides that his one way out is to marry the only girl that he knows and to accept the renunciation involved in a suburban future. Adaptation is seen to involve a dismissal of the past, and an implementation of the guiding fantasy of the deprived self; illusory desires, such as Adeline and a literary career, are distinguished from archetypal needs, as registered in Richard's obsessive picturing of a maternal wife, primitive and ordinary rather than 'artistic' or 'literary'. In effect, such a 'traditional' resolution represents a capitulation to the past: 'He had been born in the shadow, and after a fitful struggle towards emergence, into the shadow he must again retire' (p. 262). Only in rare moments of 'unreasonable' joy (p. 60) has Richard been able to feel: 'The future was his, to use as he liked' (p. 60). Veering rapidly between optimism and pessimism, Richard finally comes to a compromise.

II

A Man from the North is a typical product of the *fin de siècle*; in view of its morbid concern for death, sickness and alienation, and in spite of certain redeeming passages, it might well be termed an extremely pessimistic book. It is structured upon the progress of spiritual defeat, accepting adaptation as a process inevitably involving capitulation to process and the *status quo*. It wallows in failure and numbness and frustration. How then are we to account for its obsessions and self-indulgence in contrast with the 'cheerful' objectivity of Bennett's work in the Edwardian decade?[13] Even in 1903, only five years after publication, Bennett referred to it in terms of half-embarrassed facetiousness. Even he couldn't imagine the exigencies of that seriously pessimistic mood of 1896–8; he writes as if remembering, with paradoxical clearness, a distant and all but forgotten age:

> So I sat down to write my first novel, under
> the sweet influences of the de Goncourts,
> Turgenev, Flaubert, and de Maupassant. . . . I
> clearly remember that the purpose uppermost in
> my mind was to imitate what I may call the
> physical characteristics of French novels. . . .
> There was to be no bowing in the house of the
> Rimmon of sentimentality. Life being grey,
> sinister, and melancholy, my novel must be grey,

sinister, and melancholy. . . . It was to be the
Usual miraculously transformed by Art into the
Sublime.

The sole liberty that I might permit myself
in handling the Usual was to give it a rhythmic
contour – a precious distinction in those Yeller-
bocky days.[14]

There are historical reasons for the development from Victorian optimism to *fin-de-siècle* pessimism to Edwardian optimism
to post-World-War pessimism, but who can re-live the sense of
impending doom of the 1890s or the Edwardian sense that all
was potentially all right with the world? Wells is an example of
the way in which an individual writer, sensitive to the movement of the times, can be buffeted around by the tide of history,
can be duped and at the same time dupe others and himself, can
change and change again. Bennett and Galsworthy did not
make the final Wellsian recantation,[15] but it is obvious – if only
from these comments on his first novel – that Bennett too was
caught up in cultural changes that he could not completely
account for, imaginatively. There are, for instance, two other
conflicting versions of the Richard Larch plot, two short stories
that Bennett wrote in the early 1890s which illustrate in what
way and how far he was dominated by the pessimism of the age,
by the threat of calendar apocalypse.

The hopeless hero of 'A Letter Home'[16] is a young tubercular
down-and-out in London; but he comes from a respectable
Potteries family, and he takes a special place among the scum,
among the crowd of tramps and outcasts waiting to get into a
London park. He is isolated amidst the alienated – 'Only one
amongst them was different';[17] he might well have come straight
out of Nordau. A little later, on his deathbed, he reviews his life:
'Poor mother! No, great mother! The grandeur of her life's
struggle filled him with a sense of awe.'[18] As in *A Man from the
North*, the lack of a 'ruling relative' is interpreted as contributing
to the hero's failure: 'If Pater had only lived he might have kept
me in order.'[19] He addresses a 'Letter Home' to his mother and
gives it to a friend to deliver. But his friend, true to his degenerate type, is not much of a friend; later that night he gets drunk
and uses the letter to light his pipe. There the story ends.

The hero of 'The Artist's Model'[20] – another Richard, Richard Lacy – is an isolated, poverty-stricken, struggling young artist. At last he is given the job of illustrating a friend's novel. He chooses a simple, shy girl – another Mary – as model for the heroine. The onset of malady is registered by the most naïvely-presented wish-fulfilment:

> One day when she came he was almost
> prostrated by a more than usually severe
> headache, a complaint from which he
> frequently suffered. In the middle of the
> morning's work she suddenly jumped up.
> 'Why, Mr. Lacy, you are ill!' she cried.
> 'Only one of my headaches,' he cried,
> faintly and wearily.
> 'You know, I often have them. But I
> think I will sit down a bit ——'
> Then he fainted.
> When he recovered consciousness he found
> himself lying on the only couch which the
> studio boasted, while Mary Blackwood stood
> over him with a bottle of smelling salts.[21]

Work is avoided and motherly companionship is in the offing. Artist and model fall in love, and decide to marry when they have enough money. A portrait of Mary is destined for the Academy, but once again illness interferes:

> The eagerly-expected and much-prized
> varnishing ticket arrived, but Lacy was
> unable to make use of it, in spite of all
> Mary's nursing. His attacks of headache had
> lately become more frequent and severe, and
> on the eventful day he was incapable of move-
> ment (p. 83).

Mary suggests the doctor. The doctor suggests an oculist. The Harley Street 'great specialist' (p. 83) advises 'absolute rest for two or three years' (p. 83). Richard objects: 'But I can't – I must live!' (p. 83). But the specialist insists: 'If you don't rest, you will be blind before you are thirty-five' (p. 83).

Bennett doesn't spare his readers a melodramatic rehearsal of the full implications of the tragedy:

> Poor fellow! None but those who have
> been in the same awful predicament can realize
> his feelings. He must work or starve; yet if
> he worked darkness and black despair would
> surely overtake him (p. 83).

Fortunately, however, a solicitor recognizes the portrait of Mary Blackwood, heiress to £30,000 and a country house:

> Richard Lacy had a holiday extending over
> three years, and so saved his eyesight. He
> puts A.R.A. after his name now, and paints
> portraits of £1,000 apiece (p. 83).

There are, of course, precedents – apart from the French realists – for Bennett's 1890s fiction. There are George Moore's *A Modern Lover*[22] and *A Mummer's Wife*;[23] there are George Gissing's *The Nether World*[24] and *New Grub Street*.[25] But, using these two short stories by Bennett as a guide, we can point to an important difference in the latter's work: to a far greater extent than Moore's or Gissing's, it allows its author greater scope in the literary expression of his most fundamental wishes and fears. If we bear in mind the quality of these two short stories (with their dreamlike directness) and return to *A Man from the North*, we shall see that the latter is also an 'autistic' work (as much, in its own way, as *The Time Machine* is), and that its total effect (like that of the Wells novel) is to present an autistic critique of reality. When Bennett quotes Moore in admiration he is drawing attention to the way the *fin-de-siècle* self 'poeticizes' its own deprivation:

> . . . when Lewis, a starving and resourceless
> student, exasperated by the opulent luxury and
> dissipation around him, is walking one night
> through the West End, we read: *In his madness
> he fancied he heard the shower of gold and
> kisses that fell over the city.*[26]

This 'aesthetic-symptomatic' energy of hypochondria was not wasted in the 1890s; for after 1900 Bennett was more and more able to create characters who follow the self-assertive Rieffian therapy: 'The therapeutic mode developed by Freud is essentially alloplastic and aims . . . systematically at an externalization of human vitality.'[27] Edwin Clayhanger's consciousness is a Utopianizing flame which does not think of capitulating to the past:

> In that head of his a flame burnt that was
> like an altar-fire, a miraculous and beautiful
> phenomenon, than which nothing is more miraculous
> nor more beautiful over the whole earth. Whence
> had it suddenly sprung, that flame?
> After years of muddy inefficiency, of
> contentedness with the second-rate and
> the dishonest, that flame astoundingly
> bursts forth, from a hidden, unheeded
> spark that none had thought to blow upon.[28]

In terms of the powerful myths that determine much of literary expression between 1890 and 1910, Richard's 'malady' was the conventional prerequisite for Edwin Clayhanger's drive for health. The detour through fantasy brings post-cultural man 'back to life'.

5
Jocelyn

I

Twenty-one years after the words 'All art constantly aspires towards the condition of music' came to the attention of the English public, Galsworthy published his first and most musical novel. With its clear division into three parts, of ten, eight and ten chapters respectively, with its 'aesthetically' symmetrical deployment of hero and heroine, and its lightly involuted motifs of light and shade, of dream states and local colour, it corresponds closely to Ford's concept of the musical novel. This is Ford's version of 'an imaginary conversation with H. G. Wells':[1]

Self, I suppose then, in the matter of
Form, you arrive at the Sonata.
E.N. Yes, that's it. What *is* the
Sonata?
Self. Like this: You state your first
subject (Hero or Heroine) in the key
of the Tonic. You then state your
second subject (Heroine or Hero) in
the key of the Dominant, if the
first subject is in a major – or
in the key of the relative major,
if the first subject is in a minor
key. You repeat all that, and that
finishes the first part. Then comes

88

what is called the working out or
Free Fantasia. . . .
E.N.   Then there is some Freedom. . . .
Self.   In that you mix up themes A and B,
embroider on them in any related, or
even unrelated, keys and tempi. You
introduce foreign matter if you like. . . .
E.N.   I see. The Tertium, what is it?
Self.   You introduce foreign matter, and
generally have a good time. In the
Restatement you restate:
A emphatically in his or her key, and
B equally emphatically, but in the tonic
original key of A. That becomes the
key of the whole Sonata: Op. 232 in
E Flat Major! You *might* restate the
Foreign Matter which you introduced
into the Free Fantasia. . . .
E.N.   Ah!
Self.   But that is irregular. And you may
or may not have a Coda, a short sweet
passage of reminiscence – the children
tumbling over the Newfoundland on the
lawn.

Now any work of art that has the Aristotelian attributes of
beginning, middle and end might be interpreted by a sufficiently
officious critic in terms of this Fordian Sonata-form. The
rhythms, moreover, of a literary work may operate in a similar
way to those of music, even if the author is wholly 'unmusical'
and indifferent to this kind of analogy between art-forms. But
when *Jocelyn*, with its careful rhythms and delicate, intimate
interplay of character and *mise en scène*, is examined, the analogy
is difficult to resist. And the fact that one thus also applies the
jargon of the drama places the analogy in its right perspective;
after all, *Jocelyn* is also a typical example of the visually impressionistic 'environment novel' of the *fin de siècle*. Rather than
saying simply that this is a book which aspires to the condition
of music, we might suggest that in one historical period serious
novels constantly aspired to the condition of 'the arts', and that

Galsworthy is attempting here to cover a wide range – perhaps thinly spread – of artistic experience: plastic and pictorial, musical and poetic, dramatic and novelistic.

Jocelyn has Giles Legard for hero ('A'). The book opens with:

> A light laugh came floating into the sunshine
> through the green shutters of a room in the Hotel
> Milano. It grated on Giles Legard, who sat on
> the stone terrace outside, face to face with a
> naked fact for, perhaps, the first time in ten
> years.[2]

Chapter 1 states theme 'A', the setting and background for the hero. We learn that Giles, a reserved, refined and sun-tanned Englishman living a pleasant but sterile life on the French Riviera with his bed-ridden and chronically ill Polish wife, Irma, is awakened to 'reality' – and hence consciousness – when he falls in love with a young acquaintance called Jocelyn Ley. Jocelyn is 'Heroine' ('B'), and Chapter 3 states the heroine's theme:

> Jocelyn Ley's mother died when she was born.
> She was an only child, and her father, who was
> in the army, began immediately to idolize her
> with an abrupt and well-bred idolatry. When
> she was eighteen her father died, leaving her
> independent, and very desolate (p. 27).

We learn that Jocelyn is a type of the turn-of-the-century new child-woman. Her 'free spirit and delicate nature' – to use a phrase which Garnett chooses for the description of one of his environmental heroines in *An Imaged World*[3] – corresponds to a series of familiar idealizations: Adeline, for example, has the same quality of refined consciousness fighting against Fate (and the same kind of name); and some of the well-known young heroines of James and the early Forster follow the same pattern. Perhaps the most vivid idea of the type may be derived from Monet's (1886) *Lady with a Parasol turned towards the Right*,[4] which represents the kind of visual inspiration that lies behind these often beautiful images of light and shade. Jocelyn, like Adeline and Weena, is all light, just like the Lady with a Parasol – polarized against implied death and fate and darkness. The pattern of the 'Sonata' is that the author/hero stands in the 'Shadow', while the young girl dances in, or at least exults in, the light.

This statement of themes in Part One is followed by further elaboration of the respective situations of hero and heroine up to the point of their first kiss, upon which 'note' the first section of the novel comes to a well-defined end. Three or four quotations will show the development of this first 'movement'; the actual musical references in the text, and musical metaphor itself, help to establish the total musical status of the novel:

(*a*) The sound of a piano came from the next room . . .
. . . the little tune gripped some string in his
heart (p. 4).
(*b*) . . . the subdued strains of music . . . (p. 33).
(*c*) She was turning to the piano when her eyes
fell upon the figure of Giles (p. 45).
(*d*) She *knew* – nothing could take that from him;
she *knew*, and she had been glad to know.
Now that the keynote had been struck, all the
deep chords, unstirred for so many years in his
mind, sounded with a full consonance; all the
great, unsatisfied longing hitherto unshadowed
in his deeply affectionate nature had taken to
itself shape, all the vast gambling possibility
in him was fiercely aroused (p. 95).

After the embroilment of Part One – which ends with the words, 'Their lips met' – comes the 'working out' of Part Two. The 'Free Fantasia' of the Sonata-form is the 'accidental' death of Irma, which is clearly an imaginative rearrangement of the terms of Galsworthy's own problems with Ada and her husband. Giles comes one morning upon his wife still in morphia-induced sleep; the bottle of morphia stands at her bedside instead of her morning medicine. Giles at once sees the 'gambling possibilities' of this situation, hoping that upon waking Irma will swallow a poisonous dose by mistake. He hastily leaves the house, and on returning finds that Irma has indeed died. But meanwhile introduced 'foreign matter' has also been at work; Nielsen, the sophisticated, roulette-playing Swede, has declared his love for Jocelyn. It is he who sees Giles in bare-headed flight

from his house on the morning of Irma's death, and who –
falling short of revealing the full horror of his suspicions – tells
Jocelyn later that Irma has died of an overdose of morphia.
Jocelyn is stricken with the fear that the death was suicidal,
Irma having somehow learned of her relationship with Giles.
Giles is thus forced to confess his own ambiguous part in the
death, and at the end of Part Two Jocelyn insists that she must
go away, the two never to meet again.

In the 'Tertium' the introduced foreign matter is represented
by a drastic change of scene. Jocelyn is in London, escorted by
Nielsen. Giles is in North Africa. Exasperated at not receiving a
letter for nine weeks, he makes his way to London. He sees
Jocelyn, but she is still what one might call adamant. The 'A'
theme having been thus restated (with Giles in a state of
awakened but frustrated desire for Jocelyn), Giles departs on a
voyage to the Far East. The 'B' theme is restated equally
emphatically, but this time in 'the tonic original key of A' in so
far as Jocelyn declares her new sense of isolation and alienation,
something she has in some sense 'picked up' from Giles. She has
one last long discussion with Nielsen, who is still hanging on,
and realizes that her larger moral destiny is to take her 'natural'
place with Giles. Free Will, Fate and natural evolutionary
processes are beckoning her.

The 'Coda' comes at the end of the last chapter, when Jocelyn join Giles in Ismailia. Their moment of reunion is dreamlike,
registering the final oneness that each achieves with the other
and with the universe:

> His eyes rested on her face – and he gasped.
> He thought 'I am dreaming . . .' And now great
> shadows stalked along the cold sands, like
> the uneasy thoughts of a dream (pp. 305–7).

And Jocelyn's final whisper is lost to and taken up by
infinity: 'The wind carried the whisper away into the remote-
ness of the desert' (p. 309).

There the book ends, just as it began, with the carefully
modulated sound. The awakened consciousness has reconciled
unconscious needs with the 'superconsciousness' and so is quiet
again.

In novelistic terms, the 'reality' expressed in *Jocelyn* (the author's sense of life) is *temperamental*. Galsworthy seems more concerned with the pathology of temperament, with what might be called 'biological characterization', than he is with writing about love, say, or expressing a moral experience. He is concerned with individual consciousnesses, and his chosen aesthetic is a form of novelistic evolutionary harmonization (i.e. *musicalization*). It is possible to show that the therapeutic intent (the curing, ultimately, of Giles's and Jocelyn's sickness of the heart) coheres with Galsworthy's painstaking musical aestheticization of their experience.

As Kenneth Graham has shown, one pioneer of the musical analogy in fiction in England was George Moore,[5] and there is a very definite tradition of treating the novel in musical terms long before Ford's comments of the 1920s. In fact, the search for analogies between the arts in fiction criticism cannot be discussed separately from the Victorian concept of the 'organic fusion of the incidents into one living whole' which is the 'art of all arts'.[6] Graham claims that, for the period 1865–1900, 'the deliberate application of the principle of organic unity is one of the most remarkable and unexpected features in the whole age's criticism of fiction'.[7] It is part of his case that subsequent accounts of pre-Conradian fiction (notably by Ford himself) have tended to falsify our knowledge of earlier interest in the *art* of the novel. But if we think of the closeness of these nineteenth-century theories of organic fusion in literature – and theories of the common properties and ultimate aims of the arts – to evolving theories of racial and cosmic unity, we shall surely not remain surprised at this precociousness of the late Victorians; it is of the essence of the age.

This, then, is the first way in which the musical analogy works – it appeals to the aesthete's need for formal order and harmony between elements, to the quest for the imposed and developing rhythm. But there is another sense in which music provides a useful analogy for the processes of fiction – the sense in which both music and the novel tend towards the highest evolutionary form (in Pateresque aspiration), especially towards the widening of the range of consciousness available to the artist and hence to his audience. The emergence of a manifold sensory impressionism in the novel – tactile, visual, auditory, gustatory, and olfactory – together with the emphasis upon ultimate synthesis, parallels Herbert Spencer's concept of the evolutionary process, where the higher product is both more greatly differentiated and at the same time more completely integrated. And so we find in Conrad's 1897 Preface to *The Nigger of the 'Narcissus'* a characteristically *fin-de-siècle* vulgarization of what is already a quite vulgarized tradition:

All art, therefore, appeals primarily to the
senses, and the artistic aim when expressing
itself in written words must also make its
appeal through senses, if its high desire is to
reach the secret spring of responsive emotions.
It must strenuously aspire to the plasticity
of sculpture, to the colour of painting, and
to the magic suggestiveness of music – which is
the art of arts. And it is only through
complete, unswerving devotion to the perfect
blending of form and substance; it is only through
an unremitting never-discouraged care for the
shape and ring of sentences that an approach
can be made to plasticity.[8]

So that while music is only the highest in the hierarchy of the several arts that are 'borrowed from' in order to increase both the range of consciousness and the aesthetic 'attack' of the novel, it is the one which – with its 'magic suggestiveness' – has access to the widest range of conscious and unconscious experience.

Jocelyn, in its para-Freudian pattern of calming the sick consciousness, is a highly sophisticated work of art. It is interested both in psychologizing (with its 'tiresome psychological subtleties')[9] and the awakened consciousness, and also in aestheticizing, in what may seem a superadded 'aesthetic' appeal. But perhaps we call Galsworthy's local colour and music superadded because we miss the point that the events of the novel (out of which one demands, in an Aristotelian way, the effect of beauty to arise) are events not of action simply, but of consciousness. The whole novel is in fact about consciousness and its relation to the non-conscious elements of existence. Galsworthy's rhetoric is to take the destroyed worlds of enervated post-cultural selves, to take neurasthenic, fevered

consciousnesses, and to submit them to a process of Utopianization. Once again paraphrasing Jean Duvignaud, we might say:
Galsworthy's imaginative invention of Jocelyn is 'the fruit of a
Utopian experience, the reconstruction of a living whole in and
around a character who becomes the momentary symbol of this
assembling process'.[10] The 'assembling process' in *Jocelyn* is the
musicalization of experience presented in the novel.

Galsworthy is at this stage of his career thinking in much the
same way as Joseph Conrad (by whom he was influenced, both
personally and artistically, far more than appears to be generally accepted) when the latter extends the romantic tradition of
an unconscious affinity between the individual and the larger
harmony and unity of the created universe:

> He [the artist] speaks to our capacity for
> delight and wonder, to the sense of mystery
> surrounding our lives; to our sense of pity,
> and beauty, and pain; to the latent feeling
> of fellowship with all creation – and to the
> subtle but invincible conviction of solidarity
> that knits together the loneliness of
> innumerable hearts, to the solidarity in dreams,
> in joy, in sorrow, in aspirations, in illusions,
> in hope, in fear, which binds men to each other,
> which binds together all humanity – the dead to
> the living and the living to the unborn.[11]

At the turn of the century this kind of commitment therapy for
post-cultural man was not uncommon. Its reference to a 'global
village' form of community for man freed of cultural and societal
restrictions indicates how useful such a theory is for the rede-
ployment of human 'social instincts'. The source of such a
philosophy in existential deprivation is indicated in Conrad's
phrase, 'solidarity in dreams', and Jung's concept of the
'collective unconscious' should be seen against a prevailing
mood:

> The individual consciousness is already social,
> and all that re-echoes in our entire organism, in
> our entire consciousness, assumes a social aspect.
> Long ago the Greek philosophers found the beautiful

in harmony, or at least esteemed harmony one of the
most essential characteristics of beauty; this
harmony, too abstractly and too mathematically
conceived by the ancients, reduces, for modern
psychology, to an organic solidarité, to a conspiration of living cells, to a sort of social and
collective consciousness in the breast of the
individual. We say *I*, and we could as well say *we*.
The agreeable becomes beautiful to the measure in
which it includes more of organic harmony
(solidarité) and of sociability between all the
parts of our being and all the elements of our
consciousness, to the measure in which it is more
attributable to this *we* which is in the *I*.[12]

The basis of Galsworthy's own theorizing on the subject of
aesthetics is centrally (and often crudely) evolutionary. 'By art
alone', he wrote in 'Vague Thoughts on Art',[13] 'can true
harmony in human affairs be fostered, true Proportion revealed.
and true Equipoise preserved.'[14] Realism not only puts life into
perspective, but has an implicit evolutionary function:

What purpose then will the novelist serve?
Well! By depicting a section of life in due
relation to the whole of life without fear or
favour, he does not cure the section, but he
does throw it into proper relief for the general
eye, and indirectly fosters evolution.[15]

Art, then, is a therapy for the deranged consciousness, for what
Wells calls 'a society that has failed to develop a collective intelligence and a collective will for order commensurate with its
perplexities'.[16] R. G. Collingwood defines a related role for the
artist in his book, *The Principles of Art*:

As spokesman of his community, the secrets he
must utter are theirs. The reason why they need
him is that no community altogether knows its own
heart; and by failing in this knowledge a community
deceives itself on the one subject concerning
which ignorance means death. For the evils which

come from that ignorance the poet as prophet
suggests no remedy, because he has already given
one. The remedy is the poem itself. Art is the
community's medicine for the worst disease of
mind, the corruption of consciousness.[17]

Galsworthy's account of the role of art involves a recognition of
the new responsibility of post-Darwinian man in so far as his
own evolutionary future is involved:

The artist, they say, is not concerned with
morals, but in truth no one is more concerned
with morals if a longer view be taken. For to
the artist we look for those pictures of life
as it really is, those correlations of sectional
life to the whole, essential to the organic
moral growth of human society.[18]

The fundamental precept of Galsworthy's poetic is his determination to see both life and the novel as simultaneously 'life'
and 'art'. It is the spreading of evolution-theory into aesthetics
that enables him to claim that

. . . this essential quality of Art ['Beauty']
has also, and more happily, been called Rhythm.
And what is Rhythm if not that mysterious harmony
between part and part, and part and whole, which
gives what is called life; that exact proportion,
the mystery of which is best grasped in observing
how life leaves an animate creature when the
essential relation of part to whole has been
sufficiently disturbed. And I agree that this
rhythmic relation of part to part, and part to
whole – in short vitality – is the one quality
inseparable from a work of Art. For nothing
which does not seem to a man possessed of this
rhythmic vitality, can ever steal out of
himself.[19]

So that we are able to identify the neo-Vitalist structure of
Jocelyn. The book begins with Giles as an isolated individual, cut
off from 'life', and finding his newly-awakened consciousness

a painful embarrassment, almost as much 'malady' as Richard Larch's heightened sensitivity became. Jocelyn also possesses this sense of alienation and deprivation: 'It seemed to her that all around the pulse of life was throbbing, in herself alone it stood still' (p. 208). The melodramatic clichés emphasize the representative quality of Jocelyn's sense that life is elsewhere, away from the finite personal present, in the infinite places of the earth:

> She would sit at the window sometimes for hours,
> watching the view, longing to get away upon it to
> the sea, far away to the East, to countries
> where no one knew her, where the sun was
> bright, and she might begin her life again' (p. 211).

And Jocelyn's self-pity doesn't hide the fact that she is expressing what amounts to the spirit of the age, the sense of living divorced from any central vital current of evolving life: 'Why isn't there a place for me to fill? Why am I always alone? Everything I see has a home. . . . I am out in the cold, always in the cold' (p. 278).

But the book ends, of course, with union in the desert, and there is the transmitted sense that the achieved state of harmony works at a level above the merely conscious; hence the recourse to suggestive symbolism. The total movement of the novel becomes, in fact, a development towards the manifestation in the lives of Giles and Jocelyn of what Conrad calls 'the latent feeling of fellowship with all creation', the assumption of cosmic selfhood.

So that while there is throughout *Jocelyn* a pursuit of the sense of reality that awakened and hypersensitized consciousness brings with it, there is also the idea that the ultimate goal of human experience may only be achieved through some kind of superconsciousness, even, one might say, by the abolition of what is ultimately – by itself – *pathological* consciousness. The final decision, around which the final harmonization of experience in *Jocelyn* revolves, is the outcome of dialectic, the synthesis of the two central discussions that the heroine has with Nielsen. Firstly, there is the difference of opinion that the two have about the painting they go to see together, the 'Paolo and Francesca'. Nielsen is unable to respond to the picture, but

Jocelyn sees in it a truth that has a bearing upon her own experience:

> If ever the truth of life has been revealed
> in art, surely it is in that picture. There,
> is all the joy of life, and all its suffering,
> endless motion, and triumphant love (p. 225).

For Jocelyn there is a caught sense of 'union' in the picture, '"union" in spite of everything else' (p. 287). And the epithet which stands at the beginning of the book (as warning guardian, perhaps, of an obsession) is:

> Isolation is surely the everyday condition,
> Union that for which we strive so wildly and
> never perfectly attain; and do not these two
> between them contrive all the ups and downs
> of life?

The portrait of 'Paolo and Francesca' having initiated the movement towards 'union' in the latter part of the book, Jocelyn and Nielsen have their final and crucial discussion – on determinism, free will and morality. Nielsen makes the point that

> If you choose to do something unexpected, it
> is really the expected thing you are doing all
> the time, because the chains of your circumstances
> and your temperament would not permit you to do
> otherwise (p. 280).

And then, when he goes on to refer to the transcendent 'morality' of nature, Jocelyn realizes that she is, as it were, on to a good thing: if everything has its place – 'Nature is very moral. . . . Look at that grass' (p. 281) – then why shouldn't she assume her rightful place with Giles, even if he did practically murder his wife? It is, in effect, a ruthless Darwinism that leaves Irma dead and Nielsen abandoned in order that the final desert meeting be possible, although, of course, the lack of any true moral response to Irma's death is played down because the moral aspect is throughout defined 'psychologically'. The suicide is not so much morally as existentially disrupting for Giles and Jocelyn.

99

II

George Moore has a useful suggestion to the effect that the 'instrumentation' of a novel is 'the novelist's device of blending physical phenomena from the outer world with the inner feelings of characters at some moment, as in Flaubert and Turgenev'.[20] Following on from this we might argue that what music brings to *Jocelyn* is simply instrumented inevitability – it is the aesthetically reconciling function equivalent to the principle of Vitalism in post-Darwinian evolutionary thought. The embodiment of beauty of form in a novel is a vital part of the process which, in *fin-de-siècle* discussions of evolutionary aesthetics, takes the form of a transition from the *Unconscious* to the *Conscious*, and from the *Conscious* to the *Super-conscious*, a spiritual absolute that transcends individual and relative experience.

The neo-Vitalism which appears towards the end of the nineteenth century, and which is an essential element of the Edwardian movement, represents one of the first and most important post-Christian therapics.[21] In particular, it comprises a direct counter to the Darwinian evacuation of teleology. Hans Driesch wrote in 1914:

> Gustav Wolff's excellent critique of Darwinism
> appeared in 1890, and fully merits its great
> reputation. In spite of being (without any
> reflection on its originality) behind the times
> as a criticism of Darwinism, it is the first of
> its kind, arising, as it does, from the clear
> conviction that the fall of Darwinism will bring
> a simultaneous revival of teleology of great
> significance.
>
> In the year 1894, Wolff followed his critique
> by an experiment which was expressly undertaken
> as a solution of the question: Darwinism or
> teleology.[22]

Specifically suited to the salvation of individuals suffering cultural depletion, neo-Vitalism enabled the self to look beyond culture to 'an organic solidarité, to a conspiration of living cells, to a sort of social and collective consciousness in the breast of the individual'.

Edwin Bjorkman's version of a hierarchy of consciousness is typically neo-Vitalistic; he defines the three 'universal levels' of existence between which all life is distributed as 'unconscious energy', 'conscious life' and 'self-conscious spirit'.[23] In these terms *Jocelyn* points the way (via a satisfying of unconscious requirements and a stilling of troubled consciousness) to a potential 'union' with 'Life' – 'Where the cosmic self is,' affirms Edward Carpenter, 'there is no more self-consciousness.'[24] Carpenter and Bjorkman are writing in the same tradition; what Carpenter means by 'no more self-consciousness' is close to what Bjorkman means by 'self-conscious spirit', although the jargonizing appears on the surface to suggest a difference. There is a para-Jungian (and hence anti-Rieffian) element in this kind of commitment therapy; we can now see why Conrad made so much of 'the *secret* spring of responsive emotions' and of the '*magic* suggestiveness of music', and of the '*latent* feeling of fellowship with all creation' and of the 'solidarity *of dreams*'. The unconscious is here related to the cosmos in a very direct way and the distinction between 'Unconsciousness' and 'Cosmic Consciousness' becomes not, as in Freud's version, a battle fought out on the ground of culture, but the source of 'reunion'. Bjorkman's triadic, mystical hierarchy of consciousness, which seems to be related structurally to Freud's triadic model of unconscious 'id', conscious 'ego', and 'super-ego', is useful in understanding such Edwardian novels as Wells's *Kipps* and *Mr. Polly*. In these novels a balance is achieved not so much between id and 'cultural' super-ego, as between id and acultural cosmos. But here, as elsewhere in Edwardian fiction, the implicitly recommended mode of life, and the mode which may perhaps correspond most closely to the well-being derived from Freudian analysis, is 'self-conscious spirit', and such an attainment of cosmic spirituality (a higher 'collective consciousness') is seen to involve the renunciation of consoling super-ego injunctions and the discarding of 'civilization' and a life ordered culturally. Thus although Bjorkman's Vitalistic therapy is directly opposed to what Rieff calls Freudian neutrality with respect to teleological commitments, its cosmic pursuit of 'consciousness' involves an equally categorical step beyond culture.

The empty desert at the end of *Jocelyn* is a model of the post-cultural universe in process of cosmic repletion. When Galsworthy came to write *The Man of Property* and *Fraternity*, he was writing crisis novels in which post-cultural selves, unable to connect their animal selves with cosmic purposefulness, fall into crises of consciousness, into a fallen state between conscious life and self-conscious spirit.

Part III
Wells, Bennett and Galsworthy
as Edwardians

6
Transition

It would not, of course, be accurate to say that as soon as the year 1900 was past Wells, Bennett and Galsworthy stopped writing *fin-de-siècle* novels of consciousness in crisis, and began writing the healthily 'objective' books of the Edwardian myth. Both decades should be seen as partaking of the turn-of-the-century crisis, and, as I shall try to show in Chapters 7, 8 and 9, the shape of Edwardian novels is very much dictated by the conditions of a continuing response, gradually emerging as more positive, to existential insecurity. But by the time of the Liberal Revival, the three Edwardians had developed a new genre in the novel, a genre which surely represents a distinct and important phase in the history of English literature.[1] Instead of the widespread feeling of impending crisis in the 1890s fiction, there had appeared a confidence in living in a present time felt in some sense to be (or to have been) redeemed. There is a noticeable opening out towards society.

By the year 1910, Wells, Bennett and Galsworthy were able to write novels which worked both in and beyond what Raymond Williams has called the 'realist tradition':

When I think of the realist tradition in
fiction, I think of the kind of novel which
creates and judges the quality of a whole way
of life in terms of the qualities of persons.
The balance involved in this achievement is
perhaps the most important thing about it.
It looks at first sight so general a thing,

the sort of thing most novels do. It is what
War and Peace does; what *Middlemarch* does;
what *The Rainbow* does. Yet the distinction
of this kind is that it offers a valuing of a
whole way of life, a society that is larger
than any of the individuals composing it, and
at the same time valuing creations of human
beings who, while belonging to and affected by
and helping to define this way of life, are also,
in their own terms, absolute ends in themselves.
Neither element, neither the society nor the
individual, is there as a priority. The society
is not a background against which the personal
relationships are studied, nor are the individuals
merely illustrations of aspects of the way of life.
Every aspect of personal life is radically
affected by the quality of the general life, yet
the centre of value is always in the individual
human person – not only one isolated person, but
the many persons who are the reality of the
general life. Tolstoy and George Eliot, in
particular, often said, in much these terms, that
it was this view of life they were trying to
realize.[2]

The triumvirate (if such a term is valid for a group of writers
who would perhaps individually have denied such an implied
closeness) were so palpably committed in the 1900s to implicit
ideals of health and personal perfection that the quasi-thera-
peutic criterion of 'the qualities of persons' is peculiarly apt for
their Edwardian novels. Such an approach to Wells, Bennett
and Galsworthy draws attention to the polemical core of their
fiction as its characteristic achievement. This therapeutic 'core'
should not be separated from the 'art-content' of the novels. The
therapeutic imagination of Wells, Bennett and Galsworthy is,
on the contrary, the focusing of a distinct and original poetic.
While this Edwardian poetic is not pursued uniformly by the
three writers, it is something which critics have tended to isolate
out as a separable object of attack, so that perhaps it is not altogether new to claim this kind of affinity between the three.

Such an affinity is to be traced in the uniformity of the developments of the three writers through the turn-of-the-century period of transition. The general characteristics of this transition (in my view of it) have already been described. The novels which show Wells, Bennett and Galsworthy in process of transition from the 'subjective' 1890s to the 'objective' 1900s are *Love and Mr. Lewisham* (1900), *Anna of the Five Towns* (1902)[3] and *Villa Rubein* (1900). Lacking the supremely confident detachment of the novels published between 1905 and 1910, these works nevertheless achieve an objectivity which is a great advance on the 'obsessive' novels discussed in Chapters 3, 4 and 5. They remain more or less grim and earnest (what is missing is the comic element which appears in the Wells of five years later and in *The Old Wives' Tale* and *The Man of Property*). But *Mr. Lewisham* is the first of Wells's novels to exist totally in the realist mode, being a novel about the social 'trajectory' of the hero, his journey from 'illusion' to 'reality'. *Anna of the Five Towns*, by a simple reversal of geographical locations, deals with the intimate details of the 'Northern' milieu that Richard Larch left behind. Anna's family life, and her relationship with other families, is realized in social terms; there is a willingness to depict the terms of her cultural emigration, and the implicit (and perhaps unwitting) diagnosis of her final condition in the novel as that of precarious adaptation, is firmly grounded in a culturally plausible aetiology.

Villa Rubein, again, is the first of Galsworthy's novels 'of society'. There is admittedly a central plot element concerned with the illicit love-affair of an upper-middle-class English girl and an Austrian artist-anarchist (which thus derives in part from the iconography of *fin-de-siècle* fiction), and this is admittedly given a happy ending, but for the first time in Galsworthy's fiction there is the attempt to render the different members of the central family – in atomized extension, as it were – as the social setting of the primary story. There is also some inset discussion of social problems, foreshadowing that of *The Country House*, notably concerning the morality of marriage.

Each of the novels ends in a marriage; and although there is the sense in each case that the union is private and post-cultural, these marriages are more conventional than their equivalents in the later Edwardian fiction (the 'non-marriages' of Polly and Sophia and Soames). In each of the former cases, the threat of disruption is implicit in the conditions of the marriage, and a transitional willingness to capitulate to the stringencies of reality in this context is exhibited in all of the characters concerned. Thus Lewisham's (plausible) marriage difficulties are overcome when he 'sees' that his not loving Ethel is an illusion;[4] but this is more nearly an autoplastic mode of adaptation which will not work for Mr Polly.

The transition from *fin-de-siècle* evasion of reality (in the obsessive working out of fears and wishes) to capitulation to reality (in the 'transitional' novels) to the depiction of more enterprising characters in active creation of their 'reality' (in the 'High Edwardian' novels), appears to reflect both the general conditions of the emergence of modernism and a process of psychological maturation. The distinction between the capitulatory mode and the creative mode is of the greatest importance in any consideration of therapeutic systems.[5] The conflict of therapies defined in my first chapter (e.g. in the quarrel between existential anti-psychiatry and institutionalized psychotherapy) may reflect a conflict between alloplastic and autoplastic modes which is inevitable in all human adaptation, and which is presumably greatest at times of most drastic cultural change. Lionel Trilling diagnoses such a conflict in the very basis of Freudianism:

> . . . the essentially Freudian view assumes that the mind, for good as well as bad, helps to create its reality by selection and evaluation. In this view, reality is malleable and subject to creation; it is not static, but is rather a series of situations which are dealt with in their own terms. But beside this conception of the mind stands the conception which arises from Freud's therapeutic-practical assumptions; in this view, the mind deals with a reality which is quite fixed and static, a reality that is wholly 'given' and not (to use a phrase of Dewey's) 'taken'. In his epistemological utterances, Freud insists on this second view, although it is not easy to see why he should do so. For the reality to which he wishes to reconcile the

neurotic patient is, after all, a 'taken' and not
a 'given' reality. It is the reality of social life
and value, conceived and maintained by the human
mind and will. Love, morality, honor, esteem –
these are the components of a created reality.[6]

The present study cannot undertake to explore this problem in
the approach to Freud, but in defence of Freud we might cite
Bennett's injunction:

The facts of today, which in my regeneracy,
I regarded primarily as anxieties, nuisances,
impediments, I now regard as so much raw
material from which my brain has to weave a
tissue that is comely.[7]

Such a formulation seems to resolve the problem, for while
Bennett confirms that 'reality is malleable and subject to creation' he also insists that individuals must submit themselves
to the 'fixed' 'raw materials' which are 'given'. Such a view
leaves scope both for those whose remedy must involve a great
effort towards the mere recognition of reality, and for those
'freer' souls whose Utopianization of the conditions of existence
is more radical. There is perceptual naïveté involved in any such
simplified account of the problem, and we might well wish to
steer clear of the issue if it were not for the fact that the categories invented by Trilling, and in a sense related by Bennett,
are so closely relevant to the development of the English novel
between 1890 and 1910. The fictional characters of Wells,
Bennett and Galsworthy are, like neurotic patients, shown as
confronting a crisis in reality. In the 1890s these characters are
depicted as so much under the pressure of the *fin-de-siècle* process
that they either give up all pretensions to realistic thinking
or they give themselves up, not to Trilling's 'static' reality,
but to the ongoing process which contains them (e.g. the Time
Traveller, Richard Larch, and Jocelyn and Giles). The 'neurosis' of the characters is reflected in the tendency for the authors
to forsake realist settings and to opt for fantasy situations or
situations in which the social background for the action is depicted only partially. The next two stages in the development
take Wells, Bennett and Galsworthy into true 'realism'. The

second stage (the 'transitional') shows authors and characters at the point of having accepted reality, but as stopping short there, as it were, and leaving the 'creative' mode of adaptation to the more optimistic moment of the Liberal Revival. The great characters of the Edwardian novels, Mr Polly, George Ponderevo, Sophia Baines and Irene Forsyte, will not rest content with simple acceptance of 'the facts of today'. They make a claim for alloplastic adaptation, for the 'essential' Freudian mode, for the recreation of reality in terms which are dictated by the self in its post-cultural phase. There is no question of Mr Polly's accepting the therapy which solved Lewisham's marital problems. The rebellious Sophia is set up against the constant Constance. And Irene would hardly have claimed, as Christian does (albeit with fragile conviction) at the end of *Villa Rubein*: 'You see, I wouldn't have my life different really.'[8]

Once this principle of development is grasped, the criticism which sees the triumvirate's fiction solely in terms of its rendering of social consciousnesses must surely be reconsidered. What may be true of *Love and Mr. Lewisham* in this respect is not true of the later Wells novels. Sophia is a distinct development from Anna, not simply another version of the same prototype. And Irene refuses to become real in the world of the Forsytes because in terms of that environment she exists in a post-cultural mode.

It is interesting, however, to see just how strongly this earlier mood of renunciation, which is carried over in part from the *fin-de-siècle* submission to 'Fate', is represented in the transitional stage. It manifests itself, after 1900, in a new sense of practicality, and in realistic thinking. Mr Lewisham manages at last to accept his personal limitations; the plan for self-improvement he had constructed years before is destroyed:

He doubled the halves and tore again,
doubled again very carefully and neatly
until the Schema was torn into numberless
little pieces. With it he seemed to be
tearing his past self.[9]

As in Bennett's *The Man from the North*, Wells's hero bequeaths his over-weening ambitions to evolutionary posterity, and hence therapeutically rids himself of a tremendous existential burden:

'Come to think, it is all the Child. The
future is the Child. The Future. What are
we – any of us – but servants or traitors to
that?'[10]

The important character Chaffery expresses, in a somewhat
unpleasant allegory, the possibility of a 'compromise' mode of
adaptation which is in part alloplastic and in part autoplastic;
it is very similar to the advice given by Bennett to the readers of
his 'Pocket Philosophies' later in the 1900s:

'This cheese is as nutritious and unattractive
as Science', remarked Chaffery, cutting and
passing wedges. 'But crush it – so – under your
fork, add a little of this good Dorset butter,
a dab of mustard, pepper – the pepper is very
necessary – and some malt vinegar, and crush
together. You get a compound called Crab and
by no means disagreeable. So the wise deal with
the facts of life, neither bolting nor rejecting,
but adapting.'[11]

Chaffery's predicament, which leads him into a self-destroying
amoralism, is thus very much the Freudian predicament, and it
is a disease which *The History of Mr. Polly* sets out to cure in its
hero. We need to bear in mind Philip Rieff's insight that 'the
therapeutic mode developed by Freud is essentially alloplastic
and aims . . . systematically at an externalization of human
vitality' (p. 197). It is precisely a therapy able to permit the
healthy 'externalization of human vitality' that Chaffery is
demanding, an analytic method for relating the totality of the
self with the impulses which operate 'upon' it. Lewisham's
capitulation is, for Chaffery, too unthinking an instinctual deprivation.

Anna's decision to marry Mynors at the end of Bennett's
novel is similarly renunciatory. Like Isabel Archer in a sense,
Anna knows she does not love Mynors in the way she loved
Willie, but still feels bound to marry him. To this extent she
realizes herself through culture and not 'beyond' it.

But it is in Galsworthy that the problem is most directly
stated. In a curious coda to *Villa Rubein*, Christian, having at

last married the penniless artist, shows herself to be retreating
to a Jocelyn-style dissatisfaction. But there is a new principle of
'compromise' which makes her fit precariously into the marriage:

> Christian gave a faint sigh. Harz put his lips
> to her hand.
>   'Dearie,' he said, 'are you tired?'
>   'No, It's only – what Greta says in her letter
> about the spring, it makes one want things,'
> and, slipping her hand from his arm, she
> went back to the window.[12]

The novel finishes on a note which presents the predicament in
erms of shallow irony:

> Christian looked at Harz. Presently she
> rose and went across to him.
>   Tramper blew out a cloud of smoke. He
> stared dubiously at the sky.
>   'Well,' he muttered, 'I guess it's all a
> kind of compromise, any way!'[13]

It is that note which characterizes the intermediate novels of
Wells, Bennett and Galsworthy at the turn of the century. The
thesis of indulged fantasizing had been totally replaced by the
antithesis of instinctual renunciation. That in itself represented a
process of maturation. But the process was half complete. The
dialectic finishes for the purposes of this study with the therapeutic synthesis in the Edwardian moment, where autoplastic
and alloplastic modes are set one against the other, and an ideal,
explicit or implicit, emerges. What finally is produced is the
systematic 'externalization of human vitality' which Lawrence
was able to take up, redefine and push to extreme limits.

The new recognition of the demands of reality that the new
century brought with it is registered also in other areas of
artistic activity. The transition from *Art Nouveau*[14] to Cubism
(1907) in modern art took place over the same period, and
Picasso's early mournfully 'realistic' works at the turn of the
century perhaps correspond to the transitional novels of Wells,
Bennett and Galsworthy. In technical terms, the three have
more affinities with the Impressionists than with Picasso; but in

terms of the psychohistory of the turning of the century, their 'High Edwardian' 'externalization of human vitality', limited as it is in comparison with Lawrence's later developments in the same long dialectic, is not by 'mere chance' contemporaneous (though unwittingly) with the revolutionary work of Freud and Picasso.

7
H. G. Wells

I

H. G. Wells is the greatest of the modern global therapists;
nobody else, indeed, has seemed to want the publicity of being,
in an age of public exposure, a prophet so vulnerable. But the
millennial unity that Wells imagined and fought for is something taken almost for granted in the computerese of Marshall
McLuhan. While Wells was perhaps the last important 'thinker'
to attempt to confront a 'sequential' universe, and was caught
up to the last printed utterance of his life in the disordered conflict between fears and wishes in the face of the future, Philip
Rieff, for example, announces 'a fundamental change of focus
in the entire cast of our culture – toward a human condition
about which there will be nothing further to say in terms of the
old style of despair and hope'.[1] We may return to Rieff again
and again as we examine the therapeutic crisis of Wells, not as
to some new prophetical absolute (in whom we put all trust and
faith) but as a focus point for ironical contrast with Wells.

Perhaps Wells is more important as the writer who could be
passionately either an optimist or a pessimist than as one or the
other exclusively. For in his application of alternative fantasies
of Utopia and anti-Utopia he is the very archetype of bemused
pre-Rieffian, pre-McLuhan, man. It may be, indeed, that
Wells's 'optimism' and 'pessimism' are not separate states
indicative of some radical inconsistency, but are complement-
ary attitudes. As Frank Kermode has suggested:

In general, we seem to combine a sense of
decadence in society – as evidenced by the
concept of alienation, which, supported by a
new interest in the early Marx, has never
enjoyed more esteem – with a technological
utopianism. In our ways of thinking about the
future there are contradictions which if we
were willing to consider them openly, might
call for some effort towards complementarity.
But they lie, as a rule, too deep.[2]

Equipped as we are to trace the connection between the post-
cultural state and the mixture of freeing and alienation that it
involves, we may perhaps understand more clearly the Utopianizing role played by Wellsian characters like Bert Smallways:

Bert Smallways was a vulgar little creature,
the sort of pert, limited soul that the old
civilization of the early twentieth century
produced by the million in every country of the
world. He had lived all his life in narrow
streets, and between mean houses he could not
look over, and in a narrow circle of ideas from
which there was no escape. . . . Now by a curious
accident he found himself lifted out of his
marvellous modern world for a time, out of all
the rush and confused appeals of it, and floating
like a thing dead and disembodied between sea and
sky. It was as if Heaven was experimenting with
him, had picked him out as a sample from the
English millions to look at him more nearly and
to see what was happening to the soul of man.[3]

Bert Smallways's transcendental experience in a world
without God is the archetypal experience of Wells's post-1900
heroes. Although Wells's Edwardian novels have in common a
direct, outward-looking interest in 'society', they nevertheless
focus that interest by rendering the disengaged consciousnesses
of ordinary men. Often this discrepancy between the isolated
consciousness and the 'old-fashioned' cultural limitations of its
societal environment is the source of some excellent comedy,

which is exploited as a method for showing the pressures operating upon dissociated existence, upon existential man.

However much a Wells book may seem to be concerned with society on a large scale, as in *Tono-Bungay* or *The War of the Worlds*, it derives its force and originality from the rhythm of personal Utopianization that runs through it. Whether Wells is concerned primarily with social ideas or with the plight of an individual, he generally presents, in his pre-1910 novels, a therapeutic process containing one main character. In the early novels the process tends to be conformative, and the therapy implemented by Griffin, for example, is negative. In the post-1900 novels, and certainly in the novels from *Kipps* (1905) and *In the Days of the Comet* (1906) onwards, the therapeutic pattern tends to be positively Utopianizing and transformative.

In Bert Smallways the pattern of desocialized, 'disembodied', post-cultural existence recurs. In his deculturalized state he is 'like a thing dead', but he has a cosmic involvement unknown to the millions of 'limited' souls: 'It was as if Heaven was experimenting with him.' The analytic attitude which the narrative of the novel forthwith displays is the attitude necessary for survival in the limbo beyond culture. Only a transformative activism can effect the cosmic Utopianization which is seen to have occurred in, for example, the last pages of *Mr. Polly*:

> Polly sat beside the fat woman at one of the
> little green tables at the back of the Potwell
> Inn. . . . It was as if everything lay securely
> within a great, warm, friendly globe of
> crystal sky. It was as safe and enclosed
> and fearless as a child that has still to be
> born.[4]

II

In the Days of the Comet is divided into two parts: in the first the lower-class Leadford is driven to desperation when his beloved Nettie has a love affair with the upper-class Verrall. He sets out to murder them both. At the very climax of the murder-hunt, the apocalyptic comet effects a global 'Change' in human psychology, and a new sense of 'well-being' and rationality descends upon all the characters of the novel. A Wellsian *ménage à trois*, rationally managed, is the outcome. The new triumph of the rational ego is associated with a widespread communalization of society.

In the Days of the Comet is thus radically different from the science-fiction novels of the 1890s. It might be seen as a way of talking about the transition from pressurized *fin-de-siècle* time to the post-1900 experience of 'redeemed' time. Its time-structure is interestingly similar, in fact, to *The Winter's Tale* (which may also, of course, relate to the experience of living through the turning of an important century).

In this novel of 1906 a para-Freudian analytic therapy is set up as the cure for cultural crisis. Frank Wells has drawn attention to the existence of the characters in the book *Beyond Culture*:

> This novel is . . . a touchpaper to set off a
> rocket of discussion, ideas and argument.
> The characters are not inhabitants of the Five
> Towns, as are the living characters of Arnold
> Bennett, they are 'world' characters – strangely
> English.[5]

This usefully emphasizes H. G. Wells's sense of the incongruousness of the residual cultural characteristics of his post-cultural characters; but only in the second half of the book is Frank Wells's second sentence strictly applicable. In the first half of the book the murderous intensity with which Leadford pursues his class-hatred is depicted strictly – though, indeed, crudely – in a specifically English milieu, with the social divisions which Wells saw characterizing that milieu depicted in some 'cultural' detail. Seen in this light, Leadford is initially an *alter ego* of Kipps's. Only after the comet has effected its change does the 'citizen of the World' character of Leadford emerge.[6]

Wells's depiction of Leadford in a pre-apocalyptic state of cultural repression, driven into an irrational murderous rage by the exigencies of contemporary society, may bear resemblances to the state of Wells's mind before 1900 and indeed to the psychic condition of the late-Victorian period as a whole. Leadford, writing of an imminent fictional war with Germany from his post-apocalyptic vantage-point, defines himself in much the same way as the symptomatics of the 1890s unconsciously defined themselves:

It was like one of a flood of disease germs
that have invaded a body, that paper.[7] There I
was, one corpuscle in the big amorphous body of the
English community, one of forty-one million such
corpuscles; and, for all my preoccupations, these
potent headlines, this paper ferment, caught me and
swung me about. And all over the country that day,
millions read as I read, and came into line with me,
under the same magnetic spell, came round – how did
we say it? – Ah! – 'to face the foe'.[8]

Here Wells is defining *fin-de-siècle* crisis in terms of a disease of society, and relating the sense of apocalypse to a synthesis of war-feeling. As in much of the pre-1900 writing of Wells, Bennett and Galsworthy, Leadford's translation here of the *fin-de-siècle* experience gives the impression that men felt themselves to be under the influence of magic, as if afflicted by a voodoo charm. The words, 'magnetic spell', are suggestive of the very heavily 'determined' state of Western thinking in the years just before calendar apocalypse. In this novel of 1906 (which perhaps reflects the apocalyptic 'disconfirmation' provided to a degree by the outcome of the Boer War), news of the coming war results in the comet's being 'driven into obscurity overleaf' (p. 94), just as information about the coming freeing to be derived from passing through the year 1900 was hidden by the 'disease germs' of *fin de sièclism*.

Again, the state of Leadford after the comet has passed seems exactly to match Wells's consciousness after 1900; the transition is made in Wells's fiction from a preoccupation with isolated individuals in desperate states to a speculative concern for the quality of individual life within society as a whole. As soon as Leadford wakes up from the short sleep induced by the comet, he meets Melmount, one of the fifteen men who are supposed to have been controlling the Empire and thus have been responsible for the German war. Leadford is thus, by coincidence, introduced to the first sane (i.e. Wellsian) meeting between the statesmen:

And what a strange unprecedented thing was
that cabinet council at which I was present,
the council that was held two days later in
Melmount's bungalow, and which convened the
conference to frame the constitution of the
World State (p. 188).

Nothing could be more naïvely the projection of a writer's
own personal wishes than this, and the lack of artistic tact with
which Wells frames this section is analogous to (though not
simultaneous with) the general movement in Wells's own
development from artist to therapist impatient of art. It would
be easy to accuse the second section of the novel of being mere
discursive polemic, even less patiently 'realized' than the first
half. But if there is naïveté in Wells's account of the changes
wrought by the comet (and indeed of the initial 'spell' upon
Leadford), the naïve (in the Kermodean sense) apocalypse of
the 1890s and the sense of a beginning in the 1900s *were* absurdly, childishly, structured out of the gullibility of men pro-
jecting, as Kermode would say, their existential anxieties upon a
centurial ending. Thus, although Wells's novel is objective
enough to depict the turning into a new era with some justice, it
partakes of some of the simple-mindedness of the immediately
post-1900 period. It positively takes simple-mindedness to be a
sign of health.

It is possible to relate Leadford's sense of dispossession and his
alienation before the advent of the comet to the tradition of
alienation that has gradually come to assume a para-cultural
role, being one of the ways in which 'literate' people now make
sense of life. The concomitant of alienation is therapy, and it is
also tempting to relate Leadford's sense of 'well-being' (p. 153)
after the 'Change' to our own nostalgia for health, to the
health-ideal implicit in our own constant diagnosing of contemporary sickness. Before the change, Leadford's determination to
murder Verrall is nihilistic (involving self-destruction), similar
to Mr Polly's decision to set fire to his shop:

From that moment when I insulted old Mrs.
Verrall I became representative. I was a man
who stood for all the disinherited of the world.
I had no hope of pride or pleasure left in me.

I was raging rebellion against God and mankind.
There were no more vague intentions swaying me
this way and that; I was perfectly clear now upon
what I meant to do. I would make my protest and
die (p. 111).

Leadford's predicament seems also to parallel Griffin's in *The
Invisible Man*, and it is significant that once again conscious
man's position is seen to be that of 'the disinherited'. We have
seen how this state of mind is defined in terms of 'germs' and
'sickness'. The post-apocalyptic state of Leadford is as clearly
defined as 'well-being', and the return to health involves a
return to 'the barley-fields of God'. The intimate association of
Revelation with regained health is unmistakable:

I seemed to awaken out of a refreshing sleep.
I did not awaken with a start, but opened my eyes,
and lay very comfortably looking at a line of
extraordinary scarlet poppies that glowed against
a glowing sky. It was the sky of a magnificent
sunrise, and an archipelago of gold-beached
purple islands floated in a sea of golden-green.
The poppies, too, swan-necked buds, blazing
corollas, translucent stout seed-vessels, stoutly
upheld, had a luminous quality, seemed wrought
only from some more solid kind of light. . . .
    I felt very light, full of the sense of
physical well-being. I perceived I was lying
on my side in a little trampled space in a
weedy, flowering barley-field, that was in
some inexplicable way saturated with light
and beauty. I sat up and remained for a long
time filled with the delight and charm of the
delicate little convolvulus that twined among
the barley stems, the pimpernel that laced the
ground below. . . .
    I felt as though I was a thing in some very
luminous painted window, as though this dawn
broke through me. I felt I was part of some
exquisite painting painted in light and joy. . . .
    . . . I felt sure I was dead; no one living could

have this perfect assurance of good, this strong
and confident peace. I had made an end of the
fever called living. . . .

These, then, must be the barley-fields of
God! (pp. 153–5).

This is, aesthetically, a most complex passage, but it should be
possible to establish that the 'Luminism' which helps to define
the scene significantly as a dawning is not the style of French
Impressionism, but belongs to another tradition. The passage
surely reflects the Edwardian assimilation of the Renaissance,
and a new transfiguration of man:

I held up my left hand and arm before me, a
grubby hand, a frayed cuff; but with a quality
of painted unreality, transfigured as a beggar
might have been by Botticelli. I looked for a
time steadfastly at a beautiful pearl sleeve link (p. 154).

Such a vision exemplifies the characteristic Edwardian Utopianization of self; written in a prose-style which is a strange
mixture of stock image and pseudo-scientific originality, it
reflects a disdain for traditional cultural usage which is entirely
in keeping with its rendering of the state which exists beyond
culture. The phenomenon involved is a post-1900 infilling of the
Victorian hollow universe; and, like the Renaissance, this
man-made apocalypse is vitally concerned with revivification.
There is a connection between this vision of 'a magnificent
sunrise' and the passage from *The First Men in the Moon* which
is cited by Bernard Bergonzi in *The Early H. G. Wells*:

One after another all down the sunlit slope
these miraculous little brown bodies burst and
gaped apart, like seed-pods, like the husks of
fruits; opened eager mouths that drank in the
heat and light pouring in a cascade from the
newly-risen sun.

Every moment more of these seed coats
ruptured, and even as they did so the swelling
pioneers overflowed their rent, distended seed-
cases and passed into the second stage of growth.
With a steady assurance, a swift deliberation,

these amazing seeds thrust a rootlet downward
to the earth and a queer bundle-like bud into
the air. In a little while the slope was dotted
with minute plantlets standing at attention in
the blaze of the sun.

They did not stand for long. The bundle-like
buds swelled and strained and opened with a jerk,
thrusting out a coronet of little sharp tips,
spreading a whorl of tiny, spiky, brownish leaves,
that lengthened rapidly, lengthened visibly even
as we watched. The movement was slower than any
animal's, swifter than any plant's I have ever
seen before.[9]

Bergonzi attempts to account for the difference between this
kind of writing and the earlier 'imaginative' prose of the pre-
1900 scientific romances. He concludes: 'In describing the
imaginary panic in London following the Martian invasion,
Wells was making certain implications about the society he
lived in; in describing the equally imaginary blossoming of the
lunar flowers, he was simply exercising his imagination for its
own sake.'[10] If we search for Bergonzi's idea of the 'implications' of *The War of the Worlds*, we find this: '*The War of the
Worlds* enacts the secret fears and lack of confidence of late
Victorian bourgeois society.'[11] In the light of this explanation, it
seems unlikely that Wells's description of the moon-flowers was
an exercising of the imagination 'for its own sake', however; it
surely represents, on the contrary, an attitude to the future
strikingly opposite to that implicit in *The War of the Worlds*. It
depicts the reverse of 'lack of confidence' in its rendering of
'steady assurance'; and 'secret fears' are replaced by 'a swift
deliberation'. In place of the conformative landscapes of *The
Time Machine*, we find the transformative landscape of the moon
and the barley-fields of God. Bergonzi draws attention to a
difference between the early and later work, but his description
is more useful if the post-1900 sense of a Utopianizing beginning
is recognized:

In the lunar scenes Wells was able to describe
a strange and exotic world with the confidence in
his own powers that he had displayed in *The Time*

Machine. Indeed, many of these scenes show more exuberance of imagination – particularly visual imagination – than any other passages of Wells's writings. In *The Time Machine* the world of 802701 is vividly realized, but for all the strangeness of detail, the contemporary Southern English landscape is somehow apparent through the great cultivated garden in which the Eloi live. The lunar landscapes are, in one sense, wholly 'artificial'.[12]

Bergonzi does not deal with *In the Days of the Comet*, which he believes to be a 'very inferior novel',[13] but he might perhaps agree that there is some evidence of 'exuberance of imagination – particularly visual imagination' in the 'barley-fields of God' passage. And the special quality of the 'scientific' prose there might indeed be explained by saying that it constructed 'artificial' landscapes. After the *fin-de-siècle* depiction of post-cultural man in crisis, hollow and inhabiting a hollow universe, comes the Edwardian creation of a 'psychomorphous' universe. A willed intervention in 'creative evolution' replaces the self-depriving mode of conformative adaptation. In the section immediately preceding that quoted by Bergonzi, Bedford and Cavor undergo an experience which seems to parallel this transition from the dead, mechanical universe of Darwinian process to the Bergsonian Vitalism of the post-1900 world:

How can I describe the thing I saw? It is so petty a thing to state, and yet it seemed so wonderful, so pregnant with emotion. I have said that amidst the stick-like litter were these rounded bodies, these little oval bodies that might have passed as very small pebbles. And now first one and then another had stirred, had rolled over and cracked, and down the crack of each of them showed a minute line of yellowish green, thrusting outward to meet the hot encouragement of the newly-risen sun. For a moment that was all, and then there stirred, and burst a third!

'It is seed', said Cavor. And then I heard him whisper very softly, 'Life!'

'Life!' And immediately it poured upon us
that our vast journey had not been made in vain,
that we had come to no arid waste of minerals,
but to a world that lived and moved! We watched
intensely.[14]

Perhaps Bergonzi would want to claim a mythic content for
such a vision; in any event, it seems that this redeemed, 'artificial' landscape is still the ground of our latter-day universe. It is
true that the First World War induced a very deep disconfirmation of the Edwardian Revelation, and that we have come
to see that

April is the cruellest month, breeding
Lilacs out of the dead land . . .

but we still have a deep reverence for life itself. It might even be
argued that Wells's account of life on the moon may be a new
creation myth for post-Christian man, a moving beyond Darwinian crisis: 'immediately it poured upon us that our vast
journey had not been in vain, that we had come to no arid
waste of minerals, but to a world that lived and moved!'

Bedford is so fascinated by the lunar scene that, as he relates,
'I kept rubbing the glass before me with my sleeve, jealous of the
faintest suspicion of mist'; the clarity of the scene is essential,
and any subjectivity, any 'impressionism', might suggest a
reversion to the *fin-de-siècle* mode. Immediately before the
passage (from *In the Days of the Comet*) that describes the 'weedy,
flowering barley field, that was in some way saturated with light
and beauty', comes the section of the novel leading up to the
'Change'. Although this is a novel of 1906, it is not difficult to
recognize the element of *fin-de-siècle* 'mist'. We are reminded of
parts of *The Time Machine*:

Someone pursued me, perhaps several people – I
do not know, we left them all behind. . . .
We ran. For a space I was altogether intent
upon the swift monotony of flight and pursuit.
The sands were changed to a whirl of green moon-
shine, the air was thunder. A luminous green
haze rolled about us. What did such things matter?
We ran. Did I gain or lose? that was the question.

They ran through a gap in a broken fence that
sprang up abruptly out of the nothingness, and
turned to the right. . . .
    They were gone! Everything was going, but I
kept on running. Once more I stumbled. There
was something about my feet that impeded me, tall
grass or heather, but I could not see what it was,
only this smoke that eddied about my knees. There
was a noise and spinning in my brain, a vain
resistance to a dark green curtain that was falling,
falling, falling, fold upon fold. Everything grew
darker and darker. . . .
    . . . all things ceased to be.

Here we are in Matthew Arnold's Victorian world where all is

                . . . turning, turning,
    In mazes of heat and sound.

But the comet induces a change which moves Leadford forward
to a therapeutic renaissance:

I seemed to awaken out of a refreshing
sleep. I did not awaken with a start, but
opened my eyes, and lay very comfortably. . . .
    I felt very light, full of the sense of
physical well-being.

Following Bergonzi's suggestion about the earlier romances, we
might here identify a neglected Edwardian myth of secular apocalypse. Just as the *fin-de-siècle* myths were not merely 'fantasy',
but reflected contemporary social and psychic conditions, so
this Edwardian myth is not simply shallow Wellsian wish-fulfilment, but a vivid analogue of the actual process of psychic
rebirth that seems to have occurred in the Edwardian period.
    The primary strength of the work as model of centurial
apocalypse is its principal weakness as a conventional novel. It
has no simple sequential structure. The first half has close
affinities with the ordinary suspense novel of the Victorian
world, but just at the climax of the action, when the reader
expects Leadford to murder Nettie and Verrall, the green mist
falls. The speeded-up time of the murder-hunt makes the

strongest possible contrast with the new order of time which follows the change. There is an effect similar to the truncated hunt at the end of William Golding's novel, *The Lord of the Flies*.[15]

The transition from a hysterically rapid process of uncontrolled violence to the redeemed springtime of a pastoral world is also the pattern of *The Winter's Tale*, whose structure is similarly split and 'flawed'. In each work an apocalyptic pastoralization occurs which provides the formal opportunity for measured discourse. In the second half of *In the Days of the Comet* a form of therapeutic society is constructed out of the ruins of the old order. This is typically Wellsian, of course, but in this particular novel the discursive element is presented in satisfying formal contrast to the strict sequentiality of the first section of the narrative. *In the Days of the Comet* is, then, an interesting attempt to render the transition to what I have called a Rieffian universe. The breakdown in linear, sequential narrative, and the breakthrough into a non-sequential narrative universe, reflects a general movement towards analytic activism. Wells uses an image strikingly similar to the 'nihilistic' vision of the end of *Tono-Bungay*:

> We sat silently for a time before our
> vivisected passions.
> 'Gods!' I cried, 'and there was our poor
> little top-hamper of intelligence on all these
> waves of instinct and wordless desire, these
> foaming things of touch and sight and feeling,
> like – like a coop of hens washed overboard and
> clucking amidst the seas.'
> Verrall laughed approval of the image I had
> struck out.
> 'A week ago,' he said, trying it further,
> 'we were clinging to our chicken coops and going
> with the heave and pour. That was true enough
> a week ago. But today ——?'
> 'Today,' I said, 'the wind has fallen. The
> world storm is over. And each chicken coop has
> changed by a miracle to a vehicle that makes
> head against the sea.'[16]

This concept of post-cultural man who escapes a purposeless clucking through cognitive control of himself and his environment is akin to Rieff's idea of a Freudian analytic therapy-for-therapy's-sake, in which the aim is to 'keep going'. In his para-Freudian assertion of the power of the ego and a concomitant passing beyond culture, Wells deliberately undermines the 'cultural' content of his writing by using an image which is both banal and absurd. There is a built-in safeguard against the critic who might read such a passage and claim it to comprise a 'myth of centurial apocalypse', say, By writing in this way Wells sets out to reverse the appeal being made to the reader as he reads the first part of the book. At first, such is the physiology of reading, the reader is bodily following Leadford on his murder-hunt; then Wells devalues all the emotional involvement of the reader by offering an absurd fiction of chickens and chicken coops. The reader is forced into an analytic mode in the very act of processing his own 'literary' reactions, his fictional disappointments. The reader's vertigo is not least among the elements which come under cure when Wells deliberately destroys the cultural 'integrity' of the novel, leaves the initial action unfinished, and proceeds to analyse the sexual relations between the characters with a patience which is unwittingly Freudian. Cultural ordering, which to Wells involves conforming to an evolved state of disinheritance and existing in perpetual crisis, is replaced by therapeutic community, involvement in the ongoing activist creation of a psychomorphous universe.

III

Kipps was published in 1905, a year before *In the Days of the Comet*, and presents a vision of England before change. Kipps himself comes to represent deprived existence badgered by the conditions of cultural order:

> The stupid little tragedies of these clipped
> and limited lives!
>   As I think of them lying unhappily there in
> the darkness, my vision pierces the night. See
> what I can see! Above them, brooding over them,

I tell you there is a monster, a lumpish monster,
like some great griffin thing, like the Crystal
Palace labyrinthodon, like Coote, like the leaden
goddess of the Dunciad, like some fat, proud
flunkey, like pride, like indolence, like all that
is darkening and heavy and obstructive in life.
It is matter and darkness, it is the anti-soul,
it is the ruling power of this land, Stupidity.
My Kippses live in its shadow. Shalford and his
apprenticeship system, the Hastings Academy, the
ideas of Coote, the ideas of the old Kippses, all
the ideas that have made Kipps what he is, – all
these are a part of its shadow. But for that
monster they might not be groping among false
ideas to hurt one another so sorely; but for that,
the glowing promise of childhood and youth might
have had a happier fruition; thought might have
awakened in them to meet the thought of the world,
the quickening sunshine of literature pierced to
the substance of their souls; their lives might
not have been divorced, as now they are divorced,
from the apprehension of beauty that we favoured
ones are given, – the vision of the Grail that makes
life fine for ever.[17]

Kipps's 'clipped and limited' life is shown very much in class
terms in the novel, but the total vision of the book is not directed
by class-hostilities. The medical socialist's therapeutic imagination transcends matters of class, and turns for example to literature not for its 'cultural' embodiment of the finest values but
for its 'quickening sunshine' which 'pierces' to the very 'substance of . . . souls'. The sentimental socialism of the passage
continues:

I have laughed, and I laugh at these two people;
I have sought to make you laugh. . . .
    But I see through the darkness the souls of my
Kippses as they are, as little pink strips of
quivering living stuff, as things like the
bodies of little, ill-nourished, ailing,
ignorant children – children who feel pain,

who are naughty and muddled and suffer, and
do not understand why. And the claw of this
Beast rests upon them.[18]

Wells's cry for better births and 'a happier fruition' is fundamental to his therapeutic vision of cultural crisis. His dissociated
existences, bemused by the cultural pressures which afflict
them, constitute a means of defining a crisis in society. Even the
'Story of a Simple Soul' can become a revolutionary realization
of social fragmentation, in which the self's unwitting demands
for therapy are the source of a transformative dynamic.

Wells refers to his design to make the reader laugh; in Kipps
the comedy becomes the source of the reader's sympathy for the
hero:

'And how does it feel to have twelve hundred
a year?' asked Masterman, holding his cigarette
to his nose tip in a curious manner.
  'It's rum', confided Kipps, after a reflective
interval. 'It feels juiced rum'.[19]

Masterman's unpleasant cynicism is the mark of revolution of
the conventional kind. Kipps's innocuously inflated language,
'clipping' and 'limiting' as it is, establishes the implicit purity of
Kipps's dissociated 'soul' as a revolutionary instrument of a
more radical kind.[20] Set into the world uttering absurdly
anachronistic phrases, it undermines cultural coherence, making
through its very vulnerability and imperfection the most compelling of requests for therapy. To Masterman accrues the guilt
of putting such a therapeutic vision into words; but his vision is
only an abstraction from Kipps's predicament, and depends
upon implicit criteria of psychological well-being:

As for happiness, you want a world in order
before money or property or any of those things
have any real value, and this world, I tell you,
is hopelessly out of joint. Man is a social
animal with a mind nowadays that goes round the
globe, and a community cannot be happy in one
part and unhappy in another. It's all or nothing,
no patching any more for ever. It is the standing
mistake of the world not to understand that.

Consequently people think there is a class or
order somewhere just above them or just below
them, or a country or place somewhere that is
really safe and happy. . . . The fact is, Society
is one body, and it is either well or ill.
That's the law. This society we live in is ill.
It's a fractious, feverish invalid, gouty, greedy,
ill-nourished. You can't have a happy left leg
with neuralgia, or a happy throat with a broken
leg.[21]

We may note that cultural ordering, as in 'a class or order' and
'a country or place somewhere', is once again in Wells's thought
replaced by therapeutic ordering. Happiness derives from a co-
herent 'community' and 'This society . . . is ill'. The appeal of a
therapeutic vision which partly derives its criteria of health
from aesthetic considerations is clear in both the Beast passage
and this speech of Masterman's. The words 'ill-nourished',
which appear in both passages, suggest existential deprivation.
But more than this, such words seem to be responding to a new
kind of communal guilt or anxiety, foreshadowing the strange
fascination that photographs of Biafran children have for us. In
place of the Original Sin of the pre-Darwinian world, sickness,
physical emaciation and 'suffering' become the objects of redemption.

It is important to understand the primacy of the therapeutic
motive in Wells's sensibility, and not to confuse the money-
symbolism of *Kipps*, for example, with a thorough-going
para-Marxism. As Masterman's speech suggests, Wells is not
concerned with the historical importance of economic factors.
Kipps is just as much involved with money at the end of the
novel as at the beginning. But just as Ann's half of the sixpence
is 'redeemed', so is Kipps's money-dealing.

The symbolic structure of the novel seems simple. The divided
sixpence represents the hygienic removal of a piece of 'Muck' –
as Chaffery calls coinage in *Love and Mr. Lewisham*[22] – and the substitution of individual human union between two people rein-
forcing the 'worth' of the relationship. The sixpence when cut
through is worthless as a coin, but is infinitely valuable, since it
may symbolize mutual realization if the two halves are brought

together again. The therapeutic process which works to still
Kipps's alienated consciousness may be traced in two moments
of the novel's development. When Kipps is in the dining-room
of the Royal Grand Hotel, he is so out of place and so (as he
fancies) laughed at in his attempts to eat 'properly', that he
undergoes a rapid adaptive change and finds himself emerging
as a 'Socialist':

> The mental change Kipps underwent was, in its
> way, what psychologists call a conversion. In a
> few moments all Kipps's ideals were changed. He
> who had been 'practically a gentleman', the
> sedulous pupil of Coote, the punctilious raiser
> of hats, was instantly a rebel, an outcast, the
> hater of everything 'stuck up', the foe of
> Society and the social order of today. Here
> they were among the profits of their robbery,
> these people who might do anything with the
> world. . . .
> 'No thenks', he said to a dish.[23]

Wells catches admirably the funny-pathetic quality of the 'foe
of Society' who nevertheless makes an automatic effort to copy
the accents of 'Society', and ultimately thereby to become
Society. The scene is brought to life by the vividly idiosyncratic
language which shows the dissociated existence of Kipps precariously adopting a cultural mode of being in the world. But
from the extreme self-consciousness of his exposure in the
dining-room, Kipps moves to an ultimate stilling of consciousness, where the word 'reely' is a sign of existential authenticity,
and where the unity of the family (Kipps, Ann and their child)
is reflected in the final caught moment of union with natural
beauty:

> Out of the darkness beneath the shallow
> weedy stream of his being rose a question,
> a question that looked up dimly and never
> reached the surface. It was the question
> of the wonder of the beauty, the purposeless,
> inconsecutive beauty, that falls so strangely
> among the happenings and memories of life. It

never reached the surface of his mind, it never
took to itself substance or form; it looked up
merely as the phantom of a face might look, out
of deep waters, and sank again into nothingness.
    'Artie', said Ann.
    He woke up and pulled a stroke. 'What?' he said.
    'Penny for your thoughts, Artie'.
    'I reely don't think I was thinking of
anything', he said at last, with a smile. 'No'.[24]

In this priceless unconscious union with the universe (valued ironically at a penny) there is a kind of harmony and sense of well-being not previously depicted in Wells's novels. It is the harmony of the post-cultural self in intimate, mutually realizing relations with another self, the harmony of 'cosmic' existence. Such a harmony is available to Kipps only after he has found it possible to give up all 'cultural' pretensions, only after he and his family have established an intensely private bridge-head beyond culture.

IV

Tono-Bungay is less conventional in structure than *Kipps*, and it may be that recent accounts of the novel[25] have concerned themselves too exclusively with structural considerations. The apparently uncontrolled alternation of sexual and socio-economic episodes in *Tono-Bungay* might be interpreted as an analytic process for relating the Freudian and Marxist predicaments in an ongoing way, the activist remedy that Wells recommends at the end of the novel being implemented in the actual 'anarchic' sequence of events in the novel. The very gap or aesthetic discrepancy between the sexual and social themes is in itself, in this view, the grounds for the establishing of a remedial Freudo-Marxist dialectic. The image of individual man 'making and passing', 'striving upon a hidden mission, out to the open sea',[26] is not superadded to the novel, nor is it conflicting in spirit with the analytic-agnostic attitude implicit in the ordering of the material of the novel.

    Structural approaches to *Tono-Bungay* are, in this view,

rather wide of the critical mark. It is a novel which defines itself as it proceeds as an ongoing process; it would be proper to talk not of its structure, but of the experience it engenders during the time the reader spends reading it. The form of *Tono-Bungay* analogizes Edwardian crisis temporally. Whereas the great Victorian novels move always towards an end, *Tono-Bungay* is structured around the release of the narrator from an ending process. At the end 'through the confusion sounds another note',[27] and there is discernible 'a music beneath the noise'.[28] At first sight the narrator's opting out of contemporary decadence, and submission to historical process, may seem Marxist. But it may be a mistake to dwell on the Marxist character of Wells's Utopianization, for that Utopianization is both technological and at the same time intensely private. Wells grew more and more convinced of the programmatic need for self-submission to human racial process, but his later theorizing should not be allowed to distort our view of the Edwardian novels, which are novels of private consciousness, and make demands which are fundamentally existential.

In *Tono-Bungay* Wells's 'nihilistic' faith in the destroyer, 'X2', represents the denial of any cultural teleology, the Marxist included. The novelistic registration of the other note which sounds through confusion is the sense of redeemed private time in the modulation of tenses in the penultimate paragraph of the novel:

> Though, as a matter of fact, X2 isn't intended
> for the empire, or indeed for the hands of any
> European power. We offered it to our people
> first, but they would have nothing to do with me,
> and I have long since ceased to trouble much about
> such questions. I have come to see myself from
> the outside, my country from the outside – without
> illusion. We make and pass.[29]

The final present tense represents a temporal freeing similar to the freeing at the end of Mr Polly, a freeing from the very apocalyptic sense which has been responsible for the panicky, Mailerian structuring of events in the novel in the trajectile form. In a sense the novel depicts the process of apocalyptic Utopianization which is undertaken by all men who move

beyond culture into the existential mode; the movement in
Tono-Bungay would seem to work towards a privatism in which
the Utopian rewards include immediate release from the pressures of an unknown future. The achieved mode is no mere
'living for the present', but involves the responsible and
constant commitment of the individual to an ongoing cognitive
process.

The conventional reading of *Tono-Bungay* raises this problem:
at the beginning of the novel the narrator admits himself to be
in urgent need of self-expression, and he acknowledges the disorder of the material he will be assembling; at the end of the
novel the narrator makes large claims for a mature attitude and
a settled attitude, but doesn't seem to remember that the very
act of writing the novel has itself been a self-professed therapy –
he seems to attribute the therapeutic process to his actual
experiences and not to the confessional telling of them in the
novel. The reader, absorbed in the novel as cognitive process,
does not necessarily, however, find this a major difficulty;
the events of consciousness implicit in the first-person ordering
of the story are the events which consolidate the feeling of a final
redemption from cultural time. When Wells begins the book he
uses his narrator to take the reader with him into a world of
cultural crisis, where no assured moral response is possible:

> I want to set out my own queer love experiences
> too, such as they are, for they troubled and
> distressed and swayed me hugely, and they still
> seem to contain all sorts of irrational and
> debatable elements that I shall be the clearer-
> headed for getting on paper.[30]

When George Ponderevo claims at the end of the novel to be
'clearer-headed' and seems to forget that the writing out of the
novel has itself effected the cure, the apparent lack of novelistic
tact is positively useful in that it establishes the revolutionary
nature of the analytic process. By the end of the novel the reader
has learned to make do without the reassurance of a conventional end-oriented narrative; he has learned to live beyond the
'cultural' ordering which the narrator diagnoses as the source of
the initial confusion. George Ponderevo finally goes beyond conventional 'community' and enters the negative community of

private selves redeemed by technological process. His revolution
is similar to that described by Philip Rieff:

> . . . the modern cultural revolution has built
> into itself a unique prophylaxis: it is
> deliberately not in the name of any new order
> of communal purpose that it is taking place.
> On the contrary, this revolution is being fought for
> a permanent disestablishment of any deeply internalized
> moral demands, in a world which can guarantee
> a plenitude produced without reference to the rigid
> maintenance of any particular interdictory system.[31]

Tono-Bungay is the remarkable *tour de force* that it is for the
very reason that it engenders cultural disintegration in the
reader's experience of reading the novel. By the end of the novel
the reader is able more nearly to share the experience of 'post-
cultural' man, because he has been sharing in the process by
which a confused mind has set out, analytically, the grounds of
its confusion:

> I remember how I laughed aloud at the glimpse
> of the name of a London County Council steamboat
> that ran across me. *Caxton* it was called, and
> another was *Pepys* and another was *Shakespeare*.
> They seemed so wildly out of place, splashing
> about in that confusion. One wanted to take
> them out and wipe them and put them back in
> some English gentleman's library.[32]

And if he has read sensitively he will feel the need for the implementation of therapy:

> To my mind radio-activity is a real disease
> of matter. Moreover it is a contagious disease.
> It spreads. . . . It is in matter exactly what the
> decay of our old culture is in society, a loss
> of traditions and distinctions and assured
> reactions.[33]

The passing of the 'old cultural' mode of social organization
(where reactions were semi-automatic and 'assured') is the
signal for the initiation of a therapeutic vision as outlined in the

final paragraphs of the novel. The effect that 'quap' has upon
nearby human beings is to make them experience the kind of
neurotic symptoms from which Mr Polly suffers at the beginning
of the later novel:

> I believe that the primary influence of the
> quap upon us was to increase the conductivity
> of our nerves, but that is a mere unjustifiable
> speculation on my part. At any rate it gave a
> sort of east wind effect to life. We all became
> irritable, clumsy, languid, and disposed to be
> impatient with our langour.[34]

In *The History of Mr. Polly* Wells asks: 'Why cannot doctors
give us an antidote to the east wind?'[35] By the end of *Tono-
Bungay* the set of the reader's cultural expectations has been
so disconfirmed, his need for 'structure' and end-orientation
has been so neglected, and his own moral insufficiency has
been brought home to him that he may be pleased to leave
the public confusion of culture and enter with Wells the
cold and intensely private world of his therapeutic activism.
'Psychiatrically', as R. D. Laing has said in another context,
'this would appear as ex-patients helping future patients to go
mad.'[36]

V

The History of Mr. Polly sets out more conventionally the cognitive process which permits its hero to proceed beyond the
moral ordering of his life towards a mode which might be
described as existential. Mr Polly's arson and attempted
suicide are cognitive acts, 'mad' in terms of internalized
cultural values, but ultimately equivalent to an active mode of
enlightenment. As Wells writes in a well-known passage:

> But when a man has once broken through the
> paper walls of everyday circumstance, those
> unsubstantial walls that hold so many of us
> securely prisoned from the cradle to the grave,

he has made a discovery. If the world does not
please you, *you can change it*. Determine to
alter it at any price, and you can change it
altogether.[37]

In place of the conformative *fin-de-sièclism* of *The Wheels of
Chance*,[38] for example, which is content to remain largely in the
symptomatic mode, this later novel traces a therapeutic pattern
of development in its comic hero, and activist cognition is
specifically depicted as a therapeutic process. The book starts
with Mr Polly suffering from indigestion and 'sick of everything',[39] unable to diagnose his general malaise: 'He suffered
from indigestion now nearly every afternoon in his life, but as he
lacked introspection he projected the associated discomfort
upon the world' (p. 7). After the fire at Fishbourne, however,
his symptomatic condition emerges more clearly, and a suitable
alloplastic therapy is formulated:

> There are no circumstances in the world that
> determined action cannot alter, unless perhaps
> they are the walls of a prison cell, and even
> those will dissolve and change, I am told, into
> the infirmary compartment, at any rate, for the
> man who can fast with resolution. I give these
> things as facts and information, and with no
> moral intimations. And Mr Polly, lying awake
> at nights, with a renewed indigestion, with
> Miriam sleeping sonorously beside him, and a
> general air of inevitableness about his
> situation, saw through it, understood his
> former despair (pp. 283–4).

The moralistic, legalistic prison-walls of cultural circumstance
'dissolve' into the walls of the infirmary; we move beyond
'moral intimations' to cognition, to 'seeing through'. Mr Polly
sees himself for the first time as involved in a process of self-cure.

At the end of the novel Polly's cure is complete, and the process is specified as therapeutic, even medical, by a reference
back to the hero's initial state of health:

> One summer afternoon, about five years after
> his first coming to the Potwell Inn, Mr Polly

found himself sitting under the pollard willow,
fishing for dace. It was a plumper, browner,
and healthier Mr Polly altogether than the
miserable bankrupt with whose dyspeptic portrait
our novel opened. He was fat, but with a fatness
more generally diffused, and the lower part of his
face was touched to gravity by a small square
beard (p. 355).

The comedy may hide the fact that Mr Polly is a strikingly new
type in English fiction. His final achievement (when he has
come to benefit from the good things of life at the Potwell Inn)
is close to that of Rieffian revolution:

... this revolution is being fought for a
permanent disestablishment of any deeply
internalized moral demand, in a world which
can guarantee a plenitude produced without
reference to the rigid maintenance of any
particular interdictory system.[40]

In a sense he is a Romantic hero, but he is post-Romantic in the
transformative nature of his refusal to undertake the self-
deprivation upon which culture must depend:

I have failed in presenting Mr Polly
altogether if I have not made you see that
he was in many respects an artless child of
Nature, far more untrained, undisciplined,
and spontaneous than an ordinary savage.
And he was really glad, for all that little
drawback of fear, that he had had the courage
to set fire to his house, and fly, and come to
the Potwell Inn (p. 357).

The pre-requisite for a 'permissive society' in this context seems
to be a human type recognizable for its dissociation from
cultural modes of adaptation. Only such a subject, 'more untrained' and 'undisciplined' than a savage whose life is 'clipped'
and 'limited' by cultural loyalties, can fulfil the promise of
therapeutic activism.

The post-cultural self in the *fin-de-siècle* myth lives in a Godless universe, attenuated, flickering in a limbo of transition. The hollow universe and hollow self, and the images of emaciation and deprivation which are pervasive in 1890s literature, become polarized after 1900 into an opposite mode. The Edwardian typology as manifest in Mr Polly bears the same relation to *fin-de-siècle* man as the later Polly bears to the earlier:

> It was a plumper, browner, and healthier Mr
> Polly altogether than the miserable bankrupt with
> whose dyspeptic portrait our novel opened (p. 355).

By a striking reversal, the empty clothes of the Invisible Man are replaced by a Mr Polly who is 'fat, but with a fatness more generally diffused' (p. 355). If we return to J. Hillis Miller's version of Darwinian crisis, we shall see how closely Mr Polly's cure matches the symptoms of late-Victorian crisis:

> When God is annihilated, at the same time
> man annihilates himself and annihilates also
> the world around him. He annihilates them in
> the sense of hollowing them out, emptying them
> of any substantial presence. Human subjectivity
> comes more and more to be experienced as a lack,
> as a devouring emptiness, as an unassuageable
> hunger for some lost plenitude of being.[41]

The teleological and cultural deprivation and the devaluation of all values implicit in *fin-de-siècle* crisis become in the Edwardian revolution the very grounds for the implementation of the new therapy ('. . . this revolution is being fought for a permanent disestablishment of any deeply internalized moral demands'). And the late-Victorian nostalgia for 'some lost plenitude of being' becomes the basis for the Edwardian Utopianization of reality which 'can guarantee a plenitude produced without reference to the rigid maintenance of any particular interdictory system'.

'Plenitude' is perhaps the primary theme of the final chapter of *The History of Mr. Polly*, in which the words 'the fat woman' occur fourteen times in the seven pages. In place of *fin-de-siècle* depletion ('We need to put a living soul in the clothed body'), Wells presents an image of repletion:

Mr Polly sat beside the fat woman at one of
the little green tables at the back of the
Potwell Inn, and struggled with the mystery of
life. It was one of those evenings serenely
luminous, amply and atmospherically still, when
the river bend was at its best. A swan floated
against the dark green masses of the further
bank, the stream flowed broad and shining to its
destiny, with scarce a ripple – except where the
reeds came out from the headland, and the three
poplars rose clear and harmonious against the
sky of green and yellow. It was as if everything
lay securely within a great, warm, friendly globe
of crystal sky. It was as safe and enclosed and
fearless as a child that has still to be born.
It was an evening full of the quality of tranquil,
unqualified assurance. Mr Polly's mind was filled
with the persuasion that indeed all things whatsoever
must needs be satisfying and complete (p. 368).

'Some things I can't believe,' says Mr Polly to the fat woman,
'and one is your being a skeleton' (p. 373).

But if Mr Polly's cure foreshadows our own Rieffian therapy,
there are other elements in the novel which are directly opposed
to the Rieffian mode. If Polly's activism corresponds to a cognitive existential therapy, there are moments when Wells seems
to be recommending an adjustive therapy or a therapy centred
in society itself:

He could not grasp what was wrong with him.
He made enormous efforts to diagnose his case.
. . . for all his attempts at self-reproach and
self-discipline he felt at bottom that he
wasn't at fault.
As a matter of fact all the elements of his
troubles had been adequately diagnosed by a
certain high-browed, spectacled gentleman living
at Highbury, wearing a gold pince-nez, and
writing for the most part in the beautiful
library of the Climax Club. This gentleman
did not know Mr Polly personally, but he had

dealt with him generally as 'one of those ill-
adjusted units that abound in a society that
has failed to develop a collective intelligence
and a collective will for order commensurate
with its perplexities' (pp. 75–6).

And if this seems ironically distanced and not necessarily
corresponding with the narrator's own beliefs, there is further
evidence in Chapter 10 of the novel:

If our community was collectively anything
more than a feeble idiot, it would burn most
of London and Chicago, for example, and build
sane and beautiful cities in the place of
these pestilential heaps of private property
(p. 357).

What Wells is missing in these discursive passages is the fact that
this very societal failure 'to develop a collective intelligence
and a collective will for order' is the basis of Polly's intensely
private Utopianization of experience. His quasi-nihilistic
activism derives directly from the lack within him of any
cultural allegiance. His determination to fight off Uncle
Jim and to defend the world he has created by discovering, is
atheoretical and works simply towards sustaining 'a plenitude
of being'. More and more after 1910 these discursive passages tend to take over from the truly fictional element in
Wells's work, and the Rieffian, para-Freudian therapies of the
Edwardian fiction are replaced by a commitment therapy
directed towards the institution of a variety of global entities,
including the 'World State', the 'World Brain' and the 'World
Mind'.

VI

Kipps and Polly, though appearing in books which sporadically
recommend societal commitment therapies, extend the Dickensian consolidation of the self to the extreme point of Rieffian
privatism. Though ostensibly founded upon a Socialist theory of
the perniciousness of private property, they promote a mode of

self-possession which is nowadays implicit in the plasticity of property and the affluence and plenitude of Western life. The private linguistic worlds of Dickens's characters are well known; they might be more clearly understood if we took note of the perception that Mr Polly 'has a strange fantastic culture of his own'.[42] Deprived of access to a common societal source of cultural order, the self adopts its own parodic behaviour patterns. Mr Polly admits that he has always been the 'skeptaceous sort' (p. 370), and his distortion of language betrays his determination to exist on his own terms. He becomes the centre of 'culture' in the universe, and his decisions are existential decisions, not at all dictated by internalized moral standards. His language revolutionizes reality as defined linguistically; its transformative function may be compared with the conformative language of Uncle Jim. The latter's mythically frightening quality may in part derive from his loyalty to a primitive cultural mode:

> 'Bolls!' came the thick voice of the enemy
> behind him, as one who accepts a challenge, and,
> bleeding but indomitable, Uncle Jim entered the
> house.
>   'Bolls!' he said, surveying the bar. 'Fightin'
> with bolls! I'll showim fightin' with bolls!'
> (pp. 326-7).

Distortion of language here is an act of cultural violence, a subscription to the 'clipped' and 'limited' behaviour patterns peculiar to a definite group of people. There is no appeal to such a creature's 'higher qualities', since all the values implicit in his behaviour are registered in the conformity of his language to its lower-class pattern. The battle at the Potwell Inn then becomes a Darwinian fight for survival between cultural and post-cultural man. Polly wins because he is not limited to any kind of 'savage' culture; he ignores Uncle Jim's protestations that ducking him in the water 'ain't fair fightin'' (p. 332). Polly's privatism is well adapted to 'the private war'.

Uncle Jim may remind us of the wretched animals vivisected into semi-humans by Dr Moreau[43] and suffering the cultural fettering defined by Nietzsche:

Man, imprisoned in an iron cage of errors,
became a caricature of man, sick, wretched, ill-
disposed toward himself, full of hatred for the
impulses of life, full of mistrust of all that is
beautiful and happy in life, a walking picture of
misery.[44]

Such a cultural fettering is, in fact, the essence of Wells's definition of Leadford, Kipps and Polly before the respective
'Changes' that alter their lives. Our own sense of the power of
the myth of well-being may ultimately derive from the disgust
which Nietzschean, 'sick', 'imprisoned' man instigated in so
many Edwardian sensibilities.

8

Arnold Bennett

I

One of the most striking features of the transition in literature from the *fin-de-siècle* world to the Edwardian is the change in the simple experience of reality. Reality for Richard Larch in *A Man from the North* is an oppressive 'Fate'; and if life is to be lived instinctual renunciation is necessary. The final 'adjustment' that Bennett's hero makes at this stage is not so much a 'Triumph of the Therapeutic' as spiritual capitulation, and there is a suggestion of a sense of existential 'offence' in the book. The final paragraph of *Clayhanger* (1910) might, in the contrast it makes and the light it sheds, stand as a coda for the years of Edwardian development beyond Bennett's early gloom:

> After a whole decade his nostrils quivered
> again to the odour of her olive skin. Drowning
> amid the waves of her terrible devotion, he
> was recompensed in the hundredth part of a
> second for all that through her he had suffered
> or might hereafter suffer. The many problems
> and difficulties which marriage with her would
> raise seemed trivial in the light of her heart's
> magnificent and furious loyalty. He thought of
> the younger Edwin whom she had kissed into
> rapture, as of a boy too inexperienced in sorrow
> to appreciate this Hilda. He braced himself
> to the exquisite burden of life.[1]

It would be easy but not quite accurate to cite this as an example of Edwardian activism confronting 'reality' firmly and without illusion. In a sense it is that, but there is an indication that behind the intention to 'brace himself' there is for Edwin a self-indulgence and a cashing-in, as it were, on a kind of mother-love, a pleasurable drowning. The ambiguity is centred in the last sentence with its revealing mixture of active and passive attitudes. This qualification is important, also, for Wells and Galsworthy. Mr Polly, for example, is the Edwardian activist *par excellence*, breaking through the walls of everyday circumstance and making a stand against the almost archetypally evil Uncle Jim; but Polly's final achievement may seem to constitute a kind of self-indulgent acquiescent calm:

> They were not so much thinking, as lost in a
> smooth, still quiet of the mind. A bat flitted
> by.
>   'Time we was going in, O' Party', said Mr
> Polly, standing up. 'Supper to get. It's as
> you say, we can't sit here for ever'.[2]

Such self-assurance, such successful adaptation to temporal nextness, has the look of an orgy of complacency when it is compared with the anxiety, the defeat by time, of earlier Wellsian characters. If we think of the Time Traveller, we might remember Frank Kermode's suggestion that 'Schizo-phrenics can lose contact with "real" time, and undergo what has been called "a transformation of the present into eternity"'[3] In the later novel Mr Polly and the fat woman retain contact with present time ('Supper to get'), and yet still manage to 'transform the present into eternity'. It is the richness of that redemption[4] which is puzzling for latter-day readers of Edwardian fiction, and which may have the appearance of being superadded. Similarly, Bennett's enthusiasm ('the exquisite burden of life') may seem facile, even spurious, to the modern reader. Our scorn for the passivity of characters like Polly and Edwin may derive from our envy of their 'persuasion that indeed all things whatsoever must needs be satisfying and complete'.[5] Our dismissal of the Edwardian feeling that all is all right with the world perhaps derives from the distance between us and the redeemed decade after 1900.

The final paragraph of *Clayhanger* relates past, future and present in a way that is, according to Kermode, classic. Such a passage is a microcosm of the process in novels whereby 'mere successiveness, which we *feel* to be the chief characteristic in the ordinary going-on of time, is purged by the establishment of a significant relation between the moment and a remote origin and end, a concord of past, present, and future . . .'.[6] Just as the *fin-de-siècle* failure to pattern history in fiction resulted in autistic literature and discordance, so the Edwardian feeling of release from an ending process and sense of a beginning resulted in an extremist version of what Kermode calls 'kairos'.[7] The popular myth of the good old days of Edwardian England has thus a relation not so much to the physical character of life in the period, but to the temporal attitudes implicit in its literature and social patterns. Such a period of halcyon days at the beginning has, perhaps, become an essential factor in our making sense of the twentieth century. Our dismissal of the Christian culture and the old world, approximately to be dated from the year 1900, permits a new myth of Paradise and Fall ordering themselves around the concept of man's responsibility for world events. Thomas Hardy found the sinking of the *Titanic* poetic justice for an age of false pride and shallow confidence; but it is out of that sense of repletion and a beginning that the modern world is born.

It may be possible to accept such a partial explanation of the character of Edwardian literature, but it still may be necessary for us to condemn its confidence as 'unrealistic'. Striving for exemption from 'our insatiable interest in the future',[8] we try to uncover any instances of calendar determinism which may recur and bind us once again. In order to define a certain irrational health-consciousness in Bennett's later Edwardian novels, we might look at the journals of his friend, George Sturt, which conveniently cover the period between 1890 and 1927. In these journals may be traced a parallel development to that implicit in the movement from *A Man from the North* to *Clayhanger*. The entry for 28 November 1890 has this comment ('typical', as the editor of the 1967 edition notes, 'of what was being said . . . during the 1880s and 1890s'[9]):

I read this afternoon an essay of R. Proctor's,
on 'A menacing comet'. A huge moth-like thing,
fluttering round the sun for its candle, and
likely, thinks Proctor, to be eventually drawn
into it and consumed: when the velocity changed
into heat may cause the extinction of the human
race. It is due about '97. So argues Proctor.
I felt a sense of desolation on reading it: –
a temptation to resort to some sort of teleology,
to postulate a *purpose* to be served, in the
Existence of Man. And then, opposed to that,
the delusion of size crept in: – what could so
large an affair as this Comet and the Sun care
for us? I have no sense today for
transcendentalism. . . .[10]

Once again the coincidence of post-Darwinian teleological
deprivation and the coming twentieth century seems to be
responsible for a reaction to life that comes close to the insane.
There is here no simple faith in a *fin du globe*; but there is a
neurotic abdication from confident living in present time due to
the pressure of the future. And the year 1900 is being used,
albeit unconsciously, as a dangerous focus-point for world
doom. What is perhaps even more disturbing is the converse of
this *fin-de-siècle* mood, as expressed in Sturt's entry for 10
February 1909; it is as unbalanced in its attitude to the future as
the earlier entry:

To develop the Idea of Progress, and be aware
of the Reality of racial life (surrounding us on
all sides, visible, audible) one should cultivate
a habit exactly the reverse of that acquired by
doctors. . . . Thus, instead of seeing individuals,
they see something – a sort of influence, wide-
dispersed – that pervades individuals without
their consent, and mars them. In similar manner,
we might look for the tokens of that greater
force, which also pervades individuals without
their consent, and makes them.
   Hitherto this has been but an abstract idea
to us, and we have called it 'Health', not

perceiving that it is a very active and lively,
a very awe-inspiring force, far more potent than
that of disease. It is time to 'realize' this
abstraction; that is to say, to vitalize the
idea with sights and sounds of such realities,
so that when we see the shapes of muscle and
limb, or the beating of the pulse, or the graceful
gesture, or hear the voice timbre, we may feel that
a great influence is present, just as the doctor
feels that a dread influence is present when he
sees the alcoholist's bloated skin or the epileptic's
secretive eyes.[11]

And so we move from William James's image of the epileptic in the passage quoted in Chapter 2 ('moving nothing but his black eyes and looking absolutely non-human'), from a symptomatic vision, to a Vitalist vision which looks for the converse of that 'dread influence' a doctor senses when he sees 'the epileptic's secretive eyes'. Such Vitalism has a strong period quality, and we may not want to share in an idealism which may have been partially responsible for the unflagging efforts of both sides to promote the First World War and for the rise of Nazism. Nevertheless, the concept of 'World Health' is more centrally implicit in our latter-day thinking than we may be prepared to admit, and if there is any implicit ideal by which we order our responses to global and parochial problems, it is the criterion of well-being. Such a revolutionary reversal was necessary if the fully ateleological therapeutic mode recommended by Philip Rieff was finally to flourish. Rieff's theories are, strictly speaking, anti-Vitalist; and the various forms that post-1900 Vitalism takes in Wells, Bennett and Galsworthy are equally antagonistic to the Rieffian mode. Wells's communalism, Bennett's interest in 'synthetic' devices in fiction, and Galsworthy's fascination with 'union' are all aspects of Edwardian Vitalism, and all tend to lead towards the commitment of the self to a 'superior communal end'.[12] On the other hand, Edwardian theories of cosmic process tend not only to return to the Vitalism which opposed materialism in the scientific debates of the nineteenth century, but to attribute vital force to consciousness itself; John A. Lester quotes a passage from *The Dynasts* which relates to

Bennett's idea of making something 'comely' out of the 'raw material' of life:

> More philosophically, the literary mind could
> view consciousness as a small but growing faculty
> in living creation, but one that might steadily
> grow until it could control the Will itself,
> moving toward that joyance of the time sung by
> the Chorus of Pities which concludes Hardy's
> *Dynasts*: 'Consciousness the Will informing, till/
> It fashions all things fair!' If consciousness
> could be seen as playing such a new and exalted
> role in the evolutionary process, perhaps man
> himself could one day introduce into this process
> the sympathy, altruism, and sense of purpose
> which had been so ruthlessly banished by orthodox
> Darwinism.[13]

It is those aspects of the triumvirate's fiction which attribute value to the analytic powers of consciousness which anticipate Rieff; and the post-cultural play of freed consciousness is precisely that which clears the way for the intensely private sense of well-being achieved by Irene and Bosinney, by Kipps and Polly, and by Edwin Clayhanger. The new Vitalism (as manifest, for example, in the work of George Bernard Shaw) was revolutionary and culturally iconoclastic; its dependence upon the released consciousness involved the repudiation of cultural forms. Thus Carpenter's 'cosmic consciousness' was envisaged as the outcome of the process of curing the disease known as 'civilization'.[14] Marshall McLuhan's writing seems to relate back to these Edwardian theories of the communal, synthetic role of consciousness, while Philip Rieff's anti-communal 'Triumph of the Therapeutic' appears to derive from the existential element in the triumvirate's approach to consciousness. What connects Bennett with Rieff, in particular, is his trust in a cognitive activism.

II

The Edwardian living in redeemed time involves an achieved assimilation of Darwinism, a learning to live with human animality. The dominant pattern of the major Edwardian novels is one of permissive rather than renunciatory adaptation, and an essential element in the new liberality is the accepted presence of fleshly reality, which is no longer felt to be a threat to spiritual existence. The physical life had received sanction from the new post-cultural cosmic theory of health implicit in and distinguishing the new Vitalism. Bennett's major Edwardian novels are *The Old Wives' Tale* (1908) and *Clayhanger* (1910). The first compares Constance and Sophia Baines, who respectively adopt remissive and permissive modes of adaptation; Constance remits her instinctual rights and remains constant to the culture in which she is indigenous. The second novel deals more explicitly with the autotherapeutic process of cognition by which ontological development, full self-realization, may be recognized.

The plot of *Clayhanger* is well-known; it is concerned with the growth to manhood of Edwin Clayhanger, the son of a Five Towns printer. The story tells of Edwin's difficult relationship with his harsh, coarse and repressive father; the gradual triumphing of Edwin through his father's old age, sickness and death; and Edwin's final decision to marry Hilda Lessways. An early relationship with Hilda, though promising, ended unhappily when Hilda jilted Edwin (for what emerges as a good enough reason). Contrasted to the rough home of old Darius Clayhanger, the sweetness-and-light home of the architect, Orgreave, seems like heaven to Edwin. Mr Orgreave's mode of life specifically unites activity and instinctual fulfilment:

> It was the drawing-room of a man who had
> consistently used immense powers of industry
> for the satisfaction of his prodigal instincts.'[15]

The passage develops from this point into a *locus classicus* of Edwardian activism:

> . . . it was the drawing-room of woman whose
> placidity no danger could disturb, and who
> cared for nothing if only her husband was
> amused. Spend and gain! And, for a change
> gain and spend! That was the method. Work till
> sheer exhaustion beat you. Plan, scheme, devise!

Satisfy your curiosity and your other instincts!
Experiment! Accept risks! Buy first, order first,
pledge yourself first; and then split your head
in order to pay and to redeem! When chance aids
you to accumulate, let the pile grow, out of
mere perversity, and then scatter it royally!
Play heartily! Play with the same intentness
as you work! Live to the uttermost instant
and to the last flicker of energy! (p. 199).

Thus was Sophia's fire set up against Constance's constancy in
The Old Wives' Tale. In Chapter 9 of Book II of *Clayhanger*
Edwin reviews his attitude to pleasure and Puritanism:

He was intoxicated; not with wine, though he
had drunk wine. A group of well-intentioned
philanthropists, organized into a powerful
society for combating the fearful evils of
alcoholism, had seized Edwin at the age of
twelve and made him bind himself with solemn
childish signature and ceremonies never to taste
alcohol save by doctor's orders. He thought of
this pledge in the garden of the Orgreaves.
'Damned rot!' he murmured, and dismissed the
pledge from his mind as utterly unimportant,
if not indeed fatuous. No remorse! The whole
philosophy of ascetism inspired him, at that
moment, with impatient scorn. It was the hope
of pleasure intoxicated him, the vision which
he had had of the possibilities of being really
interested in life. He saw new avenues toward
joy, . . . and the sight thereof made him tingle,
less with the desire to be immediately at them
than with the present ecstasy of contemplating
them (pp. 213–14).

The 'pledge' is in a sense an analogue of social contract with its
inbuilt instinctual deprivation for the individual. With this
passage from *Clayhanger* in mind, we might at this point cite
Philip Rieff:

Not only our Western system but every system
of integrative moral demand, the generative
principle of culture, expressed itself in
positive deprivation – in a character ideal that
functioned to commit the individual to the group.
Culture was thus the establishment and
organization of restrictive motives. Men
engaged in disciplines of interdiction.
The dialectic of deprivation and remission
from deprivation was in the service of those
particular interdicts by which a culture
constituted itself. The analytic attitude . . .
points toward a character ideal that is in
principle anti-ascetic and therefore
revolutionary if viewed from perspectives
formed in the inherited moral demand system.
The dialectic of perfection, based on a
deprivational mode, is being succeeded by a
dialectic of fulfilment, based on the appetitive
mode.[16]

The therapy of all therapies is not to attach
oneself exclusively to any particular therapy,
so that no illusion may survive of some end
beyond an intensely private sense of well-being
to be generated in the living of life itself.[17]

It is interesting that Bennett is able to identify this anti-ascetic
interest in Edwin as, in a sense, the very opposite of activism:

But he did not reason; he felt. He was
passive, not active. He would not even, just
then, attempt to make new plans. He was in a
beatitude, his mouth unaware that it was
smiling (p. 214).

It is almost as if a scientific naturalist has managed to show us a
member of a newly discovered species in one of its interesting
states, the state, surely, not so much of mystic trance as of 'well-
being' itself. This is the redeemed time of the therapeutic's
universe, this passive mood of unconscious spiritual health
which follows upon activism as reward. Earlier in Chapter 9 of

Book II the reader is given some hint as to what lies behind this desire for 'passive' joy:

> When the front door of the Orgreaves interposed
> itself that night between Edwin and a
> little group of gas-lit faces, he turned away
> towards the warm gloom of the garden in a state
> of happy excitement. He had left fairly early,
> despite protests, because he wished to give his
> father no excuse for a spectacular display of
> wrath; Edwin's desire for a tranquil existence
> was growing steadily. . . . He wanted to be in full
> possession of himself, at leisure, and in
> freedom . . . (p. 213).

The dialectic of perfection, presented as the way of life into which Edwin first casts himself ('By a single urgent act of thought he would have made himself a man, and changed imperfection into perfection' – p. 15), is replaced as he matures by the dialectic of fulfilment, based on the appetitive mode. The final aim becomes repletion itself, in which the concept of well-being is grounded. 'Full possession' of oneself is the egocentric goal of the therapeutic who has passed beyond culture, a cure for the existential anxiety of *fin-de-siècle* myth, a complete step forward from the depletion inherent in a universe where man is the dispossessed creation of a God who no longer exists. The political inconsistencies of Kipps's choosing to run a bookshop are resolved if we understand that his tranquil existence therein derives from self-ownership, just as Polly's existence does:

> It was an evening full of the quality of
> tranquil, unqualified assurance. Mr Polly's
> mind was filled with the persuasion that
> indeed all things whatsoever must needs be
> satisfying and complete.

The 'Mrs Brown' aspect of Bennett's Edwardian work should be seen not as manifestation, simply, of an environmental or naturalistic obsession, but as part of the cognitive process by which the deculturalized individual repossesses a dispossessed universe for himself. The naturalism of the beginning of *Clayhanger* represents the alienating cultural environment from which Edwin develops into a post-cultural self ('To the east rose pitheads, chimneys, and kilns, tier above tier, dim in their own mists' – p. 3); such description does not glorify evolved cultural constructs; on the contrary, it vilifies them. The mere bringing of the landscape of the Potteries into consciousness is to render it obsolete, so that the appetitive Edwin uses the land-scape only as a field for action. The true Mrs Brownism of Bennett comes out when his hero's new house is the scene of a cosmic repossession:

> He jumped from the stillage, and went quickly
> to the doorway and saw the cellar steps. His
> heart was beating. He trembled, he was afraid,
> exquisitely afraid, acutely conscious of himself
> amid the fundamental mysteries of the universe
> (p. 216).

The 'raw material' of the given world has been taken and made 'comely'. It is a time of repossession of almost erotic intensity:

> The house seemed full of inexplicable noises.
> When he stopped to listen he could hear scores
> of different infinitesimal sounds. His spine
> thrilled, as if a hand delicate and terrible had
> run down it in a caress. All the unknown of the
> night and of the universe was pressing upon him,
> but it was he alone who had created the night and
> the universe (p. 216).

'Property' for cultural man – for the Forsytes, for example – is a therapy in the communal mode. Such is Erich Fromm's view of a clearly recognizable modern type:

> . . . the new freedom which capitalism brought
> for the individual added to the effect which
> the religious freedom of Protestantism already
> had had upon him. The individual became more
> alone, isolated, became an instrument in the
> hands of overwhelmingly strong forces outside
> himself; he became an 'individual', but a
> bewildered and insecure individual. There
> were factors to help him overcome the overt

manifestations of this underlying insecurity.
In the first place his self was backed up by
the possession of property. 'He' as a person and
the property he owned could not be separated. A
man's clothes or his house were parts of his self
just as much as his body. The less he felt he
was being somebody the more he needed to have
possessions. If the individual had no property
or lost it, he was lacking an important part of
his self and to a certain extent was not
considered to be a full-fledged person, either by
others or by himself.[18]

Edwin's 'repossession' of the universe is not a therapy of this
kind, but an active cognitive process leading towards the
achievement of cosmic consciousness. That Fromm's statement
is important for the Edwardian novel we know from the
Forsytes of *The Man of Property*, but the mere 'possession of
property' is something which the aesthetic order has left
behind. Edwin's aesthetic 'possession' of his new house establishes him, not in society, but in the cosmos, and 'privately'. It
is true that when Griffin lost his clothes and his social 'properties' had been destroyed 'he was lacking an important part of
his self and to a certain extent was not considered to be a full-
fledged person', but the process of deculturalization is irrever-
sible. Edwin's aestheticization of the cosmos in his new house
undermines the validity of the surrounding cultural environment beyond which he has passed. Robin Hill in *The Man of
Property* is not 'property' in the older, Forsyte sense – it too represents the aestheticization of the cosmos, the creation of a new
order, which repossesses the universe for man, and so places
him beyond the need for 'portable property'. The Potwell Inn
is not Frommian property, or Mrs Brownian environment, but a
self-created universe which satisfies a therapeutic's erotic and
aesthetic appetite.

The *fin-de-siècle* discomfort of self-consciousness and heightened sensation seems to have gradually polarized into the very
conditions of redemption after 1900. It might be argued that in
Bennett's definition of the 'divine *me*'[19] the stream-of-consciousness novel has its roots:

Yet, amid the multitude of his sensations –
the smarting of his chin, the tingling of all
his body after the bath, the fresh vivacity of
the morning, the increased consciousness of his
own ego, due to insufficient sleep, the queerness
of being in the drawing-room at such an hour in
conspiratorial talk, the vague disquiet caused at
midnight, and now intensified despite his angry
efforts to avoid the contagion of Mrs Hamps's
mood, and above all the thought of his father
gloomily wandering in the garden – amid these
confusing sensations, it was precisely an idea
communicated to him by his annoying aunt, an
obvious idea, that emerged clear and dramatic:
he was the only son (p. 341).

Instead of leaving his ambitions to posterity, as Richard Larch had done in *A Man from the North*, Edwin assumes a rightful inheritance. In the earlier novel, the pressure from an unknown future has its concomitant in the inscrutability of the past. In *Clayhanger* the future is realistically Edwin's, and this release from anxiety about the future is accompanied by the clear depiction of the past from which Edwin derives and beyond which he is determined to move. In such a post-cultural universe the details of the old everyday life (such as 'Mrs Hamps's mood' and 'his father's wandering gloomily in the garden') become comically incongruous, reminding us of some of the mundane fragments set into *The Waste Land*.

The release of the ego in Bennett's Edwardian novels is Husserlian. Much of the importance of Husserl (particularly in so far as Sartre's repudiation of aspects of his phenomenology is concerned) centres around his postulation of a transcendental ego separate from and presiding over consciousness. If we understand Bennett in Husserlian terms, we shall see more clearly the therapeutic relevance of the former's ideas to the *fin-de-siècle* crisis of consciousness. If the insecurity of self in the 1890s has as its co-symptom an unbearably vertiginous consciousness, Bennett's 'Pocket Philosophies' of the 1900s represent an apt therapy:

My sense of security amid the collisions of
existence lies in the firm consciousness that
just as my body is the servant of my mind, so
is my mind the servant of *me*. . . . Often have I
said to that restive brain: 'Now, O mind, sole
means of communication between the divine *me*
and all external phenomena, you are nothing
but a piece of machinery; and obey me you shall.'[20]

Such a therapy for contingency lies behind the thought of Wells,
Bennett and Galsworthy, and, indeed, characterizes an important element in Edwardian writing in general. There is an
important episode in *Clayhanger* that demonstrates very well the
new omnipotent passivity of the safe Husserlian ego 'behind'
consciousness, the point when Darius, neglecting a weak floor,
installs new machinery in his printing shop. The new printing
press (representative, in a sense, of modern consciousness)
begins to settle through the old boards (like a 'restive brain').
It threatens to crash through entirely, thereby destroying 'the
whole shop'. Darius is powerless to prevent the catastrophe. The
basis of Edwin's rescue is that of the post-cultural presiding ego,
an ego working autonomously and transcendentally:

Darius would not loose his belief in the floor. . . .
He had always held passionately that the floor was
immovable, and he always would. He had finally
convinced himself of its omnipotent strength by
the long process of assertion and reassertion. . . .
Darius said nothing. There was another cracking
sound, louder, and unmistakeably beneath the bed
of the machine. . . . They might have been under a
spell. . . .
And then Edwin, hardly knowing what he did, and
certainly not knowing why he did it, walked quickly
out on to the floor, seized the huge hook attached
to the lower pulley of the tackle that hung from
the roof-beam, pulled up the slack of the rope-
bondage of the hind-part of the machine, and stuck
the hook into it, then walked quickly back. . . .
Another and much louder noise of cracking followed,
the floor visibly yielded, and the hind-part of the

machine visibly sank about a quarter of an inch.
But no more. The tackle held. The strain was
distributed between the beam above and the beam below,
and equilibrium established (pp. 105–6).

In Edwin's universe, previously presided over by his father and
now presided over by his own transcendent ego, this assertive
act is revolutionary, an act of knowing whose very unconsciousness demonstrates the potency of the controlling ego.
Edwin might well say to his restive brain: 'Now, O mind, sole
means of communication between the divine *me* and all external phenomena, you are not a free agent; you are a subordi-
nate; you are nothing but a piece of machinery; and obey me
you shall.'

The process of knowing by which Edwin develops is a dialectical process of the aggrandizement of the self through assimilation and cognition of a hostile external reality. The ego sets up
'all external phenomena' as 'a field for action':

The absolute ego is to be conceived as
activity. And this activity is fundamentally
an infinite striving. But striving . . . implies
overcoming, and overcoming requires an
obstacle to overcome. Hence the ego must
posit the non-ego, Nature, as an obstacle to
be overcome, as a check to be transcended.
In other words Nature is a necessary field
for action.[21]

The accusation that Wells, Bennett and Galsworthy seem able
to define character only in terms of environment is clarified by
this helpful insight. The old view of the three writers might be
exemplified by Robert Liddell's:

How crude . . . is the descriptive writing of
those novelists who tackle the problem of
character presentation . . . not looking, as Mrs
Woolf does, at the external world through the
eyes of the soul, with its complicated double
and treble vision, but describing the town,
then the street, then the house, then the room,
then the clothes, and then the body that enclose

the soul. They hope they have got their net so
tightly round the soul itself that it cannot
escape them, but it always does.[22]

But the process of characterization being described here, a
static clothing with materiality for the purposes of technical
representation, is very different from the dialectical process we
have defined in Bennett's novel. The development of character
in Wells, Bennett and Galsworthy is embodied in a dialectical
assertion of the self *against* a hostile external milieu and aggrandizement of the self by means of the re-appropriation of the
terms of environment by means of the cognitive creation of a
new 'psychomorphous' world (such as that represented in
Edwin's new creation of 'house', 'night' and 'universe'). It might
be argued that it was only through the successful application of
that preliminary dialectical consolidation of the 'divine *me*' in
the Edwardian decade that the great describers of 'the soul' in
the 1920s were able to rest as it were so secure in the inner
world of consciousness.

An introduction of epistemological considerations might
seem extraneous were it not for the fact that Bennett himself
makes Edwin's maturation a process of knowing. At the very beginning of the book, just as at the beginning of *The Old Wives'
Tale*, Edwin's 'situation' is defined in epistemological terms:

Beyond the ridge, and partly protected by it
from the driving smoke of the Five Towns, lay the
fine and ancient Tory borough of Oldcastle, from
whose historic Middle School Edwin Clayhanger was
now walking home. The fine and ancient Tory
borough provided education for the whole of the
Five Towns, but the relentless ignorance of its
prejudices had blighted the district. . . . These
interesting details have everything to do
with the history of each of the two hundred
thousand souls in the Five Towns. Oldcastle
guessed not the vast influences of its
sublime stupidity (pp. 3-4).

The environment of which Edwin is in a sense the product is set
up now over against him; in the day of his first 'step into the

world' (p. 11), 'he felt that not merely his father, but the leagued universe, was against him' (p. 10). The equipment he brings to bear at this 'crucial moment' (p. 11) is his 'knowledge':

> Knowledge was . . . the armour and the weapon of
> one about to try conclusions with the world,
> and many people for many years had been engaged
> in providing Edwin with knowledge. . . .
>   He knew, however, nothing of natural history,
> and in particular of himself, of the mechanism
> of the body and mind, through which his soul
> had to express itself. . . . As for philosophy, he
> had not the slightest conception of what it
> meant. . . . Of geology he was perfectly ignorant . . .
> (pp. 11–12).

So insistent and detailed is Bennett's description of Edwin's deficiencies in 'knowledge' that many readers have perhaps wondered what the point of these long passages in Chapter 2 of Book I is. There is, we know, a comparison to be made with the nearly contemporary novels of Wells, *Kipps* and *The History of Mr. Polly*, which contain accounts of the early educa- tion of Kipps and Polly. In Wellsian terms it is easy to agree with Kenneth Newell and say: 'Only knowledge could enable Kipps to understand his "fate" and thus become free of it. But, comparatively ignorant, he was hopelessly confused. . . .'[23] And we should then be in a position to establish the defensive func- tion of Wells's search for knowledge in the face of an unknown future. Wells, with his own admission that his whole career was an attempt to sustain his 'knowledge' of life, as it were,[24] can help us see that Bennett depicts the ontological growth of Edwin Clayhanger as a process of facing the future. For Kipps upon leaving school and for Clayhanger at his 'crucial moment', the future is about to flood in with a rush. Wells has different interests from Bennett, of course; but both writers, and indeed Galsworthy also, are committed to a distinctly Edwardian form of cognitive activism. It is difficult to understand the seriousness of the Edwardian's concern with the future unless we think of Richard Larch's intuition that 'Fate was his enemy'. The fear is partly one of being 'determined', and one might interpret the Utopianizing development of the Edwardian novel in terms of its providing a cure for the fatalist situation depicted in the novels of Thomas Hardy. The final outcome of *Clayhanger* represents an equilibrium gained by Edwin in the face of the mystery of life and the mystery of Hilda herself, a cognitive state involving the whole man:

> After a whole decade his nostrils quivered
> again to the odour of her olive skin. Drowning
> amid the waves of her terrible devotion, he was
> recompensed in the hundredth part of a second
> for all that through her he had suffered or
> might hereafter suffer. . . . He braced himself to
> the exquisite burden of life (p. 574).

III

The Old Wives' Tale, 'art-novel' as it is, is an almost experimentalist study of a character who emigrates from her cultural environment and actively creates a new environment for herself elsewhere. Sophia undertakes a complete break from her Five Towns matrix, and creates an intensely private life for herself in Paris. Her sister Constance acts very much as a control factor in the experiment, for her equable, 'constant' temperament suits her for remaining immersed in the culture which has formed her and which is described in detail in the novel. Rather than living a post-cultural existence, she is one Edwardian character whose life *is* defined through an enlarged conception of culture – a conception which includes teapots and trays as cultural products. But the contrast between Sophia and Constance is more than a comparison between the alloplastic and autoplastic modes of adaptation. It appears to correspond to a neo-Hegelian dialectic which is implicit also in *Clayhanger*; Alan Sandison offers the relevant Hegelian attitude in *The Wheel of Empire*:

> The process by which spirit – altogether
> synonymous with God – reaches self-consciousness
> involves its externalization in some concrete
> form so that it may apprehend this substantial
> form as itself. In a sentence which we find

many times echoed in Carlyle's work Hegel himself
wrote: 'What powers it inherently possesses,
we learn from the variety of products and
formations which it originates.' . . .

    Man's place in this development is quite
clear. He is 'spirit in the act of becoming
conscious of itself as spirit'.[25]

Sandison proceeds to quote from Robert Tucker on Hegel.
Tucker seems to be supplying a useful model for the relation
between the encultured Constance and Sophia on the 'path of
self-discovery':

As a builder of civilizations, a creator of
culture-worlds, he is spirit in the historical
continuation of its creative, self-externalizing
phase. But in his capacity of knower, he is
spirit on the path of self-discovery. His mind,
and particularly his religious and philosophical
mind, is the organ of the world's emergent
consciousness of itself as a subjective being.
But inasmuch as this remains an incomplete,
limited consciousness, Hegel defines man as
'finite self-conscious spirit'.[26]

Constance is a 'creator', in her way, of a 'culture-world',
representing spirit in the 'historical continuation of its creative
. . . phase'. But Sophia must release herself to the cognitive act
of running away with Gerald. The strange disconformity
between the two sisters when they meet again at the end of the
novel derives from the contrast between the culture-immersed
unconscious mode of Constance and the Sophian mode of 'self-
discovered' consciousness. One sister has gone beyond the
limited state in which they are depicted at the beginning of the
novel, and the other has represented the 'historical continuation' of it.

    Just as in *Clayhanger*, the triumphing of the emergent con-
sciousness is dependent upon the ageing and sickening of a
resented parent:

It was her father who appeared tragically
ridiculous; and, in turn, the whole movement

against her grew grotesque in its absurdity.
Here was this antique wreck, helpless, useless,
powerless – merely pathetic – actually thinking
that he had only to mumble in order to make her
'understand'! He knew nothing; he perceived
nothing; he was a ferocious egotist, like most
bedridden invalids, out of touch with life, –
and he thought himself justified in making
destinies, and capable of making them! Sophia
could not, perhaps, define the feelings which
overwhelmed her; but she was conscious of their
tendency. They aged her, by years. They aged
her so that, in a kind of momentary ecstasy of
insight, she felt older than her father himself.
    'You will be a good girl', he said. 'I'm
sure o' that'.
    It was too painful. The grotesqueness of her
father's complacency humiliated her past bearing.
She was humiliated, not for herself, but for him
(p. 49).

This ageing process which occurs so suddenly is akin, in its
'momentary ecstasy of insight', to the maturation of Edwin
implicit in 'the hundredth part of a second'. Selfconsciousness in
its Edwardian, positive mode fixes its possessor securely in time,
older therefore in a sense than the unconscious agents of the old
order, and more in control of 'destinies' also. The cultural
limitations of Sophia's father are rendered in tragicomic dialect;
he becomes literally 'absurd'. He passes 'out of touch with life',
that neo-Vitalist 'living of life itself' which is so important in the
Bennettian universe.

In comparing Sophia and Constance as post-cultural and
cultural types, respectively, it is important to understand that
neither sister is allowed the centrality of consciousness which is
given to Edwin Clayhanger, and that Sophia's life in Paris
cannot be said to release her entirely from inherited behaviour
patterns. On the contrary, it is the hard-headed thriftiness she
carries with her from the Five Towns that enables her to adapt
so successfully to the siege conditions which drive the citizens of
Paris into confusion. Madame Foucault's apartment, at first

sight rich and splendid, is seen objectively at last under Sophia's
realist gaze:

> The first impression of Sophia's eye was one
> of sombre splendour. Everything had the air of
> being richly ornamented, draped, looped, carved,
> twisted, brocaded into gorgeousness. . . . There
> was an effect of spaciousness. . . .
>
> But Sophia, with the sharp gaze of a woman
> brought up in the traditions of a modesty so
> proud that it scorns ostentation, quickly tested
> and condemned the details of this chamber that
> imitated every luxury. Nothing in it, she found,
> was 'good'. And in St Luke's Square 'goodness'
> meant honest workmanship, permanence, the absence
> of pretence. All the stuffs were cheap and
> showy and shabby; all the furniture was cracked,
> warped, or broken (pp. 350–1).

For the cultural emigrant, no cultural milieu can be authentic;
like Wells's Mr Polly, Sophia carries her own culture with her
into a world of cultural fragmentation. The rooms of prostitutes
or the luxurious retaurants of Paris are equally guilty of
'pretence'. The essence of Sophia's reaction to Madame
Foucault's apartment is one of cultural nostalgia; her regurgita-
tion of Five Towns standards only reinforces the sense that she is
cut off from any communal participation in an authentic
cultural mode. In a world of impermanence and inauthenticity,
she is reduced, obsessively and regressively, to the criteria of the
culture which produced her. She is the prototype, therefore, of
modern man, who, knowing that his emigration is irrevocable,
is yet bemused by residues from a culturally formative past.
Sophia in her boarding-house in Paris is akin to Soames the
post-cultural Forsyte. Each is sentenced to a sterility unknown
to the cultural type (e.g. Constance) and to the pure therapeutic (e.g. Irene).

9
John Galsworthy

I

The Edwardian novels that represent Galsworthy's finest achievements in fiction are *The Man of Property*, *The Country House* and *Fraternity*. At first sight there seems little in these drily ironical, detached and rather cold works to match the positive worship of 'Health' and well-being exhibited in *Mr. Polly* and *Clayhanger*. But the gradually intensifying diagnostic crisis which typifies the work of Galsworthy in the decade, the predicament of the 'spiritual' Liberal, is itself a mark of the commitment to therapeutic ideals which characterizes the period. A study of Galsworthy's post-1900 fiction affords an opportunity for the more detailed analysis of the various kinds of therapeutic programmes envisaged by the Edwardians. Galsworthy himself, for example, satirizes Wellsian 'medical socialism' in *Fraternity* (see Section IV); and the placing of key characters in *The Man of Property* as detached from communal resources, lacking the therapeutic benefits of an integrated cultural life (in the wide, sociological sense), and consequently in symptomatic crisis, seems to resemble the negative community described by Philip Rieff, where, ideally (in contrast to the property-oriented commitment-therapy represented by Forsyteism) 'no illusion may survive of some end beyond an intensely private sense of well-being to be generated in the living of life itself'.

The Man of Property, it might be argued, is a more important novel than latter-day critics have recognized. It relates to modern crisis and to the long tradition of emergent 'crisis' in a direct way. Its very literary 'deficiencies' seem able to illumine a predicament universally sensed by latter-day man. If the history of the novel is the evolution of ways of rendering the experience of private living and 'intimacy' more and more closely, Soames's slamming of the door upon himself and Irene at the end of the 1906 novel (the Irene he has raped and who is intensely repelled by him) defines a new closing off of a private universe of crisis for each individual. The totally loathed Soames is an earlier version of Kafka's Gregor, finding himself inexplicably despised, suddenly changed from his security within the cultural milieu of the family and Forsyteism into a creature existing in its own world of private consciousness. Soames takes 'guilt' and 'alienation' with him behind locked doors; he is the victim of a cultural metamorphosis which will permit the deculturalized Irene and Bosinney only a brief interlude of happiness and which plunges survivors into crisis.

It is not clear, of course, that Galsworthy consciously thought of Soames as existentially detached from the culture of 'Forsyteism'. He may well have attempted, however, to depict an entirely new type in the character of Irene.[1] But in any event it is important to see Irene as polarized against, not a Forsyte husband, but a newly conscious Forsyte, in cultural crisis. The very process of cognitive analysis in the novel separates out Soames from the Forsyte matrix and forms the basic condition of his crisis (a post-cultural inability to react 'spontaneously') and the grounds upon which his possible cure must be based. Soames's cure comes from the writing out of the novel, as it were, but is unavailable to him because he is still Forsyte enough to lack a talent for psychological analysis. Soames, like us, is caught between the old culture and the new order. His inability to act 'on impulse' (the very grounds for the implementation of Freudian therapy) is equivalent to what Wells identifies in *Tono-Bungay* as 'what the decay of our old culture is in society, a loss of . . . assured reactions'.

It should, of course, be noted that there may be a class-differential at work in the relative developments of Edwardian novels. Soames's lack of self-assurance, and Hilary Dallison's in

Fraternity, may be related to the very increasing ability of Wellsian and Bennettian heroes to become 'self-possessed'. The location of expanding consciousness in English society at the turn of the century seems to have been in the process of transferring from the upper-middle to the lower-middle class, and confidence may have accrued to members of the newly dominant class. Wells's sense of being 'post-cultural' might in this light be viewed as more typical of his pre-1900 work, and the prefix 'post-' may be chronologically inaccurate in that context, simply signifying his inability in the 1890s to feel at home in the still dominant stratum. As Wells grew more and more conscious of his own articulation and of an increasingly articulate lower-middle-class movement, particularly in the new Press, and as he indeed came to take a leading part in such a 'revolution', his confidence must have grown accordingly. At the same time a conventional hostility to Victorian property-owning seems to have been pervasive at certain social levels, not at all restricted to the working-class movement; and the central consciousness of society transferred away from the Forsyte levels of society, and became invested in the Radical movement, in the widespread sense of new beginnings, and, for example, in the novels of Wells himself. Galsworthy's sense of living in a post-cultural mode may thus have been as acute as Wells's, and more disquieting, since his characters were taken from precisely that section of society whose members' vitality within society was in the process of being drained away and they could not define themselves in the new society except in terms which negated the cultural selves they were loath to leave behind. In this sense Galsworthy's characters are caught between two modes of life. In sociological terms, individuals alienated from a cultural matrix require therapy: they must be re-initiated into some culture where they may more or less regain the healthy sense of living integrated in society; or they must find some kind of transcendent 'commitment therapy' which will give them the ability to regain faith in *something*; or (according to Rieff) they must – if cultural disintegration has proceeded beyond a certain limit – give themselves up to a life in which therapy becomes absolute, an end in itself, and a constantly therapeutic living of life becomes all that 'matters'. A writer like Galsworthy had experienced the post-Darwinian depletion too intensely for there to remain the hope of unself-conscious adherence to the upper-middle-class culture, from which he was therefore partially exiled. A thoroughgoing therapeutic activism (as in his medical Socialist, Martin Stone, in *Fraternity*), in the Wellsian manner, was too crude an expedient in the face of the psychological subtlety implicit in all social problems. The only remaining therapy, a commitment to 'Fraternity' and to 'Union', while cosmically satisfying, only served to undermine the cultural residues from the segregationalist upper-middle-class life which held Galsworthy's sense of reality in stability. It would be absurd to think of Soames or Hilary Dallison being cured of their 'maladaptation' by being brought totally into line with a contemporary Radicalism; the Potwell Inn would hardly be likely to relieve Hilary of *his* existential anxieties, and the self-confidence gradually developed by Edwin Clayhanger in his suburban house in the Potteries would be only bewildering for a Galsworthy character.

There is no cosmic repletion for Hilary in *Fraternity*, though a range of specifically therapeutic recourses is ironically presented throughout the book. Hilary at the end of the novel finds himself in a position similar to Tod at the end of Nathaneal West's novel, *The Day of the Locust* (1939). He is driven to desperation by false therapies and false apocalypse. Galsworthy's novel is more 'British' than West's (*The Day of the Locust* ends in a Munchian scream), but the 'crisax'[2] that each novel nervily analyses is essentially the same, viz. the post-cultural crisis of modern man.

II

It is enlightening to trace the sources of the anxiety which resulted in the creation of a character like Bosinney; Bosinney can tell us much about Soames's problems:

> This 'very singular-looking man', as Mrs Small
> afterwards called him, was of medium height and
> strong build, with a pale, brown face, a dust-
> coloured moustache, very prominent cheek-bones,
> and hollow cheeks. His forehead sloped back towards

the crown of his head, and bulged out in bumps
over the eyes, like foreheads seen in the lion-
house at the Zoo. He had sherry-coloured eyes,
disconcertingly inattentive at times. Old
Jolyon's coachman, after driving June and
Bosinney to the theatre, had remarked to the butler:
  'I dunno what to make of 'im. Looks to me for
all the world like an 'alf-tame leopard'.
  And every now and then a Forsyte would come up,
sidle round, and take a look at him.[3]

Bosinney, the "alf-tame leopard', transcends the cultural modes
of the Forsytes and their servants; he relates to culture as the
beast-men of Wells's *Island of Dr. Moreau* (1896) relate to
'the law' with which Moreau indoctrinates them. For Wells, the
bestiality of man seems, overtly at least, to have registered
the cosmic malevolence which Huxleyan ethics were necessary to
combat:

There is no health in us, and it is only by
effort, by wisdom and continence, by the
suppression of instincts that are a part of us,
that even a sufferable equilibrium may be
maintained.[4]

But the presence of another half-tame beast-man in a post-1900
novel of social 'revolt' may clarify Wells's 'ambiguous'[5] treatment of the beast-men in the 1896 novel. For there are traces in
The Island of Dr. Moreau of an attitude quite opposite to that
which demands 'the suppression of instincts'. Moreau's 'Law',
for example, is seen from the point of view of the beasts as
mechanical and repressive; the emotional pull of Chapter 12
('The Sayers of the Law') is towards a sympathy for the beasts
and towards the desire to release them from harsh constraints to
which they are subject. Perhaps the fundamental emotional
pull is towards a desire to heal the painful misery of their lives.
What these creatures demand above all else is the sense of well-
being. And well-being in the context of that novel seems to
imply a freedom from cultural pressure, and a more perfect
application of the Moreauesque plasticizing process. Derived
from an imperfect and unstable evolutionary transformation,

the beast-men require constant adherence to a conformative mode in order to survive. They reflect in this way the state of civilized man. The curative impulse which Wells embodies by implication in the novel is towards a more thoroughgoing plastic transformation, so that the recommended course of action is transformative and not conformative. Philip Rieff quotes E. R. Dodds on Plato; and there is no doubt that Plato's influence is to be traced in the overt ethics of *The Island of Dr. Moreau*:

> As E. R. Dodds pointed out, Plato held in his *Laws* that 'the majority of human beings can be kept in tolerable moral health only by a carefully chosen diet of "incantations" – that is to say, edifying myths and bracing ethical slogans'.[6]

But Rieff also points to a more modern therapeutic situation, wherein 'there is no positive community now within which the individual can merge himself therapeutically'.[7] And this new need for a transformative therapy is the other side of the central ambiguity in Wells's novel. Wells's view of the predicament, however, is more truly 'scientific' than individualistic.

> The modern scientist [claims Rieff], *qua* scientist, . . . has tried to extricate himself from all moral demands except those imposed upon him by the internal logic of his transformative endeavour directed against the natural world, all designed to overcome those gross miseries and necessaries nature imposes upon mankind. The scientific community aspires to be supra-cultural, and is not qualified therefore to supply a creedal dynamic to that new laity, the non-scientists.[8]

The beast-men of Moreau's island are the normal products of contemporary culture, as seen from the point of view of a scientist who wishes to 'overcome those gross miseries', to extricate man 'from all moral demands', and to institute 'supra-cultural' Utopia.

Bosinney is, in his animal freedom from cultural limitations, material for the transformative mode. But Galsworthy's view of the half-tamed beast is apparently, as Lawrence pointed out in the essay, 'John Galsworthy',[9] and as Philip Rieff rephrases, 'worshipping the releases instead of the controls, and therefore more a parody of the old consolations than a genuine advance beyond them'.[10] The significance of Bosinney and Irene, however, need not lie in their ability to 'symbolize' a new order beyond Forsyteism. Irene's very refusal to become 'absolute' or 'real' in the novel may relate to her use as one term, the antithetical, of the old, deprivational dialectic; Galsworthy's universe is one polarized into control and release, and no therapy is supplied in the novels for characters like Soames, doomed to asceticism, and characters like Bosinney, doomed to freedom in the ecstatic mode. Soames and Bosinney are related in a way that parodies the dialectic of law and plasticity (as rendered earlier in *The Island of Dr. Moreau*). Soames gives Bosinney 'a free hand in the terms of this correspondence' (p. 330), which is freedom, in other words, only as defined as antithetical, or corresponding, to cultural restraint. It is not Bosinney, but Soames, however, who occupies the centre of the novel, and the former's 'anti-Forsyte' typology is no detraction if we understand the role Bosinney plays in amplifying the conditions of Soames's alienation. The Forsytes are polarized, in their cohesion and communal impulsiveness, not against Irene and Bosinney, most fundamentally, but against Soames himself. It is as if, detached from communal consolations, Soames is a prey to erotic fantasies which replace the rewards of family life. Not feeling real as the husband of Irene, he defines himself as the husband of a woman who hates him and who chooses to desire a being who is the polar opposite of his own overt self. If Irene and Bosinney made love in some supra-Forsyte way, this intense registration of the grounds of Soames's alienation would disappear, and his predicament as post-cultural man would be blurred. The conventionality of Bosinney's animality is matched by the modelled quality of Irene's 'Beauty'. Their mythic nature intensifies their power to reflect the existential anxieties of Soames.

It is arguable that Galsworthy's intellectualization of the encounter between 'Reason' and 'Love' is more Freudian than Lawrentian, and that Lawrence's objections to Galsworthy's novel are to be associated with what Rieff identifies as Lawrence's 'belief that the decisive function in man is will or desire –

not intellect'.[11] For the very process of assembling the material
of *The Man of Property* is agnostic-anarchic, and analytic, involving an analytic separation and relation of the separate elements
of the old dialectic which no longer works. There is, of course, no
para-Freudian therapy for the individual (though, in terms of
the whole of *The Forsyte Saga*, a case might be made for the view
that Soames and Irene undergo a degree of release from fixation
and erotic disappointment) in *The Man of Property*, but inherent
in the structural method is an analytic, neutral attitude which
approaches very close to the Freudian. Lawrence, himself
searching for a voluntarist type, naturally rejected Irene. For
Irene cannot stand as an absolute, separate element; her role is
as an analytic component of the novel. Galsworthy's zoological
approach to Bosinney is typical of the dry detachment of his
analytic mode, which permits no easy way out of post-cultural
crisis, in which both control and release are freed from cultural
guidance, and present an anarchic and dissonant music when
assembled as an Edwardian *ménage à trois*:

> Eros and Thanatos, spontaneity and rigidity,
> remain in eternal although alterable conflict,
> neither victorious over the other. Two forces
> and their eternal war: this defines Freud's
> pessimism.[12]

In his best Edwardian novels, in *Fraternity* and *The Man of
Property*, Galsworthy commits himself technically to what
Rieff calls 'continuity in the dialectical effort' and thereby
refuses to accept the easy solution that most critics have identified with Irene.

I have claimed that Soames is a newly conscious Forsyte, but
it is young Jolyon who is most palpably endowed with consciousness:

> It is in the nature of a Forsyte to be ignorant
> that he is a Forsyte; but young Jolyon was well
> aware of being one. He had not known it till
> after the decisive step which had made him an
> outcast; since then the knowledge had been with
> him continually (p. 233).

Such 'continuity in the dialectical effort' is the mark of the
therapeutic type, and the 'Diagnosis of a Forsyte' (Chapter 10,
pp. 233–43) comes naturally from his lips. Young Jolyon's
account is steeped in the evolutionary anthropology conventional during the Edwardian period; he defines his relationship
with Bosinney thus:

> '. . . my Uncle James . . . is the perfect specimen
> of a Forsyte. His sense of property is extreme,
> while you have practically none. Without me in
> between, you would seem like a different species.
> I'm the missing link. We are, of course, all of
> us the slaves of property, and I admit that it's
> a question of degree, but what I call a "Forsyte"
> is a man who is decidedly more than less a slave
> of property' (pp. 237–8).

Uncle Swithin is, in this terminology, not fully civilized:

> 'Ah! in Swithin there's something primeval
> still. The town and middle-class life haven't
> digested him yet. All the old centuries of
> farmwork and brute force have settled in him,
> and there they've stuck, for all he's so
> distinguished' (p. 239).

But, for Bosinney, Jolyon's account matches the character of
Soames exactly: 'Well, you've hit your cousin Soames off to the
life' (p. 239). There is hardly evidence here that Soames is
characterized by his *consciousness*. The reverse seems to be
indicated, in fact, when Jolyon sees Soames's predicament in
his marriage with Irene: 'Whence should a man like his cousin,
saturated with all the prejudices and beliefs of his class, draw the
insight or inspiration necessary to break up this life?' (p. 241).
Nevertheless, it is in Soames that we see consciousness in crisis.
   At first Soames's 'appearance of "sniff"' (p. 5) is seen to
characterize all the Forsytes ('The habitual sniff on the face of
Soames Forsyte had spread through their ranks' – p. 4), but the
very fictional concentration upon Soames emphasizes the
secrecy of his habit and thus establishes the privacy of his
existence: 'Soames Forsyte . . . with something round and secret

about his whole appearance' (p. 17). And then, in the beginning
of Chapter 4, Soames's predicament is made clearer:

> He had left his wife sitting on the sofa
> in the drawing-room, her hands crossed in her
> lap, manifestly waiting for him to go out. . . .
>   He could not understand what she found wrong
> with him. . . .
>   The profound, subdued aversion which he felt
> in his wife was a mystery to him, and a source
> of the most terrible irritation . . . .
>   Soames was forced . . . to set the blame entirely
> down to his wife. . . . 'Then why did she marry me?'
> was his continual thought. . . .
>   For the hundredth time that month he turned
> over this problem . . . (pp. 61–2).

The ground of Soames's existence is switching from incorpora-
tion within the family to marital crisis; at the same time we
realize that Soames is the true subversive element in the
metropolis, engaged as he is in a secretive pursuit of the pastoral:

> He had stopped to look in at a picture shop,
> for Soames was an 'amateur' of pictures. . . . He
> brought them home with him on his way back
> from the City, generally after dark. . . .
>   They were nearly all landscapes with figures
> in the foreground, a sign of some mysterious
> revolt against London, its tall houses, its
> interminable streets, where his life and the
> life of his breed and class were passed . . . (p. 63).

Just as the pastoral undermines the autonomy of the metropolis,
so Soames's mirror-image undermines his absoluteness. He
presents himself to himself as isolated, privatist, self-conscious,
insusceptible to communal therapy:

> In the plate-glass window of the picture shop
> his image stood and looked at him.
>   His sleek hair under the brim of the tall hat
> had a sheen like the hat itself; his cheeks, pale

and flat, the line of his clean-shaven lips, his
firm chin with its grayish shaven tinge, and the
buttoned strictness of his black cut-away coat,
conveyed an appearance of reserve and secrecy,
of imperturbable, enforced composure; but his
eyes, cold, gray, strained-looking, with a line
in the brow between them, examined him wistfully,
as if they knew of a secret weakness (pp. 63–4).

Soames establishes the principle of the vulnerability of self.
When he builds the house at Robin Hill, he realizes that he has
left the rest of the Forsytes behind:

Soames, the pioneer-leader of the great Forsyte
army advancing to the civilization of this wilder-
ness, felt his spirit daunted by the loneliness,
by the invisible singing and the hot, sweet air.

Soames's 'strained-looking' eyes and his 'secret weakness' and
his 'daunted' spirit sustain the imperializing motive. Alan
Sandison has commented on Rider Haggard, Rudyard Kipling,
Joseph Conrad and John Buchan:

The need to secure their own identity
dictated an incessant war against an alien
and chaotic nature with the elusive end in
the subjugation of the latter. This crisis,
where the principal is at once aggressive and
embattled in a foreign and menacing world which
he nevertheless seeks to appropriate, is
essentially the crisis of empire. The embarkation
of the self on its rapacious cognitive conquest
to overcome the world's 'otherness' thus finds
an equivalent physical expression in the
imperial idea.[13]

Sandison believes that these four writers, 'in describing the
tensions of political empire . . . are in fact describing . . . the
harsh moral imperialism . . . which is the condition of their
self-consciousness'.[14] Irene may thus be said to constitute
Soames's 'possession' in a political sense, and his civilizing
colonization of her becomes literally 'rapacious cognitive

conquest'. The irritating lack of responsiveness that Irene shows to Soames is the prerequisite for his 'predatory aggression':

> He had married this woman, conquered her,
> made her his own, and it seemed to him contrary
> to the most fundamental of all laws, the law of
> possession, that he could do no more than own
> her body – if indeed he could do that, which he was
> beginning to doubt (p. 76).

Soames has found himself plunged into crisis, 'Must I always go on like this?' (p. 76), and pursues what Rieff calls in another context 'the rage to be free of the inherited morality':[15]

> He had a craving for strong drink, to lull
> him to indifference, or rouse him to fury. If
> only he could burst out of himself, out of this
> web that for the first time in his life he felt
> around him. If only he could surrender to the
> thought: 'Divorce her – turn her out! She has
> forgotten you. Forget her!'
> If only he could surrender to the thought:
> 'Let her go – she has suffered enough!'
> If only even he could surrender to the sudden
> vision: 'What does it all matter?' Forget
> himself for a minute, forget that it mattered
> what he did, forget that whatever he did he must
> sacrifice something.
> If only he could act on an impulse!
> He could forget nothing; surrender to no
> thought, vision, or desire; it was all too
> serious; too close around him, an unbreakable
> cage (p. 375).

The process begun with the mirror-image in the plate-glass window ends in a complete release of Soames into the crisis of self-consciousness, the crisis of the post-cultural man who has developed no privatist therapy sufficiently effective to replace the reassurance of the culture he has left behind. As Rieff says: 'This culture, which once imagined itself inside a church, feels trapped in something like a zoo of separate cages. Modern men are like Rilke's panther, forever looking out from one cage into another.'[16] The process, in which the imperialistic mode gives way to the therapeutic, ends in Soames's taking Irene into his house with him into the full condition of private crisis; Soames will suffer no interference with the chaos of his marital life:

> Young Jolyon's glance shot past him into the
> hall, and Soames turned. There in the drawing-
> room doorway stood Irene, her eyes were wild and
> eager, her lips were parted, her hands outstretched.
> In the sight of both men that light vanished from
> her face; her hands dropped to her sides; she stood
> like stone.
>
> Soames spun tound, and met his visitor's eyes,
> and at the look he saw in them, a sound like a
> snarl escaped him. He drew his lips back in the
> ghost of a smile.
>
> 'This is my house', he said; 'I manage my own
> affairs, I've told you once – I tell you again;
> we are not at home'.
>
> And in young Jolyon's face he slammed the door
> (p. 376).

The novel has brought not the customary stilling of a resolved ending, but the gradual crystallization of a crisis which demands therapy. Soames shuts himself off snarling in the cage of 'inherited morality'; by taking Irene with him (erotically fixated as she is), behind the closed doors of private post-cultural experience, Soames defines the point at which our modern anti-communal 'culture' takes over from unconscious, integrative Forsyteism. 'Culture', in the modern sense, becomes a therapy for relationships. The polarization of such an ending and the ending of *Mr. Polly*, for example, shows the underlying similarity between Galsworthy's and Wells's ideals. Polly's intimacy with the fat woman is of an archetypal kind; she will never be a skeleton, he says, but such a statement implies a kind of X-ray vision, a replete closeness. Soames's relations with Irene betray the same kind of Utopianizing implicit in the projected anxiety. There are very powerful erotic forces at work in the process which keeps the two combatants at battle. Irene, we feel, properly belongs (in the universe of this novel, if not in the whole of *The Forsyte Saga*) inside the house with Soames; there is a symmetry about their relationship, a circuit of Eros and Thanatos.

It is as if the very bringing of the Forsytes into a cognitive process has broken up their original coherence. The first paragraph of the novel, dealing with the Forsytes in terms of 'psychological analysis', and likening them to a tree, renders them obsolete at once. An observer at a gathering of the Forsytes we are told,

> . . . has been admitted to a vision of the dim
> roads of social progress, has understood something
> of patriarchal life, of the swarmings of savage
> hordes, of the rise and fall of nations. He is
> like one who, having watched a tree grow from its
> planting – a paragon of tenacity, insulation, and
> success, amidst the deaths of a hundred other
> plants less fibrous, sappy, and persistent –
> one day will see it flourishing with bland, full
> foliage, in an almost repugnant prosperity, at
> the summit of its efflorescence (pp. 3–4).

The shifting of the grounds of reality from the family to the privacy of the marriage relationship is simultaneous with the 'fall' of the Forsyte nation; old Jolyon focuses the process:

> Slowly, surely, with the secret inner process
> that works the destruction of an old tree, the
> poison of the wounds to his happiness, his will,
> his pride, had corroded the comely edifice of
> his philosophy. Life had worn him down on one
> side, till, like the family of which he was the
> head, he had lost balance (p. 310).

Old Jolyon suffers what Philip Rieff calls a 'deconversion toward an anti-creedal analytic attitude'.[17] The analytic attitude, implicit in Galsworthy's 'ironic' structuring of events in the novel, transcends the mere opting for instinctual fulfilment that a mass audience might identify in Galsworthy. The fully conscious mind, with its achieved talent for 'psychological analysis', stands detached from the process defined by Rieff and admittedly analogous to the Edwardian situation:

In fact, evil and immorality are disappearing,
as Spencer assumed they would, mainly because our
culture is changing its definition of human
perfection. No longer the Saint, but the
instinctual Everyman, twisting his neck uncomfortably
inside the starched collar of culture, is
the communal ideal, to whom men offer tacit prayers
for deliverance from their inherited renunciations.[18]

Although Galsworthy may appear to opt for the new worship of
the instinctual Everyman (something he shares with many of the
Edwardian writers), his presentation of the polemical material
of *The Man of Property* is analytic and neutral. Perhaps uninten-
tionally he depicts Irene as erotically fixated and as 'mytho-
logized' as Soames is. In Galsworthy's dry refusal to commit
himself 'creedally' in his novels of society, there is some of
Freud's puritanical retreat from the ugly battle between
instinct and 'inherited renunciations'. The inset polemic of the
visit to the zoo ('To shut up a lion or a tiger in confinement
was surely a horrible barbarity' – p. 190), though used overtly
to reflect the restrictive brutality of the Forsytes, reveals that
'The hungrier the beast, the greater the fascination' (p. 190),
and such a zoologization of society, pervasive in the novel, con-
tributes to the detachment of the analysis. The 'baboons and
panthers' (p. 190), painfully transformed and made to con-
form, find themselves in the private cages of post-cultural
crisis.[19] A supra-cultural technological Utopia at Robin Hill is
seen as a possible alternative, and may become the prevailing
therapy of a later generation:

'Ah!' said Bosinney sarcastically. 'Your wife?
She doesn't like the cold? I'll see to that;
she shan't be cold. Look here!' he pointed to
four marks at regular intervals in the walls of
the court. 'I've given you hot-water pipes in
aluminium casings. . . .'
Soames looked suspiciously at these marks (p. 109).

But for this book the isolation out of post-cultural individuals,
denied the consolations of communal life, but suffering from
residual repressions, becomes the condition of the universe. The

door slams at No. 62 Montpelier Square amidst the interminable streets; the existence of the new psychomorphous house at Robin Hill ('I could build you a teaser here,' said Bosinney – p. 72) constitutes only a fantastic consolidation of the grounds of real crisis.

III

By dramatizing the Soamesian predicament, Galsworthy was able to present a vivid picture of late-Victorian society in transsition. The amorphousness of the social criticism in *The Island Pharisees* (1904) is avoided in *The Man of Property* by concentrating social problems in individual self-consciousness. It is perhaps because Galsworthy's method of presenting Soames is so palpably diagnostic and because we are willy-nilly drawn into the conditions of his consciousness and hence into sympathy with him that he represents for us a satisfying image of man in crisis. In *The Country House* the 'country classes' are singled out for diagnosis as suffering from 'Pendycitis'; Chapter 9, 'Definition of "Pendycitis"', thus corresponds to Chapter 10 of *The Man of Property*, 'Diagnosis of a Forsyte'. The Pendyces are not only an 'appendix', redundant in the national organism, but have become infected. Unfortunately, the sexual tension of *The Country House* cannot rival that of the earlier novel, nor indeed that of *Fraternity* (1909), which is otherwise a much more obviously sociological and less 'literary' novel. The transition in these titles from particular man to house to ideal is indicative of the general drift of Galsworthy's Edwardian development, but *The Country House* is anomalous in this sequence in so far as it lacks a central consciousness in crisis. Instead the whole sub-culture is in crisis, and its focused centre in Mr and Mrs Pendyce is not strong enough to compete with the direct involvement of the sexual crises of Soames and Hilary.

The sacrifice of poignancy is, however, counterbalanced by a sense that Galsworthy is trying to place the ideal of fully instinctual sexuality as in some sense incomplete. There is a subdued hint in *The Man of Property* that the affair with Bosinney is all very well as an antidote to Soames, but that, judged ultimately, there is still, despite Galsworthy's idealism, something 'wrong' with it. In *The Country House* the prominent part played by Mrs Pendyce, a somewhat sentimentally drawn 'good' mother, ensures that the cosmic 'rightness' of George's affair with Mrs Bellew is qualified. That affair is still presented in terms of joy, and Helen Bellew's beauty is still the subject of a kind of worship; but the values of Mrs Pendyce, who is not at all to be identified in this respect with her reactionary husband, are subtly affronted by the undeniable sordidness of certain aspects of George's liaison. A phrase from the zoo scene in *The Man of Property* seems to suggest much of the interest of *The Country House*: '"Don't go too near, mother"' (p. 190).

The Country House is characterized by its fictional presentation of a conflict of therapies. The destructive potential of George Pendyce's 'healthy' affair with Mrs Bellew is explored in some detail, and the traditional internal 'therapies' of the country-house system are finally shown as inappropriate for the conditions of modern reality. Only by adapting to modern conditions can the Pendyce family come through the predicament intact, and their coming through intact (paradoxically, in terms of the social criticism of the novel) soon becomes an emotional requirement for the reader. George's mother, split off, through her tenderness, from Mr Pendyce, has finally to stoop to confronting Helen Bellew's husband personally, and to asking him to suspend his proceedings for divorce. Much of the book is taken up with inset disputes over the proper status of marriage in society, and this divides the diagnostic interest of the novel. On the other hand, it also helps to focus on precise issues in so far as the stubborn 'Pendycitis' of the Tory country classes is concerned. The possibility of marriage reform would represent a 'new idea' for Mr Pendyce, and he has his own therapy for such a threatening eventuality:

The times were bad and dangerous. There was every chance of a Radical Government being returned, and the country going to the dogs. It was but natural and human that he should pray for the survival of the form of things which he believed in and knew, the form of things that had been bequeathed to him, and was embodied in the words 'Horace Pendyce'. It was not his

habit to welcome new ideas. A new idea invading
the country of the Squire's mind was at once met
with a rising of the whole population, and either
prevented from landing, or if already on shore
instantly taken prisoner.[20]

In his turn Mr Pendyce is treated by Paramor (the enlightened
lawyer) as if he (together with his system of autotherapeutic
defences) is sick:

The Squire broke in:
  'Don't think that I'll have any humble pie
eaten to that fellow Bellew'.
  The look Mr Paramor gave him at those words
was like that of a doctor diagnosing a disease.
Yet there was nothing in the expression of the
Squire's face with its thin grey whiskers and
moustache, its twist to the left, its swan-like
eyes, decided jaw, and sloping brow, different
from what this idea might bring on the face of
any country gentleman (p. 173).

And it is Mr Paramor who proceeds to make the central diagnosis of the book (parallel to young Jolyon's diagnosis in *The
Man of Property*):

'The country classes', said Mr Paramor quietly,
'are especially backward in such matters. They
have strong, meat-fed instincts, and what with
the county Members, the Bishops, the Peers, all
the hereditary force of the country, they still
rule the roast. And there's a certain disease –
to make a very poor joke, call it "Pendycitis" –
with which most of these people are infected.
They're "crass". They do things, but they do
them the wrong way! They muddle through with the
greatest possible amount of unnecessary labour
and suffering! It's part of the hereditary
principle (p. 117).

The diagnosis is the pretext for the implementation of therapy:

Gregory turned his face away.

'Your joke *is* very poor', he said. 'I don't
believe they are like that! I won't admit it.
If there is such a disease, it's our business
to find a remedy'.

'Nothing but an operation will cure it', said
Mr Paramor; 'and before operating there's a
preliminary process to be gone through. It was
discovered by Lister' (p. 117).

The seduction of the scientific reference is implicit in Paramor's
anti-creedal, anti-idealist position: 'men . . . are, like plants,
creatures of heredity and environment; their growth is slow.
You can't get grapes from thorns . . .' (p. 178). Out of this detached analytic, the final well-being of Mrs Pendyce emerges as
the reward for an unwittingly para-Freudian revolutionary
compromise; after she has summoned the courage to pay her
visit to Captain Bellew, she receives the reward sought by the
therapeutic:

'How happy I am!' she thought – 'how glad and —
happy I am!'
And the feeling, which was not as definite as
this, possessed her to the exclusion of all other
feelings in the rain-soaked fields (p. 294).

Her Eros has saved her husband from the effects of his Thanatos, and together they constitute some recompense for the
indignity projected upon cultural life in *The Man of Property*.
In *The Country House* Galsworthy rather more mellowly explores
the pathos of the culturally obsolete.

IV

The movement towards the direct discussion of possible therapeutic responses to social crisis culminates in Galsworthy's
Edwardian novels in *Fraternity*, which debates – albeit in a proto-
typical manner – the issue of 'pure' therapy versus commitment therapies of various kinds. We have seen in Chapter 1
that although the drift of Philip Rieff's book is to associate
Freud exclusively with the purest 'Triumph of the Therapeutic',

Rieff is willing to hint at a tradition of health-for-health's-sake
'activism' which pre-dates Freud. But he does not acknowledge
the quite striking resemblance between the activism he identifies in the most modern of therapies and that of the turn of the
century. In *Fraternity* it is Dr Martin Stone (the 'Sanitist'[21])
who plays the role of therapeutic activist, treating 'all these
people as if they were in hospital' (p. 213), and thereby escaping the somewhat different predicament of Hilary Dallison, who
confesses to attempting to find a commitment therapy:

> . . . in a private way I try to identify myself
> as much as possible with what I see about me,
> feeling that if I should ever really be at one
> with the world I live in I should be happy (p. 85).

Rieff's distinctions may help us to see more clearly the significance of the contrasts being made in a novel like *Fraternity*. At
first, for instance, it is possible to confuse Martin Stone's therapeutic programme with Hilary's. Hilary claims:

> I do not believe that chastity is a virtue
> in itself, but only in so far as it ministers to
> the health and happiness of the community (p. 86).

And it seems only a short step from that position to Rieff's:

> If 'immoral' materials, rejected under earlier
> cultural criteria, are therapeutically effective,
> enhancing somebody's sense of well-being, then
> they are useful. The 'end' or 'goal' is to
> keep going.[22]

But it is the activist last sentence here that points to the difference between Martin and Hilary; the latter, far from 'keeping going', slows down to a less than Hamletian pace:[23]

> In Hilary . . . self-consciousness had soaked
> his system through and through; permeated every
> cranny of his spirit, so that to think a
> definite thought, or do a definite deed, was
> obviously becoming difficult to him (p. 30).

Being concerned with everybody's well-being, the well-being of
the whole community, and 'selfless' in the new collectivist spirit

of the Liberal Revival, but lacking moral guidance from an integrated culture, Hilary's radical conscience renders him powerless to do anything.[24] Rieffian man sides with Martin rather
than with Hilary:

> In the absence of news about a stable and
> governing order anywhere, theory becomes
> actively concerned with mitigating the daily
> miseries of living rather than with a therapy
> of commitment to some healing doctrine of the
> universe. In fact the universe is neither
> accepted nor rejected; it is merely there for
> our use.[25]

Hilary is thus half-way between Martin the activist and old
Mr Stone, who, having abdicated from present activity, is
writing his apocalyptic 'Book of Universal Brotherhood'.
Lacking both the surrogate 'faith' of Mr Stone (the true commitment therapist) and Martin's health-for-health's-sake activism, Hilary's very altruism becomes a destructive weapon.
Hilary is typical of what Rieff calls post-Christian man ('I dis-
believe in all Church dogmas, and do not go to church' – p. 85),
in that he finds it impossible to find a purely cultural sanction
for his commitment (or even a valid object for commitment),
but he is as bitterly opposed as so negative a man may be to
Martin's highly Rieffian idea that 'we have got to shake ourselves free of all the old sentimental notions, and just work at
putting everything to the test of Health' (p. 116). Hilary's type
is familiar to us, being, as the Forsytean Mr Purcey puts it in
Fraternity, 'very what d'you call it – *fin-de-siècle* – like all these
professors, these artistic pigs . . .' (p. 20). We remember
Hilary's degeneration described in Nordau, and his growing
inability to 'do a definite deed' echoes William James's version
of the 'sentimentalist . . . who never does a manly concrete
deed'.[26] Galsworthy is careful in his sociologization of Hilary
and Bianca as characteristic of a new section of society, 'the
cultivated classes' (p. 85), 'a section of society . . . who specu-
lated in ideas' (*ibid.*). Philip Rieff refers to an evolving type,
'complete with doctrines intended to manage the strains of
living as a communally detached individual', and suggests that
'the social type most obviously so detached is the intellectual'.[27]

The 'doctrines' which enable Hilary to manage these 'strains' are presented in Chapter 9 as his 'creed' (p. 85); the liberal's pathetic attempts to involve himself with communal purpose ('I try to identify myself as much as possible with what I see about me' – p. 85) are associated with the dangerous admission: 'I really can't take myself too seriously' (p. 86). The sentimental Hilary, temperamentally altruistic, but lacking a sense of purpose, is a prototype of post-cultural man. As so often for literature of the 1900s (and indeed for all modern literature), Nietzsche had already outlined the predicament:

> 'The well-being of the universal demands the
> devotion of the individual' – but behold, there
> is no such universal! At bottom, man has lost
> the faith in his own value when no infinitely
> valuable whole works through him; i.e. he
> conceived such a whole in order *to be able to
> believe in his own value.*[28]

Hilary's attempt to believe in 'the health and happiness of the community' and his chameleon-like ongoing effort 'to identify myself as much as possible with what I see about me' (p. 85) find no correlative in the hostile world outside himself; he has generated a social conscience 'in order to be able to believe in his own value', but still he cannot take himself too seriously. As Wylie Sypher put it,

> What began as romantic assertion of the self –
> of a free wilful, often isolated self – changed
> into a mistrust of the self, a need for communion,
> adjustment, or therapy.[29]

But Martin Stone offers Hilary a criterion of health which he rejects; the latter is an existential sentimentalist, in the tradition of Saul Bellow's Herzog. Entering into 'crisax', he refuses all offers of help.

A general concept of 'medical Socialism' (p. 305) was an important element in the spectrum of therapies newly available in the Edwardian decade; the prominence of Dr Martin Stone in *Fraternity* is in itself evidence of that importance. There is a sense, however, in which Martin's attentions to the working class are not directed by class-interest, but by a purely therapeutic vision of society. The working class is the first place to begin social cure – it being there that physical and psychosociological sickness are most palpable. The neutrality of Martin's 'philanthropy' is thus to be contrasted with the vested interest of Hilary's. Martin himself points to the autotherapeutic nature of Hilary's social conscience:

'. . . a man like Hilary's interest in all
this sort of thing is simply sentimental.
It's on his nerves. He takes philanthropy
just as he'd take sulphonal for sleeplessness' (p. 212).

But neither Conrad in *The Secret Agent*,[30] of course, nor Galsworthy in *Fraternity*, sees such a 'pure' therapy as Martin's as ultimately desirable or indeed feasible. Indeed it is surely an intention of both (however 'inconclusive' one may feel these respective novels to be) to show up the absurdity in practical terms of Shavo-Wellsian 'cure'. *Fraternity* presents a spectrum of characters reacting in their various ways to social crisis, and to the problem of social reform ('"All of us want social progress in our different ways. You, your grandfather, my brother, myself"' – p. 260); most interestingly, perhaps, it sets the therapeutic against the moralist. Hilary's fear of going beyond culture is contrasted with Martin's Rieffian sense of the triumph of the therapeutic:

'Take any subject that you like. Take the
poor themselves – what's wanted? Health.
Nothing on earth but health! The discoveries
and inventions of the last century have knocked
the floor out of the old order; we've got to
put a new one in, and we're going to put it in,
too – the floor of health (p. 131).

In the same way, Edwin's support of the shifting floor of his father's printing-shop implemented an activist mode of therapeutic intervention. Hilary sees that the therapeutics are difficult to define communally:

'But who are "you"?' murmured Hilary.
'Who are we? I'll tell you one thing.
While all the reformers are pecking at each

other we shall quietly come along and swallow
up the lot. We've simply grasped this
elementary fact, that theories are no basis for
reforms' (p. 131).

Martin's theory depends upon his typology for man: 'It's
human nature to want health' (p. 131).

In its rendering of crisis, *Fraternity* is of great interest as a
modernist structure. It is interesting in its technical ability to
present what J. Hillis Miller calls 'the community' of consciousnesses[31] of the Victorian novel as a kind of mere anarchic
'negative community' of 'intersubjectivity'.[32] There is a kind of
post-Chekhovian music in the counter-pointing of its atomized
consciousnesses, a music more acutely dissonant than that of
Jocelyn. Being at an important halfway point between what one
conventionally calls the novel of 'external characterization' and
the stream-of-consciousness novel (and being riskily, but, I
think, justifiably sociological in its approach), *Fraternity* is able
to depict the dialectical irony of simultaneous outer and inner
existence with great effectiveness. Its limpness and desiccation
are undeniable, but in a sense they help to reinforce the novel's
realization of energy dissipated in deadlock. Much the same
might be said, of course, of *The Secret Agent*, but there are
reasons for arguing that Galsworthy is able to present as
tenable a view of deadlock as Conrad's, largely through the
development of the Turgenevian form used in Galsworthy's
earlier novels. *Fraternity* is written so that its elements are
always, as it were, on the point of breaking away from the
centre; it makes absorbing reading for all those who have become absorbed anew (as Rieff, for example, apparently has) in
what one might call the centre-cannot-hold myth. For example,
Hilary in a simple sense lacks all conviction, and moves away
from the centre by finally disappearing overseas; more important, there is a deliberate and thoroughgoing decentralization of
episode in the novel, so that it becomes a model of (and induces
the experience in the reader of) 'mere' process and purpose-
lessness. There is a genuine element of narrative vertigo in the
experience of reading *Fraternity* which foreshadows the magnificent vertigo of Ford Madox Ford's Tietjens tetralogy. While
people like Martin Stone (and Philip Rieff) see centrifugal

dispersion as an opportunity or pretext for the 'peaceful' use of therapeutic energy, Galsworthy is content shrewdly to depict, 'configuratively', the conditions of a crisis which is our own.

In addition to its manifold debt to the late Dickens, *Fraternity* bears a special relation to *Dombey and Son*. In both novels a parodic group of lower-class characters is used as a mirror-image of a similar set of upper-class characters to question the authenticity of all social life. In *Fraternity* two brothers, Hilary and Stephen Dallison, are married to two sisters, Bianca and Cecilia. Stephen is a lawyer, a Conservative in the Soames tradition, but more or less happily married. Hilary is a writer, an intellectual, the indecisive Liberal, more or less unhappily married to Bianca, with whom he has failed to 'assert himself'. Cecilia has a daughter, the beautiful Thyme (who is temporarily attached to Cecilia's orphaned nephew, the Sanitist, Martin Stone), and an eccentric, visionary father, Mr Stone, who lives at her home, and is customarily closeted in his room, finishing his apocalyptic 'Book of Universal Brotherhood'. Each of these pairs or individuals has a 'shadow' or equivalent in the lower world of working-class London. Thus in Chapter One Cecilia – caught at the guilty moment after she has bought a new dress in a Kensington store – meets a little Galsworthian tableau of working-class characters, consisting of Joshua Creed, an ex-butler forced by illness to stoop to selling newspapers, and his co-slum-dweller, Mrs Hughs, Cecilia's seamstress. Living in wretched 'Hound Street' with Mr and Mrs Hughs is a gallery of 'Shadows', another married couple and their grown-up son (the equivalent of Martin), a girl lodger (the increasingly important hypnotic 'little model', who is the lower equivalent of Thyme), and another lodger, old Creed (the equivalent of old Mr Stone). A similar cast-list exists, therefore, on either side of the class line. The plot of the novel, such as it is, involves the gradual estrangement of Hilary from Bianca, an estrangement largely caused by the increasing power that 'clinging' Ivy, the little model, has over him. Hilary is driven finally into a situation where he has left his wife and agreed to take the little model away with him, but when, at the moment of their first real physical contact, she 'suddenly sprang at him . . . and fastened her mouth to his' (p. 337) he is revolted, and leaving her financially consoled, goes off alone – thus reaching sexually (in Joycean terms) what Creed calls elsewhere in the novel a 'crisix' (p. 216).

Fraternity is a social novel in this sense; that while the assault on Hilary by the little model and the associated disintegration of Hilary's marriage represent the primary emotional pull, just as important an emotional interest is the upper-level sense of being haunted or put in some sense at risk by the existence of the lower classes. The Freudian tension of the erotic scenes reinforces the fine representation of class tension throughout the novel. Part of the upper-level anxiety in *Fraternity* is seen as fear or disgust, and part as guilt. Hilary is consciously or unconsciously fascinated by the little model's sexuality (though this is sublimated at first into pity for her split boots, her darned stockings, and her old underclothes); and the upper-level fear of people like Ivy perhaps follows a dynamic identified by Rieff:

> ... we have to fear ... deadly violence between
> the culture classes. But the upper culture
> classes have already lost this most fundamental
> of all class struggles by their admiration for
> the 'vitality' of the lower, that vitality
> being a mirror image of their own earlier
> dynamism.[33]

The part played by guilt in the social reactions of characters like Hilary may be less easy to understand. It is difficult for us now, perhaps, to imagine the intensity of the Edwardian 'Social Conscience'. In a way it is a kind of liberal, domestic version of the white man's burden, a 'sulphonal for sleeplessness', a kind of projection outwards of one's own need for help. The emotional opportunism of much of the Christian investigation of 'Outcast' London in the 1880s and 1890s foreshadows the communal consolation derived in the years of the Liberal Revival from social reform. Galsworthy is not unconscious of the basic existential anxiety underlying Edwardian therapies, though his period terminology involves words like 'nerves'. The *fin-de-siècle* fascination with human attenuation and 'hollowing out', which is implicit in Conrad's fascination with the skeletal Negro 'criminals' in the grove of death,[34] seems to be taken up in the Liberal Revival as the underlying pretext for a new provisional com-

munality in social therapies of various kinds. J. Hillis Miller's
version of post-Darwinian crisis is:

> This evacuation of man's nature and of
> external nature is associated with an additional
> transformation of man's sense of himself. To
> define man as a lack, as a hunger for fulfilment . . .
> is to define him as will. . . .[35]

Contributing to 'Freedom from Hunger' may thus be, more
fundamentally, therapy for the self; only by curing the others
can one cure oneself. This kind of opportunist 'philanthropy'
amounts to a substitute for communal commitment therapy:
'theory becomes actively concerned with mitigating the daily
miseries of living than with a therapy of commitment'.[36]

Edwardian social reform is ultimately dependent, therefore,
not on social condition as such, but upon a changing human
typology. In terms of the psychohistorical process the Edwardian
social conscience emerged as a therapeutic device for remedying
ontological insecurity in a world in which man had become
'invisible', 'hollowed out', defined 'as a lack'. Such a new
myth satisfied both revolutionary and reactionary elements in
the Edwardian scene; Liberals found new communal strength
in the implementation of a real-life promised land, and Tories,
diagnosing the disaster of the Boer War as indicative of the
degeneracy of the English working man, could with zest implement authoritarian programmes for revitalization. The pursuit
of 'Health' formed a common ground, though the character of
the Edwardian period may also be distinguished by its conflict
of therapies.

Also implicit in the upper-level attitude to the complex
'threat' of the lower classes is a sense of the accidence of existence. When Roger Gard asked the question, 'What are we to
make of Edwardian "Society" which read its children rhymes
about not stepping on worms and yet produced a dress "trimmed
with the plumage of 800 canaries"?'[37] he was unconsciously
pointing to two sides of imperialism. Worm-altruism is not
only Darwinian 'There-but-for-the-grace-of-chance-go-I', but
also a substantiation of the absoluteness of self by the self's
assumption of a higher, therapeutic role (the white man's
burden). Conversely, the wearing of a dress made from the

'gratuitous' destruction of 800 existences is equally evidence
that while other existences are accidental, one's own is provi-
dential. Like *The Man of Property*, *Fraternity* focuses a gradually
emerging post-imperial crisis, a crisis deriving from the recognition that although men are not equal, existences have an
equivalence which the conditions of modern life make it
difficult to deny. Soames's imperialist rape is not enough to
subdue Irene, for she has a disquieting existence of her own, as
Uncle James finds out:

> James was left alone with his daughter-in-law.
> The glow of the wine, and of an excellent liqueur,
> was still within him. He felt quite warm towards
> her. She was really a taking little thing. . . .
>
> It may have been a recognition of danger in the
> very charm of her attitude, or a twang of
> indigestion, that caused a sudden dumbness to
> fall on James. He did not remember ever having
> been quite alone with Irene before. And, as he
> looked at her, an odd feeling crept over him, as
> though he had come across something strange and
> foreign.
>
> Now what was she thinking about – sitting back
> like that?[38]

At first Irene's femininity is alluring because she is 'really a . . .
thing', but the very Edwardian modelling of her sexuality
('her body . . . swaying when she moved, as though giving to the
arms of a lover' – p. 88) sets up her vital femininity as polarized
against James's masculinity. Suddenly the old absoluteness
disappears and James experiences 'the panic of isolation'.[39]
The confrontation of the races, of the classes, and of the sexes, so
much an issue of Edwardian social thought, thus seems ultimately to result in the breakdown of the old order of cultural
absoluteness and the release of existential equivalence.

At several points in *Fraternity*, upper-level characters are described as feeling their existences threatened by their lower-
level shadows. The presence of shadows indicates that a light
has been projected on the subject, that the upper-level characters are in the limelight, as it were. Heightened awareness of
one's own cultural identity is thus the immediate consequence

of the shadows below. The little model is especially a threat, since her posing, her capitulation to a merely mimetic existence (for example in her willingness to be painted by Bianca and re-dressed from head to foot by Hilary), implicitly exposes the less overt pose of Bianca and Hilary in their '*fin-de-siècle*' roles in society. Bianca's picture of Ivy has her standing in deep shadow in the role of a whore; but the fact that Ivy is only a 'model' (and is willing to let her 'self' be modulated in this way) only reinforces one's sense of the provisional nature of the social presentation of the self amongst the upper-level people, and exposes their hollowness. Thyme, for instance, who complains of one of the poorer areas of Kensington, '"This street gives me a hollow feeling"' (p. 117), may clothe herself in charities, but she is only in so doing revealing her own covered inauthenticity:

> Thyme soon came down. She wore a blouse of some
> blue stuff bought by Cecilia for the relief of
> people in the Balkan States, a skirt of purplish
> tweed woven by Irish gentlewomen in distress . . .
> (p. 211).

Galsworthy, true to his sociological interest, is quite explicit about this threat to the social reality of his major characters. The novel begins, as we have seen, with Cecilia buying a new dress. On the second page of the novel she appears as a hesitant 'lady' looking in a shop window:

> 'And suppose Stephen doesn't like me in it!'
> This doubt set her gloved fingers pleating the
> bosom of her frock. Into that little pleat she
> folded the essence of herself, the wish to have
> and the fear of having, the wish to be and the
> fear of being, and her veil, falling from the
> edge of her hat, three inches from her face,
> shrouded with its tissue her half-decided little
> features, her rather too high cheek-bones, her
> cheeks which were slightly hollowed, as though
> Time had kissed them too much (p. 2).

Cecilia's subtle insecurity (associated with her veiled hollow-ness) is ironically highlighted by our being permitted to enter the consciousness of Joshua Creed, who is selling newspapers nearby. Under the circumstances the confidence of his identification of Cecilia – 'He knew a lady when he saw one' (p. 2) – is almost comically poignant. It is Creed's juxtaposed consciousness of knowing Cecilia as 'a lady' that is the threat; she has a great 'fear of being'. Within a minute or two she is standing stripped naked in front of a surrealistic long mirror, 'in whose bright pool there yearly bathed hundreds of women's bodies, divested of skirts and bodices, whose unruffled surface reflected daily a dozen women's souls divested of everything' (p. 3). With the rise of privacy comes the Edwardian fascination for what the butler saw; the butler's seeing, as we shall see, becomes an assault upon upper-level absoluteness, and an exciting extension of the scope of privacy. More centrally for this context, J. Hillis Miller deals with a similar use of mirror-reflection when he talks about the mirror in *Our Mutual Friend*; he quotes:

> The great looking-glass above the sideboard
> reflects the table and the company, reflects the
> new Veneering crest, in gold and eke in silver,
> frosted, and also thawed, a camel of all work . . .
> reflects Veneering: forty, wavy-haired, dark,
> tending to corpulence, sly, mysterious, filmy. . . .[40]

and comments:

> The looking-glass above the sideboard is here
> a representation of the narrator's consciousness:
> detached, neutral, objective, reflecting what
> there is to be seen, but in this reflecting
> showing what is mirrored as an insubstantial
> facade, a dreamlike mirage. This is, however,
> what the Veneerings and their guests are. . . .[41]

Miller's rhetoric is familiar, but it is important to see the existential insecurity of Cecilia established here at the very beginning of *Fraternity* in strikingly similar terms. When Cecilia leaves the store she meets up with Mrs Hughs, as we have seen, and it is apt that later on in the book, in Chapter Seven, the enigmatic Mrs Hughs should seem to represent a disquieting mirror-image of Cecilia:

> The seamstress, who had advanced into the
> middle of the room, stood with her worn hands
> against her sides, and no signs of life but the
> liquid patience in her large brown eyes. She was
> an enigmatic figure. Her presence always roused
> a sort of irritation in Cecilia as if she had
> been suddenly confronted with what might possibly
> have been herself if certain little accidents had
> omitted to occur (p. 62).

The upshot of this final thought is surely a reiteration of the anxious Edwardian's 'There-but-for-the-grace-of-chance-go-I'.

It is interesting that the image of the mirror as pastoral pool is used in a similar way by Conrad in *The Secret Agent*. The Edwardian use of the mirror (as in Galsworthy and Conrad) is an advance on the Dickensian in that it is able more directly surrealistically to cast doubt on the autonomy of metropolis. The Professor, in *The Secret Agent*, is the most extreme representative of the self threatened by mass society; if pressed too far, he will simply blow himself up (his 'self' will disintegrate). Conrad's book comprises a much richer linguistic universe than Galsworthy's, and is therefore highly susceptible to a Miller-esque interpretation. But hints from Miller may be useful if we look more closely at *The Secret Agent* (which is, after all, a central work of the Edwardian moment), and in particular at the role the Professor plays therein.

'"I walk", the little man claims, "always with my right hand closed round the india-rubber ball which I have in my trouser pocket. The pressing of this ball actuates a detonator inside the flask I carry in my pocket . . . The tube leads up. . . ."'[42] Just as Verloc is known for his wallowing and Mrs Verloc for being unfathomable and full, the Professor is established with some vocabularic force as the possessor of this ghastly tube, which simply 'leads up . . .'. But it is perhaps the following paragraph which gives the fullest force:

> With a swift, disclosing gesture he gave
> Ossipon a glimpse of an india-rubber tube,
> resembling a slender brown worm, issuing from
> the armhole of his waistcoat and plunging into
> the inner breast pocket of his jacket. His

clothes, of a nondescript brown mixture, were
threadbare and marked with stains, dusty in
the folds, with ragged button-holes. . . .[43]

To say that this is disturbing in a peculiarly Freudian way is to
raise many interesting issues in so far as immediately pre-
Freudian literature is concerned, but is at the same time to add
nothing to the transparent horror of the central image here.
One might well claim, however, that much of the horror depends upon the fact that the phrase 'resembling a slender brown
worm' is both a simile and a way of putting 'a slender brown
worm' into the vocabularic fabric of the Professor's world. The
words 'a slender brown worm' seem to possess a vocabularic life
of their own outside their function in the simile. So that the total
effect is to transform the simile into a surrealistic flash-view of
the multi-lateral 'truth' about the Professor. It is difficult to
resist the temptation to see the little man actually (and not
metaphorically) as infected with this strangely vital death-worm
snaking indiscriminately through his ragged clothes and
emaciated body. That this is not fanciful is surely shown by the
vivid vocabularic presence of that 'slender brown worm'.

A similar effect occurs soon after:

For a moment Ossipon imagined the overlighted
place changed into a dreadful black hole belching
horrible fumes choked with ghastly rubbish of
smashed brickwork and mutilated corpses. He
had such a distinct perception of ruin and death
that he shuddered again.[44]

The underground 'hall' (p. 85) is likened by fantastic extension
to a 'hole' (and by implication, to a hell) – an image of chaos
and active destruction involving a perception of ruin and death.
But Conrad incorporates the contents of the 'as if' fantasy so
equally into the run of his prose that we accept all these horrific
words not as metaphorical or imaginary but as autonomous
vocabularic elements in the total experience of Ossipon. Thus
images derived from fantasy and fear become actual vocabularic components of the world of the novel and the 'as-if-ness'
falls away. This kind of subversive surreality, like the Professor,
tends to undermine the autonomy and hence security of any one

level of socially accepted reality. It is only appropriate that the Professor, a walking threat of total destruction, should disrupt normal unilateral reality wherever he goes. Once again vocabularic definition effects the magical transformation:

> In order to reach sooner the point where he
> could take his omnibus, he turned brusquely
> out of the populous street into a narrow and
> dusky alley paved with flagstones (p. 115).

Explosively sudden action destroys the street-norm and there is instantaneous vocabularic juxtaposition of 'street' and 'dusky alley'. We may note that Galsworthy's streets have similarly atomized existences within the Metropolis of *Fraternity*. We should remember that Galsworthy also sees 'chaos' as the condition of men in the metropolis – urban chaos is the source of Martin's Sanitism: 'The peculiar chaos surrounding all young men who live in large towns . . . had made him gradually reject all abstract speculation . . . He had embraced health' (p. 210–11). 'On one side', Conrad's novel continues, 'the low brick houses had in their dusky windows the sightless, moribund look of incurable decay – empty shells awaiting demolition' (p. 115). The narrative goes on:

> From the other side life had not wholly
> departed as yet. Facing the only gas-lamp
> yawned the cavern of a second-hand furniture
> dealer, where, deep in the gloom of a sort of
> narrow avenue winding through a bizarre forest
> of wardrobes, with an undergrowth tangle of
> table legs, a tall pier-glass glimmered like
> a pool of water in a wood. An unhappy,
> homeless couch, accompanied by two unrelated
> chairs, stood in the open (pp. 115–16).

And so we may trace the origins of surrealism back through Conrad not simply to the multilateral 'realities' of 'modern life' where reality and dream achieve equality, but more significantly back to the pastoral vacuum that a great city comprises. This is a fine example of early surrealist art, not surreal in the anthropomorphic, Dickensian way, but surreal with great purity of pastoral tension. When we read that Inspector Heat's

moustaches are the 'the colour of ripe corn' (p. 116) we do not
interpret this as local colour, but as the finely ironical vocabularic juxtaposition of the Metropolis and actual ripe corn in all
its explosive pastoral autonomy. As the processes of metaphor
break down, new perspectives appear as if by magic. The
appearance of the 'tall pier-glass' is no mere whimsy; its
magic represents an undermining negation, a polarizing
mimesis similar to the imaging of Cecilia naked in the store
mirror and as-it-were naked in the eyes of the enigmatic Mrs
Hughs.

In *Fraternity* Galsworthy imagines the whole universe of
Edwardian society polarized in this kind of way, the shadows of
the lower world being in a sense the negatives of the positives
of the upper world, neither level achieving cultural absoluteness
or security of existence. One can see, too, that the interpolation
of nature-episodes in *Fraternity* (as in *The Man of Property*) goes
beyond the Turgenevian mode to become the source of a very
nervy modern kind of proto-surrealism. It is easy to miss the
originality of such a passage as the following from Chapter
Nine of *Fraternity* because in a (typically poor) Galsworthy
poem, for instance, 'Nature' would be playing a very different
role from the role it plays here:

Pondering deeply, he ascended the leafy
lane that leads between high railings from
Notting Hill to Kensington.
It was so far from traffic that every tree
on either side was loud with the Spring songs
of birds; the scent of running sap came
forth shyly as the sun sank low. Strange
peace, strange feeling of Old Mother Earth
up there above the town; wild tunes, and the
quiet sight of clouds. Man in this lane might
rest his troubled thoughts, and for a while
trust the goodness of the Scheme that gave him
birth, the beauty of each day, that laughs or
broods itself into night. Some budding lilacs
exhaled a scent of lemons; a sandy cat on the
coping of a wall was basking in the setting
sun (pp. 89–90).

Judged from a conventional point of view this might be said to be 'inadequate'. But the incipient nihilism of this introductory passage leads on to:

> In the centre of the lane a row of elm-trees
> displayed their gnarled, knotted roots. Human
> beings were seated there, whose matted hair clung
> round their tired faces. Their gaunt limbs were
> clothed in rags; each had a stick, and some sort
> of dirty bundle tied to it. They were asleep.
> On a bench beyond, two toothless old women sat,
> moving their eyes from side to side, and a
> crimson-faced woman was snoring. Under the next
> tree a Cockney youth and his girl were sitting
> side by side – pale young things, with loose
> mouths, and hollow cheeks, and restless eyes.
> Their arms were enlaced; they were silent. A
> little further on two young men in working
> clothes were looking straight before them, with
> desperately tired faces. They, too, were silent (p. 90).

The passage as a whole raises extremely complex critical issues. If I am right, the manifest inability of Galsworthy to imagine is here being exploited in a quite modern way. Ford Madox Ford may be a possible analogue, his art depending for its effectiveness (perhaps more than critics have recognized) upon certain epistemological inadequacies in the imagining consciousness. The 'Old Mother Earth' paragraph makes nature grotesquely unavailable and conventional, but this serves a useful artistic function, for the narrative then leads directly into a kind of destroyed metaphor for the conditions of Metropolitan life. The fact that the introductory passage – in its weakly imagined life – is difficult to accept as 'true' is an essential ironical prerequisite for the comedy of the absurd that follows. It is important to see these 'human beings' as clowns, and as clowns in Bennett's sense:

> God made the Country and man made the town,
> And so, man made the doctor, God the clown.[45]

Galsworthy's passage has associations with Conrad's grove of death in *Heart of Darkness*, and with William James's 'epileptic patient',[46] and, indeed, seems to depict the very landscape of modernism, the scenery of Beckett and of the early Picasso. Bennett's anti-poem points to the pastoral source of tension in Beckett's comedy, and also to Galsworthy's comedy, where human-being clowns inhabit a pastoral anti-*milieu* which is a hole in the Metropolis and where they are only marginally human. One requires some training in *fin-de-siècle* fantasy, perhaps, to see this as a kind of space-warp, with the pastoral world and the urban existing in explosive simultaneity. Galsworthy is surely clear that his clowns are 'Waiting for God':

> In the centre of the lane a row of elm-trees
> displayed their gnarled, knotted roots.
> Human beings were seated there. . . . On a bench
> beyond, two toothless old women sat, moving
> their eyes from side to side.

The mere fact of the close vocabularic coexistence of pastoral and Metropolis is a threat to total 'reality', just as Thyme's insights into cultural relativity make her feel threatened. When she goes down among the lower-level people she feels a sapping of life and energy from herself and her class down into the newly conscious level below:

> With contemptuous movements of their lips
> and bodies, on that doorstep they proclaimed
> their emphatic belief in the virtue and reality
> of their own existences and in the vice and
> unreality of her intruding presence (p. 119).

Such is what Rieff calls the violence of the struggle between the culture-classes; it is a war of mutual annihilation. As Alan Sandison says of *An Outcast of the Islands*:

> . . . native life, with its incomprehensibility
> and organisation unrecognisable as such to the
> alien, subtly destroys the white man's faith
> in his fellow-white man – in fact in White Man
> as an exclusive and self-identifying group.[47]

More directly to the point, Sandison claims of Conrad and Kipling:

The antagonism of the environment is subtly
amplified in the invaders' confrontation with
the native race. Together they question the
Europeans' belief in their own action, compelling
them to the demoralising realisation that their
code is not, after all, universal.[48]

In its analysis of dialectically related positive and negative
existences, upper and lower classes, male and female, pastoral
and Metropolitan, *Fraternity* represents a characteristic Edwardian response to what was literally a crisis of social reality;
Wells, Bennett and Galsworthy were interested in *social realism*
because social reality was precisely what they felt to be at stake.
It might be argued that the more socially real novels became,
the more fictional contemporary society was seen to be.

The dialectic of Eloi and Morlocks is made socially explicit in
Fraternity. Cecilia's imagined sense of 'aesthetic' upper-class life
is strikingly similar to Wells's depiction of the Eloi:

Did her little daughter, so young and pretty,
seriously mean to plunge into the rescue work
of dismal slums, to cut herself adrift from
sweet sounds and scents and colours, from music
and art, from dancing, flowers, and all that
made life beautiful? (p. 303).

It is not mere 'conservatism', the wish to conserve one's property, or the traditions of one's culture, which makes Cecilia so
unsettled, though these are the overt symptoms of what R. D.
Laing would call her ontological insecurity. Nor are these
'cultivated' attributes ('music and art . . .') simply, being more
nearly a kind of proto-Bloomsburyesque therapy for purpose-
lessness. If men of one mode, unconscious of their modality, are
confronted with an alternative human mode, it may be that the
more symmetrically a negation of themselves that new mode is,
the more insecurity and loss of autonomy will result. (As we
have seen, Darwin's theory was a particularly sharply focused
assault upon the 'amodal' consciousness.) The converse is also
true, as Alan Sandison's book implies. By denying modal
equivalence with an easily recognizable infra-culture, a 'master-
race' might experience a tremendous influx of (temporary, sick

and unstable) power and 'security'. This is the basis of both imperialism and the Superman myth, which counter-exploit the
very modality that Darwin so triumphantly detailed.

It is important for a right reading of *Fraternity* that one sees
fashion (or 'mode') to be a way of adapting to pervasive
modality, to modal existence. Hence the little 'model' becomes
Galsworthy's image of modality and is (for Cecilia, for instance)
quite dangerously modal. For Hilary any acceptance of the
existential modality of human beings, of 'fraternal' equivalence,
brings about a sapping of personal security. He is not, simply, a
weak type, but an anomalous member of a culture-class whose
security depends precisely upon *not* being altruistic, upon *not*
seeing all men as brothers. I am thinking here of Hilary's
anomalous belonging to a community of liberal intellectuals in
view of his place in the larger, upper-level stratum. The
'strength' of High Victorian Britain seems to have partly depended upon the institutionalized denial of existential equivalence (the novels of Dickens are perhaps centrally concerned
with this problem); the problem at the turn of the century was
that consequently any attempt at altruism, at fraternal reform,
seemed fraught with danger – in such a situation the best would
naturally lack conviction. Erich Fromm has much that is useful
to say about the existential difficulties of living without sado-
masochistic symbiosis,[49] and this problem is partly what
Fraternity is about. It is also, conversely, about the difficulties of
freedom. When Hilary analyses his reasons for not (freely)
consummating his relations with Ivy, he claims: 'Class has
saved me' (p. 342).

What Hilary means is that when the 'touch of her lips' was
'moist and hot' he opted for 'crisax' rather than climax because
he could not 'take' the sexual and existential equivalence that
Ivy was offering (p. 337). Galsworthy is, in a sense, writing a
Freudo-Marxist critique of his hero:

The scent of stale violet powder came from
her, warmed by her humanity. It penetrated
to Hilary's heart. He started back in sheer
physical revolt (p. 337).

The 'it' apparently refers back to 'The scent', but it refers
also, more revealingly, to 'her humanity'. The recognition of

common humanity (or Fraternity) is what really makes the altruistic Hilary 'start back in sheer physical revolt'. The high point of the novel comes when, with heavy irony, Galsworthy has Hilary regress to the therapy of the cash nexus. Since Hilary cannot 'take' Ivy's self as its own modal equivalent, he uses an institutionalized signal to establish a more bearable relationship:

> Snatching from his pocket a roll of notes,
> Hilary flung them on the bed.
>   'I can't take you!' he almost groaned (p. 337).

A residual commitment to communal values saves him. The final irony is that in being morally saved and in doing 'best', in refusing to accept Ivy's sexuality (by turning down her quite genuine offer) he realizes her as a whore. With Freudo-Marxist logic she finally wears his money next to her heart. It is noteworthy that Stephen's collection of coins is 'his creative work, his history of the world' (p. 229), 'links of the unbroken chain of authority' (p. 229).

Bianca's marriage to Hilary also suffers from what is presented in the novel as a pathological diversion of desire:

> And suddenly he began to kiss her face and
> neck. He felt her answering kisses; for a
> moment they were clasped together in a fierce
> embrace. Then, as though by mutual consent,
> their arms relaxed; their eyes grew furtive,
> like the eyes of children who have egged each
> other on to steal; and on their lips appeared
> the faintest of faint smiles. It was as though
> those lips were saying: 'Yes, but we are not
> quite animals!' (p. 106).

This is a new and strikingly Freudian version of the Fall, and the therapy of redemption indicated, instead of the Christian, is an implicit, and complex, psychosociological therapy, a therapy which, in terms of this novel, may only be available in an impossible Utopia beyond culture. In Chapter Four we learn that Bianca had changed her mind about painting the little model 'half-draped'; her reaction to Ivy's sexuality is precisely that of Hilary:

... though she discussed the nude, and looked
on it with freedom, when it came to painting
unclothed people, she felt a sort of physical
aversion (p. 38).

It is the slow gelation of sexual confrontation and disgust which
sets the tempo of the novel, and the little model (as Eros) is
really the central character. *Jocelyn* ended with a clearly defined
climax, and its music was that of achieved orgasm; *Fraternity* is
a crisis-novel, fictionalizing the predicament of gentility in
process of replacement by therapeutic gentility, and, as in the
tradition established retrospectively by Ford in *The Good Soldier*
and the Tietjens tetralogy, climax is replaced by 'crisax' and
there is no definable orgasm. *Fraternity* untendentiously analyses
the corruption of consciousness in terms of post-cultural crisis.

Conclusion

There is something obliviously optimistic about the Edwardian novels of Wells, Bennett and Galsworthy. But works like *Tono-Bungay*, *The Old Wives' Tale* and *The Man of Property*, while naïvely partaking of a new therapeutic revelation, are still primarily concerned with post-cultural crisis, with the existential predicaments of individuals living beyond the cultures which nurtured them. The view which sees the Edwardian period as characterized by an out-moded neo-Vitalism soon to be repudiated by advances in scientific thought and by the advent of the First World War, must be respected;[1] but the underlying problem of disengaged consciousness, tending through its very intensity to render culture obsolete, must also be understood. The triumphant Vitalism of the Edwardian moment, which may in fact have contributed in large measure to the initiation and prolonging of the First World War, was not simply an interesting new development in Edwardian thought: it must be seen as one aspect of the centurial apocalypse which in a sense did occur around about the year 1900. The symmetry of the decades of 1890s *fin de sièclism* and Edwardian neo-Vitalism must be recognized, so that the emergent Edwardian belief in a 'Life Force' and in 'cosmic consciousness' is seen to develop out of a pervasive late-Victorian mood of devitalization, of depletion, of hypochondria. All the lacks of the 1890s are precisely what Edwardianism remedied: *Angst* was replaced by confidence; the sense of an ending by the sense of a beginning; insecurity by security; invisibility by visual repletion; emptiness by filling. Anticipation of apocalypse had already by the 1890s provided suggestions as to a possible mode beyond Darwinism, and a new view of the soul beyond the merely positivist, but only after the year 1900 did the processes of man-made apocalypse produce a wide substantiation of such beliefs. While we hold on to the view that the whole dialectical process of the turn-of-the-century apocalypse, including the excesses of the *fin de siècle* and the naïveties of Edwardianism, gave rise to highly 'determined' and in a sense obsessive literatures, we still retain our inheritance of the therapeutic imagination – indeed, it is, according to Rieff, to be our new salvation.

Instead of judging the Edwardians from a 1920s viewpoint, perhaps we should try to understand the ways in which we share their inner perception of a new order of human experience beyond culture. The Edwardians lacked the finesse of the generation which followed them, but in their very 'vulgarity' is implicit the grounds of our own alienation from the old order. The Edwardians invented a commitment therapy which worked beyond the communal mode, linking private souls in a cosmic harmony which has resemblances to Marshall McLuhan's, latter-day Utopia. The new post-1900 vision of man, like McLuhan's, involved the perception that associations of consciousness, rather than association in unconsciousness (as in cultural ordering), are the appropriate form for modern man.

Wells, Bennett and Galsworthy stand as three novelists who helped to institutionalize the therapeutic imagination of modern man. After the initial focusing malaise of the 1890s, their new positive view of health tended to replace God:

Am I, a portion of the Infinite Force that
existed billions of years ago, and which will
exist billions of years hence, going to allow
myself to be worried by any terrestrial
physical or mental event? I am not.[2]

We accept their therapeutic sensibility, but wish now to live with no more deluding teleologies beyond that of personal well-being; such, at least, is the view of Philip Rieff:

In the absence of news about a stable and
governing order anywhere, theory becomes
actively concerned with mitigating the daily

miseries of living rather than with a therapy
of commitment to some healing doctrine of the
universe.[3]

It is interesting to trace the gradual emergence of therapy-for-
therapy's-sake through the nineteenth century, the centurial
apocalypse of 1900, and the holocaustic 'disconfirmations' of
twentieth-century wars and weapons and genocide. The extent
to which the Edwardians instituted a teleological transference
from religion to therapy should not be minimized:

> Formerly physicians went to Philosophy to
> get help for their own special problems and
> to enable them to frame vast systems which
> should be co-extensive with the universe;
> now it will be rather the custom for Philosophy
> to come to Medicine, and taking from her all
> the truths which through the ages she has been
> slowly winning from ignorance and chaos, gather
> them up into one vast generalized truth which
> will at length enable men to lead the lives of
> intellectual moral beings.[4]

We have now become accustomed to organizing our activities,
not around a theoretical pursuit of 'one vast generalized truth',
but around crises which threaten the well-being of individuals.
Churchillian and Wellsian views of 'world crisis', for example,
helped to implement the founding of the League of Nations and
the United Nations; as Frank Kermode has emphasized, we
seek for images of crisis and derive our sense of direction from
them. The Edwardians represent an important transitional
stage in the development towards the 'therapy of all therapies',
which is 'not to attach oneself exclusively to any particular
therapy, so that no illusion may survive of some end beyond an
intensely private sense of well-being to be generated in the
living of life itself'.[5]

Wells, whose equipment of evolution-theory and prediction
normally enabled him to feel secure between a beginning and an
end, was the writer who left the modern world with the terms of
its new crisis, the loss of the future. In *Mind at the End of Its
Tether*, Wells describes his own recent experiences:

He did his utmost to pursue the trends, that
upward spiral, towards their convergence in a
new phase in the story of life, and the more
he weighed the realities before him the less he
was able to detect any convergence whatever.
Changes had ceased to be systematic, and the
further he estimated the course they were taking,
the greater their divergence. Hitherto events
had been held together by a certain logical
consistency, as the heavenly bodies as we
know them have been held together by the pull,
the golden cord, of Gravitation. Now it is as
if that cord had vanished and everything was
driving anyhow to anywhere at a steadily increasing velocity.

The limit to the orderly secular development
of life had seemed to be a definitely fixed one,
so that it was possible to sketch out the pattern
of things to come. But that limit was reached
and passed into a hitherto incredible chaos.
The more he scrutinised the realities around us,
the more difficult it became to sketch out any
Pattern of Things to Come. Distance had been
abolished, events had become practically
simultaneous throughout the planet, life had to
adapt itself to that or perish, and with the
presentation of that ultimatum, the Pattern of
Things to Come faded away.[6]

Much of *Mind at the End of Its Tether* is incomprehensible, and in
it Wells makes absurd claims of an imminent ending ('It is the
end'),[7] but in passages like this one there is a suggestion that
Wells senses the need for adjustment to a non-sequential universe, in which the 'Pattern of Things to Come' will be no longer
relevant, and in which events are 'practically simultaneous
throughout the planet'. Wells, in fact, defines the universe in
which James Bond has made himself mythically at home, and
in which McLuhan relaxes at his ease ('The cinema sheet stares
us in the face. That sheet is the actual fabric of being').[8] Wells
describes finally a world in which 'our deep need for intelligible

ends'[9] is eternally frustrated. Having himself benefited from the concordances derived from the centurial apocalypse of 1900, Wells lived on into our own time, unwittingly sharing our movement 'toward a human condition about which there will be nothing further to say in terms of the old style of despair and hope'.[10]

Appendix

Previous accounts of
Wells, Bennett and Galsworthy

It may be claimed that the grouping together of Wells, Bennett and Galsworthy is traditional, but in the nature of things there is an approximate date marking the first such grouping definition. At the turn of the century the 'great novelists' were Meredith, Hardy and Stevenson, but there was a definite feeling that these were passing, as it were, out of production; in 1902, Bennett wrote:

> If neither Meredith nor Hardy write another
> line, we have six novelists whose work is not
> for this generation only. I mean Joseph Conrad,
> George Gissing, Rudyard Kipling, George Moore,
> Eden Phillpotts, and H. G. Wells. With such
> work as theirs in hand, those who talk of the
> decadence of the modern novel talk nonsense.[1]

It was only after Butler's *The Way of All Flesh* was published posthumously in 1903 that the way was clear for writers interested in the positive potential of the individual in a society demonstrably in evolution. By 1909, after the publication of the respective masterpieces of the triumvirate (*The Man of Property*, 1906; *The Old Wives' Tale*, 1908; *Tono-Bungay*, 1909), the field had cleared a little, and although Bennett doesn't register as one of Ford Madox Ford's chosen six major contemporaries[2] in his 1909 *English Review* article,[3] the latter is disposed to discuss the three in the same breath, as it were:

> Some of this frigidity [Moore's] is present
> in the work of Mr Galsworthy the novelist;

211

none of it at all in that of Mr Wells, though
there is one writer, Mr Arnold Bennett, who,
with a view of life singularly similar to that
of Mr Wells in his more serious work, has
assimilated in everything but style almost as
closely the methods of our great French pre-
cursors as Mr James, Mr Conrad, Mr Moore and
Mr Galsworthy.[4]

In Ford's article it is again Kipling who is ousting a member of the
triumvirate out of his place among the great, but let it be said that
Ford is apparently more interested in Bennett than in Kipling.
Earlier in 1909 Bennett makes no attempt to associate Wells and
Galsworthy directly, although both appear in his list of 'the novelists
who have impressed themselves at once on the public and genuinely
on the handful of persons whose taste is severe and sure'.[5] In this
second part of an article on the 'Middle-Class' and its relation to
contemporary literature, Bennett puts Wells second to Hardy (in
order of mention, not merit) in a list which includes also Hale White,
Rudyard Kipling (still), J. M. Barrie, W. W. Jacobs, Murray
Gilchrist, Joseph Conrad, Leonard Merrick, George Moore, George
Meredith, and Henry James, and, 'in a rank lower than these',[6]
William de Morgan and John Galsworthy. Evidently Bennett's
relationship with Galsworthy was not in 1909 that which one would
associate with literary partnership; his journal for 9 April has:
'Wednesday. Dinner at Ford Madox Hueffer's. John Galsworthy
and wife there. Slight gêne on my part on first encounter with Galsworthy, seeing my recent articles on him.'[7] The entry proceeds,
however, to a more sanguine note: 'However, we did well together,
and he asked me to dinner. . . .'[8] At any rate, Galsworthy makes no
qualification to his inclusion of Bennett in his own defining list of
prominent contemporary novelists, written out on Christmas Day,
1910:

The book [*The Patrician*] discloses me finally
as an impressionist working with a realistic or
naturalistic technique. Whereas Wells is a realist
working with an impressionistic technique, Bennett
a realist with a realistic technique, Conrad an
impressionist with a semi-impressionistic, semi-naturalistic
technique, and Forster an impressionist
with a realistically impressionistic technique.[9]

But again Galsworthy seems to be lined up with the 'impressionists', and there is no hint that he sees Wells and Bennett and

himself as forming a separable triumvirate. But it is interesting to see
Wells, Bennett and Galsworthy gradually emerging as dominant
figures.

Wells's 1914 article, 'The Contemporary Novel',[10] again constitutes no call for an *esprit de corps*, for while Wells is quick to define
the English and French styles of Bennett (allegedly represented by
The Old Wives' Tale and *Clayhanger* respectively) and to praise both,
he isn't so clearly in support of the 'cold, almost affectedly ironic
detachment . . . which distinguishes the work of Mr John Galsworthy'.[11] The sheer fact of confronting the literary existence of
these two writers is inherent in Wells's position and in his own case,
so that at least there is common ground enough for dissent of mutual
significance, but still the differences and not the similarities are
stressed.

While Wells saw cause for identifying with Bennett and keeping
well away from Galsworthy, others thought of Bennett as the odd
man out, as the literary purist with no social axe to grind. Thus
Jane Findlater's article 'Three Sides To a Question'[12] (published in
January 1910), chooses to discuss Wells, Galsworthy and Stephen
Reynolds on social conditions, but makes no mention of Bennett. It
is difficult to imagine exactly how Bennett's novels might be fitted
into her sociological analysis of the novelist as deliberate social re-
former. Henry James, on the other hand, sees Bennett and Wells as
partners in crime, with Galsworthy as not so central a figure of the
'Younger Generation':

> We bracket together Mr Wells and Mr Bennett for
> the particular reason that with the sharpest
> differences of character and range they yet come together
> under our so convenient measure of value by
> Saturation. Each is ideally immersed in his own
> body of reference, in a close notation, a sharper
> specification of the signs of life and consciousness
> in the human scene than the three or four
> generations before them had at all been used to
> insist on. They had insisted, these generations,
> on almost nothing whatever. . . .[13]

We may perhaps take James's 'The Younger Generation' as the
first *locus classicus* in which the triumvirate appears as exclusive
literary entity. James, in his Ivory Tower, seems to have been able to
look down upon the Edwardians as if from a distance, with the kind
of detachment that only emerged generally elsewhere with the rise of
the Georgian novelists in the 1920s. It is really from the 1920s (when
the older generation were typified and marked down as 'Wells,

Bennett and Galsworthy') that the 'traditional' triadic grouping originates.

The pejorative spirit of the 1920s in this context is neatly registered in the collection of iconoclastic *Scrutinies*,[14] which contained the first publication of Lawrence's well-known essay on 'John Galsworthy'.[15] All three of the triumvirate come under heavy fire in this typical expression of the 1920s mood; and the inclusiveness of the Edwardian area for attack is indicated by the co-victims, viz. James Barrie, G. K. Chesterton, De La Mare, Kipling, Masefield, and Shaw. Neither the order of printing in this book nor anything in the individual essays, however, points to a special separability in the case of Wells, Bennett and Galsworthy. But Edwin Muir's book on *The Structure of the Novel*,[16] published in the same year, very clearly isolates the triumvirate (though still not quite completely, since Dreiser is included with them), and demonstrates the Georgian scornful outlook on a previous and old-fashioned age:

> . . . first it is necessary to deal with a kind
> of novel which has many superficial resemblances
> to the chronicle, which a generation ago had an
> immense vitality, but which now seems to be sinking
> into a decline.
>
> It is the kind of novel which is represented
> most brilliantly by the Clayhanger trilogy, *The
> Forsyte Saga, The New Macchiavelli*, and Mr
> Dreiser's records of American life. . . . The period
> novel does not try to show us human truth valid
> for all time; it is content with a society at a
> particular stage of transition, and characters
> which are only true in so far as they are
> representative of that society. It makes everything
> particular, relative and historical. . . .
>
> The bondage of the novel to period has naturally
> degraded it. . . .[17]

Muir proceeds to make final differential adjustments between the three, but the grouping and the long perspective are established. And Virginia Woolf – despite the fact of her choosing one name only for the title of the famous *Mr. Bennett and Mrs. Brown* – is quite unequivocal in her exclusive association of 'the books that Mr Wells, Mr Bennett, and Mr Galsworthy have written'[18] when she complains:

> . . . what odd books they are! Sometimes I
> wonder if we are right to call them books at all.
> For they leave one with so strange a feeling of

incompleteness and dissatisfaction. In order to
complete them it seems necessary to do something –
to join a society, or, more desperately, to write
a cheque. That done, the restlessness is laid, the
book finished; it can be put upon the shelf, and
need never be read again.[19]

Lastly, W. L. Myers, in his important *The Later Realism* (Chicago,
1927), does not hesitate in citing his 'Group II novelists' as, exclusively, a separated triumvirate of Wells, Bennett and Galsworthy.[20]
Subsequent writers and critics have been willing (or forced) to accept
the grouping either unquestioningly or with minor quibbles or with
more significantly differentiating comments whose invocation of
varying exceptions (with one writer excepting Wells, another
Bennett, and another Galsworthy) has generally served only to prove
the rule.

Since the 1920s, when there was a vested interest on the part of
critics, and especially of novelists, to 'deal with' the Edwardians,
less important work (whether historical or critical) has been undertaken. But one might distinguish three major movements in the
development of more recent attitudes towards the topic. Between
1930 and 1950 there was a period of relative quiescence in so far as
the triumvirate is concerned. Towards the end of the 1940s, with the
publication of one of the few articles that have been written specifically on the Edwardian novel,[21] and with Walter Allen's short
book on Bennett appearing in 1948,[22] the way was made clear for the
appearance in the early 1950s of a movement (which seems to have
been associated with the neo-Edwardianism of the Wain-Braine-
Amis group of novelists and the Movement poets) of renewed
interest in the triumvirate. John Wain's essay on Bennett was
written between 1949 and 1953,[23] and very clearly there was a debt
in Wain's novels to be acknowledged. Reginald Pound's biography of
Bennett appeared in 1952[24] and the main concern of this second
period does, indeed, seem to have been Bennett. Angus Wilson's
article, 'Arnold Bennett's Novels', appeared in 1954 in a fashionable
place.[25] Frank Swinnerton published his *Arnold Bennett* in 1950.[26]
Bennett is best represented, too, in the relatively few dissertations
dealing with members of the triumvirate during these years.

With the approach of the fifty-year time-gap, the 1960s have gone
on and provided the third and latest wave of modern interest in, and
reappraisal of, the Edwardian novel. Initiated in a sense by the
English Institute Essays of 1959[27] but also a development of the
interest reaffirmed in the 1950s, the present critical movement has

produced a new means of approach to Wells in Bernard Bergonzi's book, *The Early H. G. Wells*. It has also resulted in the publication of useful works like Ingvald Raknem's *H. G. Wells and His Critics* (Oslo, 1962), Yury Kagarlitsky's *Life and Thought of H. G. Wells* (translated by M. Budberg, London, 1966), and David Lodge's excellent essay on *Tono-Bungay*.[28] Lovat Dickson has recently published his *Life and Times of H. G. Wells* (London, 1969), and two important books have been produced by W. W. Wagar – *H. G. Wells and the World State* (New Haven, 1961) and *H. G. Wells: Journalism and Prophecy* (London, 1965). Two books on Bennett have recently been published in the United States, James Hall's *Arnold Bennett: Primitivism and Taste* (Seattle, Wash., 1959), and James Hepburn's *The Art of Arnold Bennett* (Bloomington, Ind., 1963). No critical account of Galsworthy has recently appeared in the form of a book, but two biographies, mainly in line with the current English interest in the televized and publicized *Forsyte Saga*, have been published.[29]

Since Richard Buckstead's 1960 dissertation on 'H. G. Wells, Arnold Bennett, John Galsworthy: Three Novelists in Revolt Against the Middle Class', no dissertation or published work has appeared dealing with the three novelists as a group.

The general achievement of recent work, and indeed of most critical and historical approaches to the Edwardian novel so far, has not been high. The fact of the intensive unit for studying the period 1880–1920 at Purdue has not really helped the situation, for while Richard Ellmann took time off, as it were, to comment on 'The Two Faces of Edward', others among the more able critics have been content to leave the pedestrian work to the professors of Purdue, and have seemed unwilling to descend to the out-of-fashion and downgraded Edwardians. That there has been an historical (if not evaluative) gap to repair is indicated by the recent publication in the United States of two characteristic works of the present moment, Samuel Hynes's *The Edwardian Turn of Mind* (Princeton, 1968) and John A. Lester's *Journey Through Despair: Transformations in British Literary Culture, 1880–1914* (Princeton, 1968). Neither of these works is the definitive study the period deserves. John A. Lester's is particularly disappointing in that it fails to live up to the promise implicit in its title, and treats the period 1880–1914 largely *en bloc*, as if it were a static sub-division of English history. However, the study of the period must begin from the position established by these two works.

Notes

Notes to chapter 1

1 *H. G. Wells and the World State*, New Haven, 1961, 1.
2 See his *The Early H. G. Wells,* Manchester, 1961.
3 Edgell Rickword (ed.), London, 1928.
4 *Mr. Bennett and Mrs. Brown*, London, 1924, 4.
5 'A Note on Paul Bourget', reprinted in Havelock Ellis, *News and Reviews*, London, 1932, 60.
6 'Modern Fiction', in *The Common Reader*, London, 1925, 188.
7 Virginia Woolf's reaction to 'the books that Mr. Wells, Mr. Bennett, and Mr. Galsworthy have written' was to complain that 'they leave one with so strange a feeling of incompleteness and dissatisfaction' (*Mr. Bennett and Mrs. Brown*, London, 1924, 12).
8 D. H. Lawrence, 'Nullus', in *The Complete Poems*, London, 1957, ii, 243.
9 *Prophets of Yesterday*, London, 1963, 248.
10 'Technique as Discovery', in William Van O'Connor (ed.), *Forms of Modern Fiction*, Minneapolis, 1948, 18.
11 See Philip Rieff on Lawrence's therapy in *The Triumph of the Therapeutic*, London, 1966, 189–231.
12 'Freud: Within and Beyond Culture', in *Beyond Culture*, London, 1966, 118.
13 *Change at Shebika*, translated by Frances Frenaye, London, 1970, 302.
14 Cited in John A. Lester, *Journey Through Despair*, Princeton, N.J., 1968, 79.
15 *Ibid.*
16 Preface, *Plays*, Manaton Edition, London, 1923–6, viii.
17 *The Triumph of the Therapeutic*, London, 1966.
18 *Ibid.*, 261.
19 In the penultimate paragraph of the novel.
20 'Technique as Discovery', in William Van O'Connor (ed.), *Forms of Modern Fiction*, Minneapolis, 1948, 17.

21 It is unlikely that Wells knew of Freud's work in 1906.

22 *The Triumph of the Therapeutic*, 67.

23 P. L. Berger and T. Luckmann, *The Social Construction of Reality*, London, 1967, 130.

24 C. H. Cooley, R. C. Angell, and L. J. Carr, *Introductory Sociology*, New York, 1933, 81.

25 *The Disappearance of God*, Cambridge, Mass., 1963.

26 Notably in Frank Kermode, *The Sense of an Ending*, New York, 1967.

27 Although it is explored in *The Sense of an Ending* and related to Wells in Bernard Bergonzi, *The Early H. G. Wells*, Manchester, 1961.

28 It will be noted that this view differs from one like John A. Lester's in *Journey Through Despair*, Princeton, New Jersey, 1968. Lester takes no special account of the year 1900, and treats the period 1880–1914 *en bloc*.

29 We may note the contrast in Huxley's novel between the primitive Mexican culture and the 'therapeutic community' in which Bernard Marx feels so uncomfortable.

30 See, for example, Nietzsche's reiteration of Goethe's prophecy of the global hospital (the latter is cited in *The Triumph of the Therapeutic*, 24, n. 17):
'Nothing would be more costly than virtue: for one would in the end have turned the earth into a hospital: and ultimate wisdom would be "everyone as everyone else's nurse". To be sure, one would then possess that much-prized "peace on earth"! But how little "delight in each other"! How little beauty, high spirits, daring, danger!' (*The Will to Power*, translated by Walter Kaufmann and R. J. Hollingdale, London, 1967, 213.)
Jacques Barzun sees 'philanthropy' as an enemy of intellect:
'Though the genius of Freud was unswervingly intellectual, it has given birth to a large progeny of adapters who, from generous as well as selfish motives, put philanthropy first. They mean to cure, or at least to "help" at any cost. They respect, certainly, no intellectual limits or principles, and one by one the chief elements of our culture have fallen within the area of their devastation. Thus the school is not to teach but to cure; body and mind are not to use for self-forgetful ends but to dwell on with Narcissus' adoring anxiety; the arts, not to give joy and light but to be scanned for a "diagnosis" of some trouble, a solution of some "problem", or else exploited for the common good in occupational therapy . . .' (*The House of Intellect*, London, 1959, 23–4.)

31 *The Triumph of the Therapeutic*, 261. Further page-references to this book are put in parenthesis in the text.

32 Cited by Helen Thurber in her 'Foreword' to James Thurber, *Credos and Curios*, Harmondsworth, Middlesex, 1969, 10.

33 *The Sense of an Ending*, New York, 1967, 94.

34 '. . . although for us the End has perhaps lost its naïve *imminence*, its shadow still lies on the crises of our fictions; we may speak of it as immanent' (*The Sense of an Ending*, 6).

35 *Journey Through Despair*, 67.

36 *The Human Machine*, London, 1909, 108.
37 *How to Live on Twenty Four Hours a Day*, London, 1908.
38 New York, 1964.
39 *The History of Mr. Polly*, London, 1910, 283.
40 *Ibid.*, 284.
41 *The Time Machine*, London, 1895, 86.
42 *A Man from the North*, London, 1896, 262.
43 Galsworthy's first published work was a collection of short stories, viz. *From the Four Winds*, London, 1897.
44 *The Early H. G. Wells*, Manchester, 1961.
45 Frank Kermode, *The Sense of an Ending*, New York, 1967, 97.
46 'The resurgence of liberal England was the political aspect of a spiritual awakening which found expression in a remarkable literary revival' (V. de Sola Pinto, *Crisis in English Poetry: 1880–1940*, London, 1967, 106).
47 The original title of a serial written during 1898–9, and revised and published as *The Ghost* in 1907.
48 1898.
49 *Ibid.*
50 *Ego Psychology and the Problem of Adaptation*, translated by David Rapaport, London, 1958, 17.
51 *Ibid.*, 18–19.

Notes to chapter 2

 1 Frederick Greenwood, 'Gospel of Content', *Yellow Book*, 1894, ii, 27. Cited by Lester in *Journey Through Despair*, 79.
 2 Bernard Bergonzi's book, *The Early H. G. Wells*, relates the *fin-du-globe* myth to Wells's scientific romances.
 3 London, 1897, 128–9.
 4 *The Form of Victorian Fiction*, Notre Dame, Ind., 1968, 32.
 5 See above, 2.
 6 1898.
 7 Arnold Bennett, *A Man from the North*, London, 1898, 262.
 8 John A. Lester's *Journey Through Despair* documents this mood in detail, but is mistaken, I believe, in attributing it to the total period 1880–1914.
 9 C. S. Lewis, 'Kipling's World', in *Selected Literary Essays*, edited by Walter Hooper, London, 1969, 246.
10 *Ibid.*, 249.
11 Derek Stanford points out that 'these fictions of the 'nineties are significant as being examples of a new thing in English writing: the short story conceived as a *genre* on its own – a fresh art-form conscious of itself' (Preface, *Short Stories of the 'Nineties*, London, 1968, 11).
12 See T. Schudi Madsen, *Art Nouveau*, London, 1967, 232.
13 First published in *The Yellow Book*, 1895, vi, 93–102.
14 See Section II of this chapter.
15 Introduction, *The Country of the Blind*, London, 1911, iv–vi.

16 Leon Edel, *Henry James. The Treacherous Years: 1895–1900*, London, 1969, 251–2.
17 *The Men of the Nineties*, London, 1920, 62.
18 'Introduction', *The Country of the Blind*, London, 1911, iv.
19 *Degeneration* (Popular Edition), London, 1913, 21.
20 'Introduction', *The Country of the Blind*, London, 1911, iv.
21 Max Nordau, *Degeneration* (Popular Edition), London, 1913, 5.
22 1600 seems to be the most important 'modern' centurial ending before 1900, and it is tempting to speculate on Hamlet's (1600–1) crisis and its relation to that of *fin-de-siècle* man.
23 III, ii 34–5.
24 'The Middle Years', first published in 1893, reprinted in Leon Edel (ed.), *The Complete Tales of Henry James*, London, 1965, ix, 55.
25 *The Early H. G. Wells*, Manchester, 1961, 4–8.
26 Popular edition, London, 1913, 15.
27 P. L. Berger and T. Luckmann, *The Social Construction of Reality*, London, 1967, 130.
28 *Loss of the Self*, New York, 1964, 35.
29 *Ibid.*, 41.
30 2 vols, London, 1890, i, 125.
31 *Ibid.*, 125–6.
32 Shaw's article, 'A Degenerate's View of Nordau', *Liberty*, New York, 1895, was revised and reprinted as *The Sanity of Art*, London, 1908.
33 Preface, *Three Plays For Puritans*, London, 1901, xix.
34 *Degeneration* (Popular Edition), London, 1913, 37.
35 *Ibid.*, 39.
36 *Ibid.*, 27.
37 *Ibid.*
38 *Ibid.*
39 *The Renaissance*, 4th edition, London, 1888, 247–8.
40 *Collected Poems, 1909–1962*, London, 1963, 86.
41 *Appearance and Reality*, London, 1893, 346. Virginia Woolf is another writer of the 1920s who returns to this aspect of the *fin-de-siècle* predicament; her novelistic characterization seems to be founded upon a Bradleyan view of consciousness.
42 *Degeneration* (Popular Edition), London, 1913, 21.
43 *Ibid.*
44 *Ibid.*
45 *Pheonix*, London, 1936, 541.
46 *Pioneer*, 1889, i, 9–36.
47 *Ibid.*, 30–1.
48 *Degeneration* (Popular Edition), London, 1913, 22.
49 *The Human Machine*, London, 1909, 108.
50 At the end of *Gulliver's Travels* a 'dissociation of sensibility' alienates Gulliver from humanity. A similar pattern is to be distinguished in Wells's scientific romance, *The Island of Dr. Moreau* (1896); see Chapter 3, below.
51 *The Unconscious Before Freud*, London, 1962, 34.

52 *Degeneration* (Popular Edition), London, 1913, 21.
53 *Man, Morals and Society*, London, 1945, 237–8.
54 Harmondsworth, Middlesex, 1967.
55 *The Principles of Art*, Oxford, 1938, 336.
56 William James, *The Varieties of Religious Experience*, London, 1902, 160–1. This passage, though cited by James as his translation of the written evidence of a Frenchman (160), has been attributed by his son to James himself. See Henry James, Jr., *Letters of William James*, 2nd edition, London, 1926, 145.
57 *Ibid.*, 161.
58 London, 1896, 218.
59 *Fraternity*, London, 1909, 90.
60 *The Wheel of Empire*, London, 1967, viii.
61 *Conrad: The Psychologist as Artist*, Edinburgh, 1968, 61.
62 *Ibid.*, 78.
63 The title of Chapter II of *Conrad: The Psychologist as Artist.*

Notes to chapter 3

1 *The Early H. G. Wells*, Manchester, 1961, 46–7.
2 *Ibid.*, 25–61.
3 *Ibid.*, 200–2.
4 20 of the 1st, London, edition. Further page-references in this edition are put in parenthesis in the text.
5 C. S. Lewis, 'Kipling's World', in *Selected Literary Essays*, edited by Walter Hooper, London, 1969, 246.
6 *Ibid.*, 249.
7 Wells presumably intends a sense of 'running down' in the numeral 802, 701.
8 See *The Early H. G. Wells*, Manchester, 1961, 61.
9 The dinner-parties are characterized by an appropriately 'masculine' bickering rivalry: '"Is not that rather a large thing to expect us to begin upon?" said Filby, an argumentative person with red hair' (p2).
10 Cf. David Daiches's perception in *Some Late Victorian Attitudes* (London, 1969) that 'Aestheticism and stoic activism can be seen as opposite sides of the same medal. It is an over-simplification to say that both represent attempts to compensate for a lost world of absolute value. Yet it is an over-simplification worth asserting . . .' (44–5).
11 'The Philosophy of a Bacteriologist', 1903, *Speaker*, ix, 112–14.
12 *The Politics of Experience*, Harmondsworth, Middlesex, 1967, 131.
13 *First and Last Things*, London, 1908, 14.
14 Cf. John A. Lester: 'What impinged on the literary mind of the 1880–1914 period was a disposition which I think marks most existential thought, a resolve that, however bleak, hostile, or incomprehensible man's predicament is, nevertheless man must *be* and must *find significance in being* (*Journey Through Despair*, Princeton, N.J., 1968, 178).
15 *Fortnightly Review*, 1 (1891), 106–11.

16 *Ibid.*, 111.
17 *Ibid.*
18 London, 1905.
19 *Ibid.*, 379.
20 *Ibid.*, 380.
21 *Ibid.*, 380–1.
22 *Ibid.*, 381.
23 *Ibid.*, 382.
24 *Ibid.*, 386–7.
25 *Ibid.*, 387.
26 The title of this Appendix.
27 *Ibid.*, 391.
28 *Ibid.*
29 *Ibid.*
30 *Ibid.*, 392.
31 *The Plattner Story and Others*, London, 1897, 201.
32 *Ibid.*, 196.
33 *Ibid.*
34 *Ibid.*, 212.
35 We may compare the latter-day use of hallucinogenic drugs in 'existentialist' psychotherapies.
36 Colin Wilson claims that Wells 'was very definitely an Insider most of his life' (*The Outsider*, London, 1956, 19).
37 *First and Last Things*, 2nd revised edn., London, 1917, 79.
38 This is what Bernard Bergonzi calls Wells's 'heuristic method' (*The Early H. G. Wells*, Manchester, 1961, 160).
39 *The Island of Dr. Moreau*, London, 1896, 215–16.
40 *Ibid.*, 218.
41 In *The Outsider*, reprinted in *The Collected Fiction of Albert Camus*, translated by Stuart Gilbert, London, 1962, 3–68. See especially 31–4.
42 In effect Wells has managed to penetrate back to an archetypal mode of experience by making a kind of inner journey. Compare an actual account of a 'psychotic episode' cited by R. D. Laing in his chapter of *The Politics of Experience* entitled 'A Ten-Day Voyage':

> I had at times a feeling of an enormous journey in front, quite, – er – a fantastic journey, and it seemed that I had got an understanding of things which I'd been trying to understand for a long time, problems of good and evil and so on, and that I had solved it in as much that I had come to the conclusion, with all the feelings that I had at the time, that was more – more than I had always imagined myself, not just existing now, but that I had existed since the beginning – er – in a kind of – from the lowest form of life to the present time, and that that was the sum of real experiences, and that what I was doing was experiencing them again (126–7).

Laing gives us the hint that the Time Traveller's black object is now placed not only far in the future, but more fundamentally far in the past. The relation between the Time Traveller and the Psychologist is very like what Laing sees as the relation between the schizophrenic and the psychiatrist:

> Instead of the mental hospital, a sort of reservicing factory for human breakdowns, we need a place where people who have travelled further and consequently, may be more lost than psychiatrists and other sane people, can find their way further into inner space and time, by people who have been there and back again. Psychiatrically, this would appear as ex-patients helping future patients to go mad (105-6).

This 'inner journey' that the Time Traveller makes is divided into three distinct stages. The first penetrates to the social level, and the Time Traveller, having been thrust into a world of what is at last meaningless horror, makes sense of it in terms of an explanation which points to the social and political insanity (the split personality, in a sense) of contemporary society. In order to reach that understanding he has to endure what Laing calls 'confusion, partial failure, even shipwreck' (104), and there are 'many terrors, spirits, demons to be encountered, that may or may not be overcome' (104). The second stage penetrates to the 'zoological' insight into the human situation provided by the monstrous crab of the future and the screaming butterfly, an insight parallel to Keats's nausea at the edge of the finite world: 'But I saw too distinct into the core/Of an eternal fierce destruction,/And so from happiness I far was gone./Still am I sick of it . . . ('To J. H. Reynolds, Esq.', lines 96-9). By the time the Time Traveller has reached the third stage, the near-dead world of the distant future, the reader has been taken, albeit by a somewhat melodramatic *fin-de-siècle* route, to the extreme edge of finite things, beyond recognizable violence into the almost abstract world of the absurd. So terrifying and horrifying is this actual participation in ultimate reality that the Time Traveller simply cannot stand it, and sustained by 'a horrible dread of lying helpless in that remote and awful twilight' (141), he manages to clamber back on to the saddle of his machine and return. We might compare his return with that of Laing's cited case:

> One morning I decided that I was not going to take any more sedatives, and that I had got to stop this business going on because I couldn't cope with it any more. . . .

The Return

> I sat on the bed, and I thought, well, somewhere or other I've got to join up with my present – er – self, very strongly . . . (131).

43 Bernard Muddiman, *The Men of the Nineties*, London, 1920, 135.

Notes to chapter 4

1 See 148 of the London, 1898, edition. Further references to this book are put in parenthesis in the text.
2 London, 1903, 64.

3 See Geoffrey Clive. *The Romantic Enlightenment*, New York, 1960, 132–49.
4 London, 1908.
5 See Malcolm Erwin's account of the novel in his *Old Gods Falling*, London, 1939, 345.
6 See J. C. Flugel, *Man, Morals and Society*, London, 1945, 245.
7 *Human Nature in Politics*, London, 1908, 81. Cited in Flugel, *ibid.*, 255.
8 This contrast between cognitive and emotional experience forms a marked feature of the fiction of the period. There is a parallel distinction between cognition and emotional excitement in *The Time Machine*.
9 Newman Flower (ed.), *The Journals of Arnold Bennett, 1896–1931*, 3 vols, London, 1932–3, i, 293. The entry is dated 25 May 1908.
10 Cf. Nordau: '. . . every scene we perceive through the window of the flying express, sets in activity our sensory nerves and our brain centres', *Degeneration* (Popular Edition), London, 1913, 39.
11 *Ego Psychology and the Problem of Adaptation*, translated by David Rapaport, London, 1958, 17.
12 In *The Way of all Flesh*, London, 1903.
13 'Never have I known anyone so cheerfully objective as Bennett . . .' (H. G. Wells, *Experiment in Autobiography*, 2 vols, London, 1934, ii, 626).
14 *The Truth about an Author*, London, 1903, 63–4.
15 *Mind at the End of Its Tether*, London, 1945.
16 *Yellow Book*, 1895, vi, 93–102.
17 *Ibid.*, 94.
18 *Ibid.*, 100.
19 *Ibid.*
20 *Tit-Bits*, 1893, xxiv, 82–3.
21 The attractions of therapy are here made maternal-erotic in the mode of *A Man from the North*.
22 London, 1883.
23 London, 1885.
24 London, 1889.
25 London, 1891.
26 *Fame and Fiction*, London, 1901, 252.
27 Philip Rieff, *The Triumph of the Therapeutic*, London, 1967, 197.
28 *Clayhanger*, London, 1910, 16.

Notes to chapter 5

1 Following the quotation by Richard Cassell from Ford's *Thus to Revisit*, London, 1921, 45–6, in his *Ford Madox Ford*, Baltimore, Md., 1961, 47–8.
2 1 (London, 1898). Hereafter page references in the text will refer to this edition.
3 London, 1894, 71.
4 Louvre.

5 *English Criticism of the Novel 1865–1900*, Oxford, 1964, 119–20.
6 *Ibid.*, 115, citing an unsigned article in the *Westminster Review*, 1873, xliv, 258.
7 *Ibid.*, 113.
8 The Uniform Edition of the Works, London, 1923, ix.
9 The phrase appears in a review of the novel in the *Saturday Review*, lxxxvi (6 August 1898), 184.
10 *Change at Shebika*, translated by Frances Frenaye, London, 1970, 302.
11 'Preface', *The Nigger of the 'Narcissus'*, the Uniform Edition of the Works, London, 1923, viii.
12 H. B. Alexander, *Poetry and the Individual*, New York, 1906, 92–3.
13 *The Inn of Tranquillity*, London, 1912, 252–78.
14 *Ibid.*, 263.
15 'Faith of a Novelist', in *Castles in Spain*, London, 1928, 184.
16 *The History of Mr Polly*, London, 1910, 76.
17 *The Principles of Art*, Oxford, 1938, 336.
18 'Faith of a Novelist', in *Castles in Spain*, London, 1927, 186.
19 'Vague Thoughts on Art', *ibid.*, 257.
20 'Turgueneff', *Fortnightly Review*, xlii (1888), 244.
21 'The newest phase in the history of Vitalism has been termed Neo-vitalism' – Hans Driesch, *The History and Theory of Vitalism*, translated by C. K. Ogden, London, 1914, 170.
22 *Ibid.*, 174–5.
23 *Is there Anything New under the Sun?*, London, 1913, 84.
24 Hilary Dallison, in *Fraternity*, suffers most acutely from this disease of civilization:

> In Hilary . . . self-consciousness had soaked his system through and through; permeated every cranny of his spirit, so that to think a definite thought, or do a definite deed, was obviously becoming difficult to him – (*Fraternity*, London, 1909, 30).

Notes to chapter 6

1 There is a definition of this 'phase' in W. L. Myers, *The Later Realism*, Chicago, 1927. According to Myers, the development of the 'Later Realism' consists in the progression from 'I', George Eliot and Meredith, to 'II', Bennett, Galsworthy and Wells, to 'III', Dorothy Richardson, Joyce, Lawrence and May Sinclair.
2 *The Long Revolution*, London, 1961, 278–9.
3 The first of Bennett's post-1900 novels.
4 See Kenneth B. Newell, *Structure in Four Novels by H. G. Wells*, The Hague, 1968, Chapter I.
5 Such a distinction may also prove useful in an amplification of the transition from mimetic to post-mimetic theories of art, and indeed of the general movement from the pre-Romantic to the post-Romantic world.

6 'Freud and Literature', in *The Liberal Imagination*, London, 1951, 44–5.
7 *The Human Machine*, London, 1909, 108.
8 London, 1900, 257. *Villa Rubein* was published under the *fin-de-siècle* pseudonym, 'John Sinjohn'.
9 London, 1900, 323.
10 *Ibid.*, 322.
11 *Ibid.*, 202.
12 *Villa Rubein*, London, 1900, 256.
13 *Ibid.*, 257.
14 'The decline of *Art Nouveau* was swift. The popularity enjoyed by the style in 1900 evaporated within two years: in Turin in 1902 it was clear to everyone that it had already passed its peak. One by one artists abandoned the style, each altering his form-language and striving towards simplicity, a more practical approach and less emphasis on decoration. In England the reaction developed more rapidly and more sharply than in other countries' (T. Schudi Madsen, *Art Nouveau*, London, 1967, 232).

A related movement beyond the cult of line and 'decoration' is to be traced in the novels of Wells, Bennett and Galsworthy in the same period.

Notes to chapter 7

1 *The Triumph of the Therapeutic*, London, 1966, 261.
2 *The Sense of an Ending*, New York, 1967, 100.
3 *The War in the Air*, London, 1908, 67–8.
4 *The History of Mr. Polly*, London, 1910, 368.
5 Collins edition, London, 1954, 15.
6 I should want, also, to suggest that Edwin Clayhanger is presented by Arnold Bennett as, in a sense, quite as much a 'world' character as Wells's Leadford. Edwin's 'culturation', his 'Five-Townsiness', is as incongruous in him, finally, as Leadford's Englishness is in Leadford. It is not in culture but by revolutionizing a private universe beyond culture that Edwin finds salvation in life. And to suggest that the 'living' characters of Arnold Bennett are *more* living than Leadford is to make a critical decision that requires some testing.
7 The *'New Paper'*.
8 Collins edition, 94. Further references to this book are put in parenthesis in the text.
9 *The First Men in the Moon*, London, 1901, 88–9.
10 *The Early H. G. Wells*, Manchester, 1961, 160.
11 *Ibid.*, 144.
12 *Ibid.*, 159.
13 *Ibid.*, 75.
14 *The First Men in the Moon*, London, 1901, 87.
15 London, 1955.
16 *In the Days of the Comet*, 211.

17 *Kipps*, London, 1905, 392.

18 392–3.

19 288.

20 There may be a parallel in this context between Kipps's 'Simple Soul' and Stevie in Conrad's novel, *The Secret Agent*.

21 290.

22 London, 1900, 207.

23 306.

24 424–5.

25 Notably in Kenneth B. Newell, 'The Structure of H. G. Wells's *Tono-Bungay*', *English Fiction in Transition*, iv (1961) 1–8; Laurence Poston, '*Tono-Bungay*: Wells's Unconstructed Tale', *College English*, xxvi (1965), 433–8; David Lodge, '*Tono-Bungay* and the Condition of England', *The Language of Fiction*, London, 1966, 214–42; Bernard Bergonzi, Introduction, *Tono-Bungay*, Boston, Mass., 1966, v–xxviii; Richard H. Costa, 'H. G. Wells's *Tono-Bungay*: Review of New Studies', *English Literature in Transition*, x (1967), 89–96.

26 The last lines of the novel, London, (1909), 493.

27 *Tono-Bungay*, London, 1908, 491.

28 Bliss Carman, *The Making of Personality*, London, 1908, v.

29 *Tono-Bungay*, 492–3.

30 6.

31 *The Triumph of the Therapeutic*, London, 1966.

32 489.

33 413.

34 415.

35 London, 1909, 12.

36 *The Politics of Experience*, Harmondsworth, Middx., 1967, 106.

37 *The History of Mr. Polly*, London, 1910, 283.

38 London, 1896.

39 London, 1910, 7. Further references to this book are put in parenthesis in the text.

40 *The Triumph of the Therapeutic*, London, 1966, 239–40.

41 *The Form of Victorian Fiction*, Notre Dame, Ind. 1968, 32.

42 'Notes on Nelson's New Novels', appended to *The History of Mr Polly*, London, 1910.

43 See *The Island of Dr. Moreau*, London, 1896.

44 *The Will to Power*, translated by Walter Kaufmann and R. J. Hollingdale, London, 1968, 214.

Notes to chapter 8

1 *Clayhanger*, London, 1910, 574.

2 *The History of Mr. Polly*, London, 1910, 374.

3 *The Sense of an Ending*, New York, 1967, 55.

4 Kermode refers to the 'time-redeeming' character of the 'concords that can be arranged in a narrative' (*The Sense of an Ending*, 52).

5 *The History of Mr. Polly*, London, 1910, 368.

6 *The Sense of an Ending*, 50.

7 *Ibid.*, 35–64.
8 *Ibid.*, 52.
9 E. D. Mackerness, *The Journals of George Sturt: 1890–1927*, 2 vols., Cambridge, 1967, i, 93.
10 *Ibid.*
11 ii, 587. It should be noted that Edward Carpenter had produced a very similar account of positive 'Health' in 1889, when he rejected the contemporary *fin-de-siècle* obsession with disease, and suggested what the future might bring in its place:

> It seems that we have lost the tradition of what health is. The state of modern civilised man in this respect – our coughs, colds, mufflers, dread of a waft of chill air – is truly pitiable. . . . This clinging of disease about man, and its connection with a certain stage of man's development, is a subject which has always attracted attention, and which has been associated with legends of the Fall. Man's mere *intellectual* superiority over the animals does not seem to guard him against this danger. . . . Anyhow doubtless this failure of health (and happiness) serves some purpose; there are indications that it is temporary, and we may fairly look forward to a time when man will reconquer these kingdoms that he has lost.
>
> The peculiarity about our modern conception of Health is that it seems to be a purely negative one. . . .
>
> But looking back, far back, into the past there dawns upon us a different conception . . .
>
> Wholeness, holiness . . . 'if thine eye be single, thy whole body shall be full of light' . . . 'thy faith hath made thee *whole*'.
>
> The idea seems to be a positive one . . . ('Civilisation: Its Cause and Cure', *Pioneer*, i (1889), 10.)

We may note that Carpenter (very acutely) prophesies a future apocalyptic state of positive health, and that Sturt uses the *present* tense when, in 1909, he says, 'It is time to realize this abstraction'.
12 Philip Rieff, *The Triumph of the Therapeutic*, London, 1966, 261.
13 *Journey through Despair*, Princeton, 1968, 84–5.
14 Edward Carpenter, 'Civilisation: Its Cause and Cure', *Pioneer*, i (January 1889), 9–36.
15 *Clayhanger*, London, 1910, 199. Further page-references to this book are put in parenthesis in the text.
16 *The Triumph of the Therapeutic*, London, 1966, 49–50.
17 *Ibid.*, 261.
18 *Freedom from Fear*, London, 1942, 104.
19 *The Reasonable Life*, London, 1907, 57.
20 *The Reasonable Life*, 56–7.
21 Frederick Copleston, *A History of Philosophy*, London, 1946—, vii, 54.
22 Robert Liddell, *A Treatise on the Novel*, London, 1947, 125–7.
23 *Structure in Four Novels by H. G. Wells*, The Hague, 1968, 47.
24 Wells wrote of himself in *Mind at the End of Its Tether*: 'The habitual interest in his life is critical anticipation. Of everything he asks: "To

what will this lead?" . . . He did his utmost to pursue the trends . . .'
(*The Last Books of H. G. Wells*, London, 1968, 69).

25 *The Wheel of Empire*, London, 1967, 56.

26 Sandison citing Robert Tucker, *Philosophy and Myth in Karl Marx*, Cambridge, 1961, 34–5 (*The Wheel of Empire*, 56).

Notes to chapter 9

1 I would question Lawrence's identification of Irene as a 'social being' ('John Galsworthy', in *Phoenix*, London, 1939, 539–50); in a sense she is a non-character, waiting to be defined as concretely asocial by Lawrence in the women of his novels, and required in a sense by Lawrence as a prototype for modification. The Lawrentian demand for freedom of the self is echoed in *The Man of Property* in Irene's refusal to become real in such a universe.

2 *Fraternity*, London, 1909, 203.

3 *The Man of Property*, London, 1906, 9–10. Further page-references in this book are put in parenthesis in the text.

4 'The Philosophy of a Bacteriologist', *Speaker*, ix (1903), 112–14.

5 See Bernard Bergonzi, *The Early H. G. Wells*, Manchester, 1961, 112. Bergonzi points out that Moreau owes something to Nietzsche's influence, but does not point to the passage in *The Will to Power* which most closely relates to Moreau's position:

> Morality is a menagerie; its proposition is that iron bars can be more profitable than freedom, even for the prisoners; its other presupposition is that there exist animal-trainers who are not afraid of terrible means – who know how to handle red-hot iron. This frightful species which takes up the fight against the wild animals is called 'priest'.
>
> Man, imprisoned in an iron cage of errors, became a caricature of man, sick, wretched, ill-disposed toward himself, full of hatred for the impulses of life, full of mistrust of all that is beautiful and happy in life, a walking picture of misery. . . .
>
> In order to be fair to morality, we must put two zoological concepts in its place: *taming* of the beast and breeding of a particular species.
>
> The priests have pretended at all times that they want to "improve" – But we others would laugh if an animal trainer spoke of his 'improved' animals. In most cases, the taming of a beast is achieved through the harming of a beast. . . . (*The Will to Power*, translated by Walter Kaufmann and R. J. Hollingdale, London, 1968, 214).

(The source of Moreau's name might perhaps be traced to François-Armand Moreau, whose *Mémoires de physiologie* was published in Paris in 1877.)

6 *The Triumph of the Therapeutic*, London, 1966, 67.

7 *Ibid.*, 71.

8 *Ibid.*, 256.

9 Reprinted in *Phoenix*, London, 1939, 539–50. Lawrence repeatedly refers to Irene as an 'anti-Forsyte'.

10 *The Triumph of the Therapeutic*, 78.
11 *Ibid.*, 231.
12 *Ibid.*, 171.
13 *The Wheel of Empire*, London, 1967, 62.
14 *Ibid.*
15 *The Triumph of the Therapeutic*, 5.
16 *Ibid.*
17 *Ibid.*, 7.
18 *Ibid.*, 8.
19 Cf. Nietzsche's foreshadowing of Soames's predicament: 'Man, imprisoned in an iron cage of errors, became a caricature of man, sick, wretched, ill-disposed toward himself, full of hatred for the impulses of life, full of mistrust of all that is beautiful and happy in life, a walking picture of misery' (*The Will To Power*, translated by Walter Kaufmann and R. J. Hollingdale, London, 1968, 214).
20 *The Country House*, London, 1907, 129. Future page-references in this book are put in parenthesis in the text.
21 *Fraternity*, London, 1909, 140. Future page-references in this book are put in parenthesis in the text.
22 *The Triumph of the Therapeutic*, 27.
23 Cf. 'Oh, this psychological analysis! It is the curse of the age; it has made Hamlets of us all. We reason and argue, and examine our deeds, instead of going straight on doing, and never doubting what we do must be right just because we must do it' (John Davidson and C. J. Wills, *Laura Ruthven's Widowhood*, 3 vols, London, 1892, iii, 157. Cited in John A. Lester, *Journey Through Despair*, Princeton, 1968, 65–6.)
24 Cf. Rieff's view: 'A culture will lose its therapeutic effect on the individual if it loses its primary power of integrating an individual under the sway of its communal purposes' (*The Triumph of the Therapeutic*, 72).
25 *Ibid.*, 86.
26 *Principles of Psychology*, 2 vols, London, 1890, i, 125.
27 *The Triumph of the Therapeutic*, 74.
28 *The Will to Power*, translated by Walter Kaufmann and R. J. Hollingdale, London, 1968, 12.
29 *The Loss of the Self*, New York, 1964, 41.
30 Conrad takes us to the heart of the Edwardian crisis:
   'And so Michaelis dreams of a world like a beautiful and cheery hospital'.
   'Just so. An immense charity for the healing of the weak', assented the Professor sardonically.
   'That's silly', admitted Ossipon. 'You can't heal weakness. But after all Michaelis may not be so far wrong. In two hundred years doctors will rule the world. Science reigns already. It reigns in the shade maybe – but it reigns. And all science must culminate at last in the science of healing – not the weak, but the strong. Mankind wants to live'.

'Mankind', asserted the Professor with a self-confident glitter of his iron-rimmed spectacles, 'does not know what it wants' (*The Secret Agent*, London, 1907, 432–3).

31 See *The Form of Victorian Fiction*, Notre Dame, Indiana, 1968, 67–8.

32 *Ibid.*, 5–7.

33 *The Triumph of the Therapeutic*, 11.

34 'Heart of Darkness', in *Youth – a Narrative: and Two Other Stories*, London, 1902, 75.

35 *The Form of Victorian Fiction*, Notre Dame, Ind., 32–3.

36 *The Triumph of the Therapeutic*, 86.

37 'Be Kind to Your Four-footed Friends', *Delta*, No. 35 (Spring, 1965), 35.

38 *The Man of Property*, 88–9.

39 *The Triumph of the Therapeutic*, 192.

40 Cited in *The Form of Victorian Fiction*, Notre Dame, Ind., 1968, 37–8.

41 *Ibid.*, 39.

42 *The Secret Agent*, London, 1907, 92.

43 *Ibid.*, 92–3.

44 *Ibid.*, 94.

45 The first lines of a poem, 'Town and Country', included in a letter to Eden Phillpotts, 27 August 1907, printed in James Hepburn (ed.) *Letters of Arnold Bennett*, London, 1968, ii, 217.

46 'He sat there like a sort of sculptured Egyptian cat or Peruvian mummy, moving nothing but his black eyes and looking absolutely non-human'. See above, Chapter 2, Section II.

47 *The Wheel of Empire*, London, 1967, 124.

48 *Ibid.*, 122.

49 *The Fear of Freedom*, London, 1942.

Notes to conclusion

1 E.g. '. . . the notions of a 'Life Force' and a self-consciousness dissociated from the laws and energies of a materialistically monist universe simply could not be accommodated within the scientist's world at all. Within the early years of the twentieth century, neo-Lamarckianism, and the optimistic view of evolution to which it had provided hope, was dead' (John A. Lester, *Journey Through Despair*, Princeton, 1968, 86).

2 Arnold Bennett, *The Reasonable Life*, London, 1907, 58.

3 *The Triumph of the Therapeutic*, 86.

4 R. A. Moon, *The Relation of Philosophy to Medicine*, London, 1909 221.

5 *The Triumph of the Therapeutic*, 261.

6 *The Last Books of H. G. Wells*, London, 1968, 69–70.

7 *Ibid.*, 69.

8 *Ibid.*, 71.

9 Frank Kermode, *The Sense of an Ending*, New York, 1967, 8.

10 *The Triumph of the Therapeutic*, 261.

Notes to Appendix

1 'English and French Fiction in the Nineteenth Century', *Academy*, lxii (15 February 1902), 174.

2 Viz. James, Conrad, Moore, Galsworthy, Wells, Kipling.

3 'English Literature of Today' (signed 'E.R.'), *English Review*, iii (1909), 655–72.

4 *Ibid.*, 659.

5 'Books and Persons', *New Age*, iv (11 February 1909), 325.

6 *Ibid.*

7 Newman Flower (ed.), *The Journals of Arnold Bennett*, 3 vols, London, 1932–3, i, 316.

8 *Ibid.*

9 Diary entry cited in H. V. Marrot, *The Life and Letters of John Galsworthy*, London, 1935, 308.

10 Originally a talk given to the Times Book Club in 1911 under the title 'The Scope of the Novel'. Reprinted with new title in *An Englishman Looks at the World*, London 1914, 148–69.

11 *Ibid.*, 157.

12 *National Review*, liv, 799–811.

13 'The Younger Generation', originally published in *The Times Literary Supplement* (19 March and 2 April 1914, 133–4 and 137–8), and reprinted in L. Edel and Gordon N. Ray (eds), *Henry James & H. G. Wells*, London, 1958, 178–215: quotation from 180.

14 Collected by Edgell Rickword' (London, 1928).

15 52–72. Reprinted in D. H. Lawrence, *Phoenix*, London, 1936, 539–50.

16 London, 1928.

17 115–18.

18 *Mr. Bennett and Mrs. Brown*, London, 1924, 12.

19 *Ibid.*

20 See the first two chapters of *The Later Realism*.

21 'The Edwardian Novel', *The Times Literary Supplement* (28 June 1947), 322.

22 *Arnold Bennett*, London, 1948.

23 'The Quality of Arnold Bennett', *Preliminary Essays*, London, 1957, pp. 121–56.

24 *Arnold Bennett: A Biography*, London, 1952.

25 *London Magazine*, i (November 1954), 59–68.

26 London.

27 Collected in Richard Ellmann (ed.), *Edwardians and Late Victorians*, New York, 1960.

28 '*Tono-Bungay*' and the Condition of England', in David Lodge, *The Language of Fiction*, London, 1966, 214–42.

29 R. H. Mottram, *For Some We Loved*, London, 1956, and R. D. Barker, *The Man of Principle*, London, 1963.

Selected bibliography

A *Wells, Bennett and Galsworthy*

1 WELLS

(i) *Fiction*

'A Tale of the Twentieth Century', *Science Schools Journal*, i (1887), 187–91, reprinted in Bernard Bergonzi, *The Early H. G. Wells* (*q.v.*), 181–6.

'A Vision of the Past', *Science Schools Journal*, i (1887), 206–9.

'The Chronic Argonauts', *Science Schools Journal*, ii (1888), 312, 336, 367, reprinted in *The Early H. G. Wells*, 187–214.

'The Pure and Natural Man', *Pall Mall Gazette*, lvii (16 October 1893), 3.

'The Inert Person', *ibid.*, lix (18 April 1894), 3.

'The Transfiguration of Porchuck', *ibid.* (25 May 1894), 3.

'The Remarkable Case of Davidson's Eyes', in *The Stolen Bacillus and Other Incidents* (London, 1895), 168–91.

'A Catastrophe', in *The Plattner Story and Others* (London, 1897), 239–51.

'Pollock and the Porroh Man', *ibid.*, 142–64.

'The Sad Story of a Dramatic Critic', *ibid.*, 262–73.

'The Cone', *ibid.*, 179–95.

'The Purple Pileus', *ibid.*, 196–212.

Select Conversations with an Uncle (London, 1895).

The Time Machine (London, 1895).

The Wonderful Visit (London, 1895).

The Stolen Bacillus and Other Incidents (London, 1895).

The Wheels of Chance (London, 1896).

233

The Island of Dr. Moreau (London, 1896).
The Plattner Story and Others (London, 1897).
The Invisible Man (London, 1897).
The War of the Worlds (London, 1898).
When the Sleeper Wakes (London, 1899).
Tales of Space and Time (London, 1900).
Love and Mr. Lewisham (London, 1900).
The First Men in the Moon (London, 1901).
The Sea Lady (London, 1902).
The Food of the Gods (London, 1904).
Kipps (London, 1905).
In the Days of the Comet (London, 1906).
The War in the Air (London, 1908).
Tono-Bungay (London, 1909).
Ann Veronica (London, 1909).
The History of Mr. Polly (London, 1910).
The Country of the Blind and Other Stories (London, 1911).
The Door in the Wall and Other Stories (New York, 1911).
The New Machiavelli (London, 1911).
Marriage (London, 1912).
The Passionate Friends (London, 1913).
The Research Magnificent (London, 1915).
Bealby (London, 1915).
Joan and Peter (London, 1918).
The World of William Clissold, 3 vols. (London, 1926).
Mr. Bletsworthy on Rampole Island (London, 1928).
Collected Short Stories (London, 1927).
   20th impression (London, 1966).

(*ii*) *Material other than fiction*

'The Rediscovery of the Unique', *Fortnightly Review*, 1 (July 1891), 106–11.
'The Limits of Individual Plasticity', *Saturday Review*, lxxix (1 May 1895), 89–90.
'Human Evolution. An Artificial Process', *Fortnightly Review*, lx (October 1896), 590–5.
'The Novel of Types', *Saturday Review*, lxxxi (4 January 1896), 23–24.
'On Morals and Civilization', *Fortnightly Review*, lxi (February, 1897), 263–8.
'The Philosophy of a Bacteriologist', *Speaker*, ix (31 October 1903), 91.
A Text Book of Biology, 2 vols (London, 1893).

Honours Physiography, in collaboration with A. R. Gregory (London, 1893).
A Text Book of Zoology, in collaboration with A. M. Davies (London, 1898).
Anticipations (London, 1901).
The Discovery of the Future (London, 1902).
Mankind in the Making (London, 1903).
A Modern Utopia (London, 1905).
First and Last Things (London, 1908).
   revised edition (London, 1917).
The War That Will End War (London, 1914).
An Englishman Looks at the World (London, 1914). Includes 'The Contemporary Novel', 148–69.
Boon (London, 1915).
The Outline of History (London, 1919).
The Science of Life, in collaboration with Julian Huxley and G. P. Wells (London, 1929–30).
Experiment in Autobiography, 2 vols (London, 1934).
The Anatomy of Frustration (London, 1936).
Mind at the End of its Tether (London, 1945).
The Last Books of H. G. Wells (edited by G. P. Wells, London, 1968).
Edel, Leon, and Ray, Gordon N. (eds), *Henry James and H. G. Wells* (London, 1958).
Wilson, Harris (ed.), *Arnold Bennett and H. G. Wells* (London, 1960).
Gettmann, Royal A. (ed.), *George Gissing and H. G. Wells* (London, 1961).

(iii) Writing on Wells

Barber, Otto, *H. G. Wells' Verhältnis zum Darwinismus* (Leipzig, 1935).
Bennett, Arnold, 'H. G. Wells', *New Age*, iv (4 March 1909), 484–5.
Bergonzi, Bernard, *The Early H. G. Wells* (Manchester, 1961).
   Introduction, *Tono-Bungay* (Boston, Mass., 1966), pp. v–xxviii.
Brome, Vincent, *H. G. Wells* (London, 1951).
   Six Studies in Quarrelling (London, 1958).
Brooks, Van Wyck, *The World of H. G. Wells* (London, 1915).
Costa, Richard H., 'H. G. Wells's *Tono-Bungay*: Review of New Studies', *English Literature in Transition*, x (1967), 89–96.
Kagarlitsky, Yury, *The Life and Thought of H. G. Wells*, translated by Budberg, M. (London, 1966).
Lodge, David, 'Tono-Bungay and the Condition of England', *The Language of Fiction* (London, 1966), 214–42.

Newell, Kenneth B., 'The Structure of H. G. Wells's *Tono-Bungay*', *English Fiction in Transition*, iv (1961), 1–8.

Nicholson, N. C., *H. G. Wells* (London, 1950).

Poston, Laurence, '*Tono-Bungay*: Wells's Unconstructed Tale', *College English*, xxvi (1965), 433–8.

Raknem, Ingvald, *H. G. Wells and His Critics* (Oslo, 1962).

Ray, Gordon N., 'H. G. Wells Tries To Be A Novelist', in Richard Ellmann (ed.), *Edwardians and Late Victorians* (New York, 1960), 106–59.

West, Anthony, 'H. G. Wells', *Encounter*, viii (February, 1957), 52–9.

West, Anthony, 'The Dark World of H. G. Wells', *Harper's Monthly*, cciv (May, 1957), 68–72.

(iv) Bibliography

Wells, Geoffrey H., *A Bibliography of the Works of H. G. Wells: 1893–1925* (London, 1925).

H. G. Wells Society, *H. G. Wells: A Comprehensive Bibliography* (London, 1966; 2nd edition, London, 1968).

II BENNETT

(i) Fiction

'The Artist's Model', *Tit-Bits*, xxiv (6 May, 1893), 82–3.

'A Letter Home', *The Yellow Book*, vi (1895), 93–102.

Love and Life, serial written during 1898–9, bought by Tillotson's syndicate in 1899, revised and published as *The Ghost* (London, 1907).

A Man from the North (London, 1898).

The Grand Babylon Hotel (London, 1902).

Anna of the Five Towns (London, 1902).

new ed. (London, 1912).

The Gates of Wrath (London, 1903).

Leonora (London, 1903).

A Great Man (London, 1904).

Tale of the Five Towns (London, 1905).

The Ghost (London, 1907).

The Grim Smile of the Five Towns (London, 1907).

The City of Pleasure (London, 1907).

Buried Alive (London, 1908).

The Old Wives' Tale (London, 1908).

Clayhanger (London, 1911).

Hilda Lessways (London, 1911).

The Card (London, 1911).
The Matador of the Five Towns (London, 1912).
These Twain (London, 1916).
Riceyman Steps (London, 1923).
Imperial Palace (London, 1930).

(ii) Material other than fiction

'The Fallow Fields of Fiction', *Academy*, lx (15, 29 June 1901), 517–18, 557–8.
'English and French Fiction in the Nineteenth Century', *ibid.*, lxii (I, 8, 15 February 1902), 117–19, 146–7, 173–4.
'The Isolation of English Fiction', *ibid.*, lxiii (8 November 1902), 505.
'Books and Persons', *New Age*, iii (19 September 1908), 412.
'Books and Persons', *ibid.*, iv (11 February 1909), 325–6.
'H. G. Wells', *ibid.*, iv (4 March 1909), 484–5.
Journalism for Women (London, 1898).
Fame and Fiction (London, 1901).
The Truth about an Author (London, 1903).
How to Become an Author (London, 1903).
The Reasonable Life (London, 1908).
The Human Machine (London, 1909).
Literary Taste (London, 1909).
The Plain Man and His Wife (London, 1913).
Books and Persons (London, 1917).
Self and Self-Management (London, 1918).
How to Make the Best of Life (London, 1923).
The Savour of Life (London, 1928).
Flower, Newman (ed.), *The Journals of Arnold Bennett, 1896–1931*, 3 vols (London, 1932–3).
Wilson, Harris (ed.), *Arnold Bennett and H. G. Wells* (London, 1960).
Hepburn, James (ed.), *The Letters of Arnold Bennett*, Vol. I, *Letters to J. B. Pinker* (London, 1966), Vol. II, *1889–1915* (London 1968).

(iii) Writing on Bennett

Allen, Walter, *Arnold Bennett* (London, 1948).
Bennett, Mrs Arnold, *Arnold Bennett* (London, 1925).
Davis, Oswald, *The Master* (London, 1966).
Hall, James, *Arnold Bennett: Primitivism and Taste* (Seattle, Wash. 1959).
Hepburn, James, *The Art of Arnold Bennett* (Bloomington, Ind., 1963).

Lafourcade, Georges, *Arnold Bennett* (London, 1939).

Massoulard, Elizabeth, 'Die Romantischen Elemente in Arnold Bennett', *Bonner Studien zur Englischen Philologie*, xxxiv (1938).

Pound, Reginald, *Arnold Bennett: A Biography* (London, 1952).

Swinnerton, Frank, *Arnold Bennett* (London, 1950).

Wain, John, 'The Quality of Arnold Bennett', *Preliminary Essays* (London, 1957), 121–56.

West, Geoffrey, *The Problem of Arnold Bennett* (London, 1932).

Wilson, Angus. 'Arnold Bennett's Novels', *London Magazine*, i (1954), 59–68.

Woolf, Virginia, *Mr. Bennett and Mrs. Brown* (London, 1924).

III GALSWORTHY

(*i*) *Fiction*

Sinjohn, John [pseud.], *From the Four Winds* (London, 1897).

Jocelyn (London, 1898).

Villa Rubein (London, 1900).

A Man of Devon (London, 1901).

The Island Pharisees (London, 1904).

The Man of Property (London, 1906).

The Country House (London, 1907).

Fraternity (London, 1909).

The Patrician (London, 1911).

The Dark Flower (London, 1913).

In Chancery (London, 1920).

Awakening (London, 1920).

To Let (London, 1921).

The Forsyte Saga (London, 1922).

The Manaton Edition of the Works, 30 vols (London, 1923–6).

(*ii*) *Drama*

The Pigeon (London, 1912).

The Eldest Son (London, 1912).

The Fugitive (London, 1913).

A Bit O'Love (London, 1915).

Windows (London, 1922).

A Family Man (London, 1922).

Loyalties (London, 1922).

The Little Man (London, 1924).

The Silver Box (London, 1930).

(*iii*) *Material other than fiction or drama*

A Commentary (London, 1908).
A Motley (London, 1910).
The Inn of Tranquillity (London, 1912).
Castles in Spain (London, 1927).
Garnett, Edward (ed.), *Letters from John Galsworthy: 1900–1932* (London, 1934).

(*iv*) *Writing on Galsworthy*

Barker, R. D., *The Man of Principle* (London, 1963).
Bjorkman, Edwin, 'John Galsworthy: An Interpretation of Modernity', *Review of Reviews*, lxiii (1911), 634–6, reprinted in *Is there Anything New Under the Sun?* (London, 1913), 183–200.
Liddell, Robert, 'The Upholstery of Galsworthy, contrasted with Henry James', *A Treatise on the Novel* (London, 1947), 125–7.
Marrot, H. V. *The Life and Letters of John Galsworthy* (London, 1935).
Mottram, R. H., *For Some We Loved: An Intimate Portrait of Ada and John Galsworthy* (London, 1956).

(*v*) *Bibliography*

Marrot, H. V., *A Bibliography of John Galsworthy* (London, 1928).
Fabes, G. H., *John Galsworthy: His First Editions* (London, 1932).

IV WRITING ON WELLS, BENNETT AND
     GALSWORTHY AS TRIUMVIRATE

Buckstead, Richard Chris., 'H. G. Wells, Arnold Bennett, John Galsworthy: Three Novelists in Revolt against the Middle Class', Dissertation, State University of Iowa, 1960.

B *All other material*

Abercrombie, Lascelles, 'Literature', in F. J. C. Hearnshaw (ed.), *Edwardian England* (*q.v.*), 185–203.
Alexander, Hartley Burr, *Poetry and the Individual* (New York, 1906).
Allen, G. A., *William James* (London, 1967).
Allen, Grant, *The Evolutionist at Large* (London, 1881).
  Science in Arcady (London, 1892).
  Physiological Aesthetics (London, 1893).
  The British Barbarians (London, 1895).
Allen, Walter, *The English Novel* (London, 1954).
  Tradition and Dream (London, 1964).

Allott, Miriam, *Novelists on the Novel* (London, 1959).

Andersson, Ola, *Studies in the Prehistory of Psychoanalysis* (Stockholm, 1962).

André, G., *Les Nouvelles Maladies neruveuses* (Paris, 1892).

Arnold, Matthew, 'The Function of Criticism at the Present Time', *Essays in Criticism* (London, 1865), 1–41.

'Art and Life', *Academy*, lxi (27 July, 1901), 75. Unsigned article.

Ash, Edwin, *Mind and Health* (London, 1910).

Baker, Ernest, *A History of the English Novel*, 10 vols. (London, 1924–39).

Baring-Gould, Sabine, 'Colour in Composition', in *On the Art of Writing Fiction* (editorship unascribed, London, 1894), 35–46.

'The Bankruptcy of Science', *Saturday Review*, lxxix (19 January 1895), 91. Unsigned article.

Bateson, F. W. *A Guide to English Literature* (London, 1965).

Batho, E., and Dobrée, B., *The Victorians and After: 1830–1914* (London, 1938).

Beach, J. W., *The Twentieth Century Novel* (New York, 1932).

Beck, William S., *Modern Science and the Nature of Life* (London, 1958).

Becker, G. J., *Documents of Modern Literary Realism* (Princeton, N.J. 1963).

Beer, J. B., *The Achievement of E. M. Forster* (London, 1962).

Belloc, Hilaire, *Mr. Clutterbuck's Election* (London, 1908).

A Change in the Cabinet (London, 1909).

Berg, Charles, *Madkind* (London, 1962).

Berger, P. L., and Luckmann, T., *The Social Construction of Reality* (London, 1967).

Bergson, Henri, *Essai sur les données immédiates de la conscience* (Paris, 1888).

Matiére et mémoire (Paris, 1896).

L'Evolution creatrice (Paris, 1907).

Booth, C. Wayne, *The Rhetoric of Fiction* (Chicago, 1961).

Bodkin, Maud, *Archetypal Patterns in Poetry* (Oxford, 1934).

Bradley, F. H., *Appearance and Reality* (London, 1893).

Bridges, John Henry, *Illustrations of Positivism* (London, 1907).

Brunetière, Ferdinand, *Le Roman naturaliste* (Paris, 1885).

Burrow, J. W., *Evolution and Society* (Cambridge, 1966).

Burrow, Trigant, *The Social Basis of Consciousness* (London, 1927).

Bush, Douglas, *Science and English Poetry* (New York, 1967).

Butler, Samuel. *Erewhon* (London, 1872).

Life and Habit (London, 1877).

Evolution Old and New (London, 1879).

Unconscious Memory (London, 1880).

Luck or Cunning (London, 1887).

Erewhon Revisited (London, 1901).

The Way of All Flesh (London, 1903).

Camus, Albert, *The Collected Fiction of Albert Camus* (translated by Stuart Gilbert, London, 1962).

Cannan, Gilbert, *The Anatomy of Society* (London, 1919).

Carpenter, Edward, 'Civilisation: Its Cause and Cure', *Pioneer*, i (1889), 9–36.

Cassell, Richard, *Ford Madox Ford* (Baltimore, Md. 1961).

Chesterton, G. K., *The Napoleon of Notting Hill* (London, 1904).

The Man Who Was Thursday (London, 1908).

Chevalley, A., *Le Roman de notre temps* (Paris, 1921).

Churchill, R. C. 'The Age of T. S. Eliot', in George Sampson, *The Concise Cambridge History of English Literature*, 2nd enlarged edition (Cambridge, 1961), pp. 944–1,030.

Churchill, Winston L. S., *Liberalism and the Social Problem* (London, 1909).

Clive, Geoffrey, *The Romantic Enlightenment* (New York, 1960).

Conrad, Joseph, *Almayer's Folly* (London, 1895).

The Nigger of the 'Narcissus' (London, 1897).

Tales of Unrest (London, 1898).

Lord Jim (London, 1900).

Youth – A Narrative: and Two Other Stories (London, 1902).

Nostromo (London, 1904).

The Secret Agent (London, 1907).

Under Western Eyes (London, 1911).

Victory (London, 1915).

The Uniform Edition of the Works, 23 vols (London, 1923–8).

Crane, Stephen, *The Open Boat and Other Stories* (London, 1898).

Daiches, David, *Some Late Victorian Attitudes* (London, 1969).

Dangerfield, George, *The Strange Death of Liberal England* (London, 1936).

Darwin, Charles. *The Origin of Species* (London, 1859).

The Variation of Animals and Plants under Domestication (London, 1868).

The Descent of Man (London, 1871).

The Expression of the Emotions (London, 1872).

Dickens, Charles, *Oliver Twist* (London, 1837–8).

Dostoevsky, Fyodor, *Letters From the Underworld* (translated by C. J. Hogarth, London, 1913).

Doyle, Arthur Conan, *The Adventures of Sherlock Holmes* (London, 1892).

Driesch, H., *History and Theory of Vitalism* (New York, 1914).

Edel, Leon, *The Psychological Novel: 1900–1950*, 2nd revised edition (London, 1961).

'The Edwardian Novel', *Times Literary Supplement* (28 June 1947), 322

Eliot, T. S., *Selected Essays* (London, 1951).
Collected Poems, 1909–1962 (London, 1963).

Ellis, Havelock. 'A Note on Paul Bourget', reprinted in *News and Reviews* (London, 1932), 48–60.
The New Spirit (London, 1890).
Man and Woman (London, 1894).
'The Colour Sense in Literature', *Contemporary Review*, lxix (May 1896), 714–29.
The World of Dreams (London, 1911).
The Task of Social Hygiene (London, 1912).
Impressions and Comments (London, 1914).
The Dance of Life (London, 1923).
News and Reviews (London, 1932).

Ellman, Richard (ed.), *Edwardians and Late Victorians* (New York, 1960).
'The Two Faces of Edward', *ibid.*, 188–210.

Ensor, R. C. K., *England, 1870–1914* (Oxford, 1946).

Erwin, Malcolm, *Old Gods Falling* (London, 1939).

Findlater, Jane, 'Three Sides to a Question', *National Review*, liv (1910), 799–811.

Flournoy, Théodore, *William James* (Geneva, 1911).

Flugel, J. C., *A Hundred Years of Psychology* (London, 1933).
Man, Morals and Society (London, 1945).

Ford, Ford Madox, *The Fifth Queen* (London, 1905).
Privy Seal (London, 1907).
The Spirit of the People (London, 1907).
The Fifth Queen Crowned (London, 1908).
Collected Poems (London, 1914).
The Good Soldier (London, 1915).
Thus To Revisit (London, 1921).
Joseph Conrad (London, 1924).
Some Do Not (London, 1924).
No More Parades (London, 1925).
A Man Could Stand Up (London, 1926).
The English Novel (London, 1930).
Mightier Than the Sword (London, 1938).

Forster, E. M., *Where Angels Fear to Tread* (London, 1905).
The Longest Journey (London, 1907).
A Room With a View (London, 1908).
Howards End (London, 1910).
Aspects of the Novel (London, 1927).

Foucault, Michel, *Madness and Civilization* (translated by R. Howard, London, 1967).

Frazer, J. G., *The Golden Bough*, 12 vols (London, 1890–1915).

Freeman, R. Austin, *Social Decay and Regeneration* (London, 1921).

Freud, Sigmund. *Studies on Hysteria* (translated by J. Strachey, London, 1956).

   The Psychopathology of Everyday Life (translated by J. Strachey, London, 1966).

   Introductory Lectures on Psychoanalysis (translated by J. Rivière, London, 1930).

   Civilisation and Its Discontents (translated by J. Rivière, London, 1930).

   Beyond the Pleasure Principle (translated by J. Strachey, London, 1950).

   The Interpretation of Dreams (translated by J. Strachey, London, 1956).

Frierson, W. C., *L'Influence du naturalisme français sur les romanciers anglais: 1885–1900* (Paris, 1929).

   The English Novel in Transition: 1880–1940 (Norman, Okla., 1942).

Fromm, Erich, *Freedom From Fear* (London, 1942).

Garnett, Edward, *An Imaged World* (London, 1894).

Gerber, Helmut E., 'The Nineties; Beginning, End or Transition?', in Richard Ellmann, *Edwardians and Late Victorians* (*q.v.*), 50–79.

Gissing, George, *The Unclassed* (London, 1884).

   Demos (London, 1886).

   The Nether World (London, 1889).

   New Grub Street (London, 1891).

   Born in Exile (London, 1892).

   The Odd Woman (London, 1893).

   Human Odds and Ends (London, 1898).

   The Private Papers of Henry Ryecroft (London, 1903).

Gosse, Edmund, *Father and Son* (London, 1907). The authorship is unascribed in the first edition.

Granville-Barker, H., *Waste* (London, 1907).

   The Madras House (London, 1910).

Graham, Kenneth, *English Criticism of the Novel: 1865–1900* (Oxford, 1965).

Greene, Graham, *The Lost Childhood* (London, 1951).

Greenwood, Frederick, 'Gospel of Content', *Yellow Book*, ii (1894), 11–33.

Hake, A. E., *Regeneration: A Reply to Max Nordau* (London, 1895).

Hardy, Thomas, *Under the Greenwood Tree* (London, 1872).

   Far From the Madding Crowd (London, 1874).

   The Return of the Native (London, 1878).

The Mayor of Casterbridge (London, 1886).
Tess of the D'Urbervilles (London, 1891).
Satires of Circumstance (London, 1914).
Hartmann, Heinz, *Ego Psychology and the Problem of Adaptation* (translated by David Rapaport, London, 1958).
Hauser, Arnold, *The Social History of Art*, 2 vols (London 1951).
The Philosophy of Art History (London, 1959).
Hearnshaw, F. J. C. (ed.), *Edwardian England* (London, 1933).
Henkin, L. J., 'Evolution and Darwinism in the Victorian Novel', Dissertation, New York University, 1940.
Darwinism in the English Novel: 1860–1910 (New York, 1963).
Hicks, Granville S., *Figures of Transition* (New York, 1939).
Hillegas, M. R., *The Future As Nightmare* (New York, 1967).
Hobhouse, L. T., *Mind in Evolution* (London, 1901).
Morals in Evolution (London, 1906).
Hobson, J. A., 'The Task of Realism', *English Review*, iii (1909), 543–54.
The Crisis of Liberalism (London, 1909).
Hodin, J. P., *The Dilemma of Being Modern* (London, 1956).
Hoffmann, Frederick J., *Freudianism and the Literary Mind* (Baton Rouge, La., 1945).
Hough, Graham, *The Last Romantics* (London, 1949).
Howells, W. D., *Literature and Life* (New York, 1902).
Hudson, W. H., *Herbert Spencer* (London, 1908).
Hughes, H. Stuart, *Consciousness and Society* (London, 1959).
Huxley, Sir J. S., *Evolution: The Modern Synthesis* (London, 1948).
Evolution as a Process (London, 1954).
The Science of Life, in collaboration with G. P. Wells and H. G. Wells (London, 1929–30).
Huxley, T. H., *Man's Place in Nature* (London, 1863).
Science and Culture (London, 1881).
The Physical Basis of Life (London, 1868).
Evolution and Ethics (London, 1893).
Hynes, Samuel. *The Edwardian Turn of Mind* (Princeton, N.J., 1968).
Jackson, Holbrook, *Romance and Reality* (London, 1911).
The Eighteen Nineties (London, 1913).
James, Henry, *The Tragic Muse* (London, 1890).
The Lesson of the Master (London, 1892).
Terminations (London, 1895).
Embarrassments (London, 1896).
The Spoils of Poynton (London, 1897).
What Maisie Knew (London, 1897).
The Two Magics (London, 1898).
The Awkward Age (London, 1899).

The Wings of the Dove (London, 1902).

The Ambassadors (London, 1903).

The Golden Bowl (London, 1904).

Notes on Novelists (London, 1914).

'The Younger Generation', *The Times Literary Supplement* (19 March, 2 April 1914), 133–4, 137–8 reprinted in L. Edel and Gordon N. Ray (ed.), *Henry James and H. G. Wells* (*q.v.*), 178–215.

The Notebooks of Henry James (edited by F. O. Matthiessen and Kenneth B. Murdock, New York, 1947).

Henry James and H. G. Wells (edited by L. Edel and Gordon N. Ray, London, 1958).

James, Henry, Jr., *Letters of William James*, 2nd edition, 1 vol. (London, 1926).

James, William, *Principles of Psychology* (London, 1890).

Varieties of Religious Experience (London, 1902).

Pragmatism (London, 1907).

A Pluralistic Universe (London, 1909).

Jastrow, J., *The Subconscious* (London, 1906).

Jean-Aubry, G. (ed.), *The Life and Letters of Joseph Conrad* (London, 1927.

'Jocelyn', *Saturday Review*, lxxxvi (6 August 1898), 184. Unsigned review article.

Jones, Ernest, *Essays in Applied Psychoanalysis* (London, 1923).

Hamlet and Oedipus (London, 1949).

Jones, Maxwell, *Beyond the Therapeutic Community* (New Haven and London, 1968).

Joyce, James, *Dubliners* (London, 1914).

A Portrait of the Artist as a Young Man (London, 1917).

Ulysses (Paris, 1922).

Ibid., Bodley Head edition (London, 1960).

Jung, C .G., *Modern Man in Search of a Soul* (translated by W. S. Dell and C. F. Baynes, London, 1933).

Kaplan, B. (ed.), *The Inner World of Mental Illness* (New York, 1964).

Kennedy, J. M., *English Literature 1880–1905* (London, 1912).

Kermode, Frank, *The Sense of an Ending* (New York, 1967).

Kettle, Arnold, *An Introduction to the English Novel*, 2 vols (London, 1951–3).

Kidd, Benjamin, *Individualism and After* (Oxford, 1908).

Kierkegaard, Soren, *The Sickness Unto Death* (translated by W. Lowrie, London, 1941).

Repetition (translated by W. Lowrie, London, 1942).

Kipling, Rudyard, *The City of Dreadful Night* (London, 1890).

The Light That Failed (London, 1890).

Life's Handicap (London, 1891).

Many Inventions (London, 1893).

The Jungle Book (London, 1894).

Kris, Ernst, *Psychoanalytic Explorations in Art* (London, 1953).

Krook, Dorothea, *The Ordeal of Consciousness in Henry James* (Cambridge, 1962).

Laing, Ronald, *The Divided Self* (London, 1960).

The Politics of Experience (Harmondsworth, Middlesex, 1967).

Lang, A., and Richardson, J., *Social Origins* (London, 1903).

Lawrence, D. H., *The White Peacock* (London, 1911).

Sons and Lovers (London, 1913).

The Rainbow (London, 1915).

Women in Love (London, 1921).

'John Galsworthy', in Edgell Rickword (ed.), *Scrutinies* (London, 1928), 52–72, reprinted in *Phoenix* (*q.v.*), 539–50.

Phoenix (London, 1939).

The Complete Poems, ii (London, 1957).

Leavis, Q. D., *Fiction and the Reading Public* (London, 1932).

Lee, Vernon [i.e. Violet Page], *The Beautiful. An Introduction to Psychological Aesthetics* (London, 1913).

The Handling of Words and Other Studies in Literary Psychology (London, 1923).

Le Gallienne, Richard, *The Life Romantic* (London, 1901).

The Romantic Nineties (London, 1925).

Lester, John A., *Journey Through Despair: Transformations in British Literary Culture 1880–1914* (Princeton, N.J., 1968).

Lewes, G. H., *Problems of Life and Mind* (London, 1873–9).

Liddell, Robert, *A Treatise on the Novel* (London, 1947).

'Literature and Life', *Saturday Review*, lxxxix (6 January 1900), 9–11. Unsigned article.

Lubbock, Sir John, *The Origin of Civilization* (London, 1870).

Lubbock, Percy, *The Craft of Fiction* (London, 1921).

Lucas, F. L., *The Decline and Fall of the Romantic Ideal* (Cambridge, 1936).

Psychology and Literature (London, 1951).

Lyell, Sir Charles, *The Antiquity of Man* (London, 1863).

MacDougall, William, *Social Psychology* (London, 1908).

Mackerness, E. D. (ed.), *The Journals of George Sturt: 1890–1927*, 2 vols (Cambridge, 1967).

Madsen, S. Tschudi, *Art Nouveau* (London, 1967).

Mallock, W. H., *The New Republic* (London, 1877).

Marshall, Henry Rutgers. *Consciousness* (London, 1909).

Masterman, C. F. G., *In Peril of Change* (London, 1903).

The Condition of England (London, 1909).

Masur, Gerhard, *Prophets of Yesterday* (London, 1963).

Maudsley, Henry, *The Physiology and Pathology of Mind* (London, 1867).

Body and Mind London, 1870).

The Pathology of Mind (London, 1897).

Maugham, W. Somerset, *Liza of Lambeth* (London, 1897).

Maurois, André, *King Edward* (translated by Hamish Miles, London, 1933).

Mazlish, Bruce, 'Old Critics, New Research', *Encounter*, xxix (December 1967), 93–4.

Melville, Herman, *Typee*, (New York, 1848).

Meredith, George, *The Ordeal of Richard Feverel* (London, 1859).

Modern Love (London, 1862).

Rhoda Fleming (London, 1865).

The Egoist (London, 1879).

One of Our Conquerors (London, 1891).

Lord Ormont and His Aminta (London, 1894).

The Amazing Marriage (London, 1895).

Meyer, Bernard C., *Joseph Conrad: A Psychoanalytic Biography* (Princeton, N.J., 1967).

Miller, J. Hillis, *The Disappearance of God* (Cambridge, Mass., 1963).

The Form of Victorian Fiction (Notre Dame, Ind., 1968).

Minney, R. J., *The Edwardian Age* (London, 1964).

Moon, R. O., *The Relation of Medicine to Philosophy* (London, 1909).

Moore, George, *A Modern Lover* (London, 1883).

A Mummer's Wife (London, 1885).

A Drama in Muslin (London, 1886).

Confessions of a Young Man (London, 1886).

'Turgueneff', *Fortnightly Review*, xlii (1888), 244.

Impressions and Opinions (London, 1891).

Modern Painting (London, 1893).

Esther Waters (London, 1894).

Celibates (London, 1895).

Moreau, François-Armand, *Mémoires de physiologie* (Paris, 1877).

Morell, J. D., *Elements of Psychology* (London, 1853).

An Introduction to Mental Philosophy (London, 1862).

Morgan, C. Lloyd, *Psychology for Teachers* (London, 1894).

Morris, William, *News From Nowhere* (London, 1891).

Morrison, Arthur, *A Child of the Jago* (London, 1896).

Muddiman, Bernard, *The Men of the Nineties* (London, 1920).

Muir, Edwin, *The Structure of the Novel* (London, 1928).

Myers, W. L., *The Later Realism* (Chicago, 1927).

Nerval, Gérard de, *Aurélia*, first published in *La Revue de Paris* (1 January, 15 January 1855).

Nietzsche, Friedrich, *The Will to Power* (translated by Walter Kaufmann and R. J. Hollingdale, London, 1967).

Nordau, Max, *Degeneration* (London, 1895).

Ibid., (popular edition, London, 1913).

Paradoxes (London, 1896).

Norris, Frank, *The Responsibilities of the Novelist* (London, 1903).

On the Art of Writing Fiction (London, 1894). Editorship unascribed.

Pater, Walter, *The Renaissance* (London, 1873).

Marius the Epicurean (London, 1885).

Appreciations (London, 1889).

Phelps, W. L., *The Advance of the English Novel* (New York, 1916).

Rapaport, Robert, *Community as Doctor* (London, 1960).

Reynolds, Stephen, *A Poor Man's House* (London, 1908).

Richardson, Dorothy, *Pilgrimage*, 4 vols (London, 1938).

Richardson, Maurice, 'Views', *The Listener* (29 August 1968), 260.

Rickwood, Edgell. (ed.), *Scrutinies* (London, 1928).

Rieff, Philip, *Freud: The Mind of the Moralist* (London, 1960).

The Triumph of the Therapeutic (London, 1966).

Robert, Sir Sydney, *Edwardian Retrospect*. The English Association Presidential Address for 1963 (London, 1963).

Roppen, Georg, *Evolution and Poetic Relief* (Oslo, 1956).

Rossetti, D. G., *Poems* (London, 1870).

Roubiczek, Paul, *Existentialism: For and Against* (Cambridge, 1964).

Routh, H. V., *Towards the Twentieth Century* (Cambridge, 1937).

Sandison, Alan, *The Wheel of Empire* (London, 1967).

Schorer, Mark, 'Technique as Discovery', *Hudson Review*, i (Spring, 1948), 67–87, reprinted in W. Van O'Connor (ed.), *Forms of Modern Fiction* (Minneapolis, Minn., 1948, 9–29).

(ed.), *Society and Self in the Novel* (New York, 1956).

Shaw, George Bernard, *The Quintessence of Ibsenism* (London, 1891).

'A Degenerate's View of Nordau', *Liberty* (New York, 27 July 1895), revised as *The Sanity of Art* (London, 1908).

The Perfect Wagnerite (London, 1898).

Three Plays For Puritans (London, 1901).

Man and Superman (London, 1903).

John Bull's Other Island and Major Barbara (London, 1907).

Socialism and Individualism (London, 1908).

Back To Mesthuselah (London, 1921).

Prefaces (London, 1934).

Spencer, Herbert, *The Development Hypothesis* (London, 1852).

Principles of Psychology (London, 1853).

First Principles (London, 1862).

Ibid. (6th edition, London, 1900).

New Principles of Psychology (1870–2).

Principles of Sociology (London, 1876–96).

The Man Versus the State (London, 1884).

Factors of Organic Evolution (London, 1887).

Stanford, Derek (ed.), *Short Stories of the 'Nineties* (London, 1968).

Stang, Richard, *The Theory of the Novel in England: 1850–1870* (London, 1959).

Stevenson, Lionel, *Darwin Among the Poets* (Chicago, 1932).

The English Novel (London, 1960).

Stevenson, R. L., 'A Gossip on Romance', *Longman's Magazine*, i (1882), 69–79.

'A Humble Remonstrance', *ibid.*, v (1884), 139–47.

Treasure Island (London, 1883).

The Strange Case of Dr. Jekyll and Mr. Hyde (London, 1886).

Kidnapped (London, 1886).

Island Nights' Entertainments (London, 1893).

Stocker, R. D. *Subconscious* (London, 1905).

Swinnerton, Frank, *Background with Chorus* (London, 1956).

Sypher, Wylie, *Loss of the Self* (New York, 1964).

Szasz, T., *The Myth of Mental Illness* (London, 1962).

Tate, Allen, 'Techniques of Fiction', in J. W. Aldridge (ed.), *Critiques and Essays on Modern Fiction, 1920–1951* (New York, 1952).

Tindall, W. Y., *Forces in Modern British Literature* (New York, 1947).

Toynbee, A., 'Poetic Truth and Scientific Truth in the Light of History', *International Journal of Psychoanalysis*, xxx (1949), 134–52.

Trilling, Lionel, *The Liberal Imagination* (London, 1951).

Beyond Culture (London, 1966).

Tuke, D. H. *Illustrations of the Influence of Mind Upon the Body in Health and Disease* (London, 1872).

Chapters in the History of the Insane in the British Isles (London, 1882).

(ed.), *Dictionary of Psychological Medicine* (London, 1892).

Tuke, John Batty, *The Insanity of Over-Exertion of the Brain* (Edinburgh, 1894).

Wagar, W. W., *H. G. Wells and the World State* (New Haven, 1961).

H. G. Wells: Journalism and Prophecy, 1893–1946 (London, 1965).

Wallas, Graham, *Human Nature in Politics* (London, 1908).

Warbasse, J. P., *Medical Sociology* (New York and London, 1909).

Weber, J. Sherwood, Afterward to the 'Signet' edition, *The Way of All Flesh* (New York, 1960), 378–84.

Westermarck, E., *The Origin and Development of Moral Ideas* (London, 1906).

Whitcomb, S. L., *The Study of a Novel* (London, 1906).

White, W. H., *The Autobiography of Mark Rutherford* (London, 1881).

Whyte, W. L., *The Unconscious Before Freud* (London, 1962).

Wilde, Oscar, *Intentions* (London, 1891).

The Picture of Dorian Gray (London, 1891).

'The Soul of Man Under Socialism', *Fortnightly Review*, xlix (1891), 292–319.

De Profundis (London, 1905).

Willey, Basil, *Nineteenth Century Studies* (London, 1949).

More Nineteenth Century Studies (London, 1956).

Darwin and Butler (London, 1960).

Williams, Raymond, *Culture and Society: 1780–1950* (London, 1958).

The Long Revolution (London, 1961).

Wilson, Colin, *The Outsider* (London, 1956).

Wingfield-Stratton, E., *The Victorian Aftermath* (New York, 1934).

Woolf, Virginia, *Mr. Bennett and Mrs. Brown* (London, 1924).

'Modern Fiction', *The Common Reader* (London, 1925), 184–95.

Wright, W. F. (ed.), *Joseph Conrad on Fiction* (Nebraska, 1964).

Yeats, W. B., *Responsibilities* (London, 1916).

Introduction, *Oxford Book of Modern Verse* (Oxford, 1936), v-xlii.

Index

Index